The Organized Teacher's Guide to

Setting Up a Terrific Classroom

The Organized Teacher's Guide to
Setting Up a Terrific Classroom

THIRD EDITION

Steve Springer, MA
Brandy Alexander, MFA
Kimberly Persiani, EdD

New York   Chicago   San Francisco   Athens   London
Madrid   Mexico City   Milan   New Delhi
Singapore   Sydney   Toronto

1 2 3 4 5 6 7 8 9 LHS 24 23 22 21 20 19

ISBN   978-1-260-44193-2
MHID   1-260-44193-8

e-ISBN   978-1-260-44194-9
e-MHID   1-260-44194-6

Interior illustrations copyright © Steve Springer and Brandy Alexander

McGraw-Hill Education books are available at special quantity discounts to use as premiums and sales promotions or for use in corporate training programs. To contact a representative, please visit the Contact Us pages at www.mhprofessional.com.

Bonus Templates

In order to access the online templates, please go to http://www.mhprofessional.com/mediacenter. Enter the ISBN of this book: 978-1-260-44193-2

For further assistance, please see the instructions on the inside front cover ad to access the templates.

Contents

Contents

Contents

Foreword

It has been over a decade since we first wrote *The Organized Teacher*. From the time it was published, we have used this book in countless classroom management courses, national and international conferences, and school district workshops and have heard directly from hundreds of teachers in the field who have used content from this book in their own classrooms. We are excited to have incorporated their ideas and suggestions into this new edition. Many of the changes you will find include everything from new rewards, updated certificates, current teacher and student websites, a refreshed children's literature bibliography, updated technology ideas, and user-friendly templates found throughout the book.

The third edition of *The Organized Teacher's Guide to Setting Up a Terrific Classroom* is an improved version of the first two, which is more aligned to the twenty-first century classroom. Many of the changes come directly from the thoughts and needs of current classroom teachers in the public and private sector in rural, urban, and suburban areas. There are a variety of alterations to be found in the illustrations, accessibility to teacher resources, and updated checklists and user-friendly templates stemming from the voices of reflective practitioners.

Teachers are inundated and overwhelmed with standards-based curriculum, high stakes testing, the pressures and responsibilities of accountability issues, and the everyday tasks of teaching; it's a wonder that teachers are as committed and determined to make a difference as they are. This is no truer than when walking into the classroom of Mr. Steve Springer or Mr. Brandy Alexander in Los Angeles, CA. On any given day, you can walk into their classrooms and observe a variety of activities from center rotations, felt storyboards, students helping one another, stories being read on the rug, the teacher's aide reading with small groups, hands-on projects taking place, and the teacher working one-on-one with students. In addition to the very busy goings-on of their rooms, bulletin boards are filled with student work samples scored with accompanying rubrics, art projects cover tabletops and walls, and computer games and student technology projects are being worked on throughout the day.

In January 2003, I had the pleasure of supervising student teachers from California State University, Los Angeles, during their Directed Teaching portion of the credential program. Two of my student teachers were placed under the guidance of Mr. Springer and Mr. Alexander. My first stop was Mr. Springer's classroom. Upon entrance, one could see that the children owned the room. The space was personalized with pictures of those residing in this class while their newest narrative writing was securely in place, the children were talking to one another, and learning was obviously occurring. English learners made up a large part of this class, and they were tended to in every lesson while advanced learners and those with special needs were also accommodated. Steve's attention to his audience is what makes much of the planning and incentive ideas in this book as strong as they are. I couldn't have asked for a better place in which to watch the professional growth of my student teacher.

The next stop was Mr. Alexander's room. I felt as though I went from one ideal venue to another. It was unbelievable to me that my student teachers were being placed in such extraordinarily positive circumstances during a time, which is often scary and unfamiliar to these teacher candidates. Seeing that technology was a key element in Mr. Alexander's class and that electronic (academic) games, group discussions, and student input were all honored, only solidified the fact that our teacher candidates were in good hands.

Mr. Springer and Mr. Alexander offered classrooms where not only the students thrive, but so did my student teachers that were placed under their guidance for eleven weeks. Toward the end of the winter quarter, as the student teachers finished their final observations, I noticed a three-ring binder full of unique ideas from lesson planning, to bulletin board ideas, to classroom discipline procedures, assessment concepts, portfolio ideas, and the like. When questioned, my student teachers admitted that Mr. Springer and Mr. Alexander provided them with these materials. Immediately, I asked Mr. Springer and Mr. Alexander why they hadn't published such materials for all new and existing teachers. From that time on, the preparation of this book was in motion.

The three of us worked diligently for several months in order to pull together the makings of a practical, no-nonsense book full of blackline masters and usable resources. It is without question that Steve Springer and Brandy Alexander are of the group of dedicated teachers who show up each day with a smile on their faces, have a classroom prepared for all learners, and materials available for each child to be successful. It is with great honor that I had the opportunity to be a part of this amazing book in which new and existing teachers will benefit from our years of experience. Through this experience, several other books in the The Organized Teacher series have emerged. In addition, Steve and Brandy have both taken on part-time lecturer positions at CSU, Los Angeles, where they teach courses in classroom management, subject-specific pedagogy, and portfolio preparations. The Organized Teacher series of books have become staples in these courses. More important, the three of us find our role as educators, satisfying, challenging, and a serious venture.

The most rewarding career is that of a teacher. While there are many aspects to the job that are less than desirable, the hugs, the smiles, the shared snacks, and the constant love from the children make up for any of the frustrating parts of the job. Having a classroom that has been carefully planned, organized, and maintained allows for more of the hugs, smiles, snacks, and love that will be generously showered upon you given the right circumstances. It is the goal of this book that you will have your classroom management in place at the beginning of your school year so that you too can enjoy the rewards of teaching.

Kimberly Persiani, EdD
Professor
California State University, Los Angeles

School Overview

The following is a breakdown of several members of a school community. Get to know many people at your school site. Each member of this community plays an important role in your success and the success of your students. Schools vary depending on the site and the number of students enrolled.

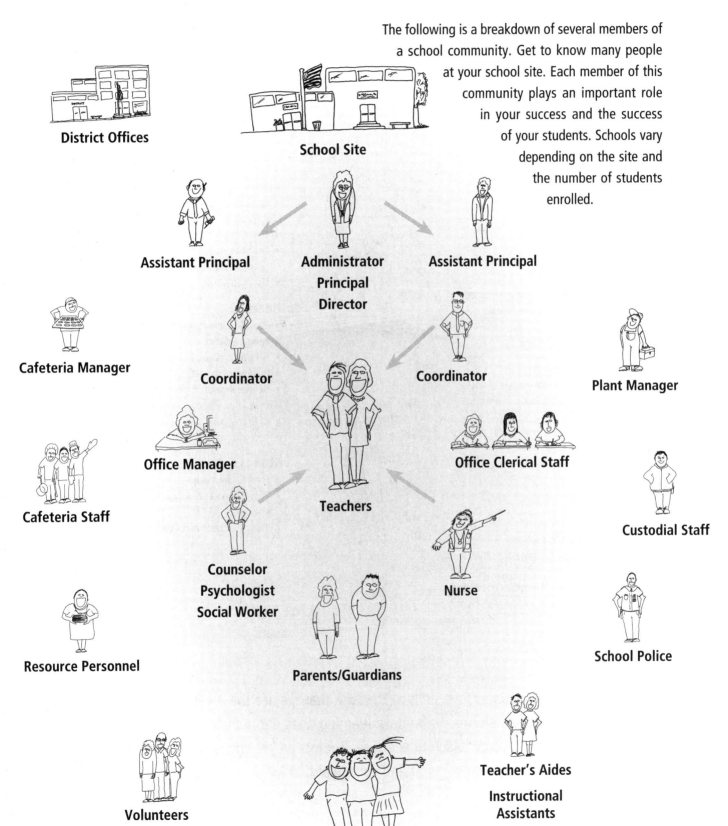

District Offices

School Site

Assistant Principal

Administrator
Principal
Director

Assistant Principal

Cafeteria Manager

Coordinator

Coordinator

Plant Manager

Cafeteria Staff

Office Manager

Office Clerical Staff

Custodial Staff

Teachers

Counselor
Psychologist
Social Worker

Nurse

Resource Personnel

Parents/Guardians

School Police

Volunteers

Students

Teacher's Aides

Instructional Assistants

Anatomy of a Teacher

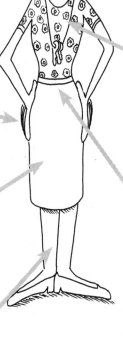

Eyes
- Watch and protect your students.
- Perceive—awareness of school surroundings and the "culture" of the school.
- Observe—"read" students' faces and emotions.

Voice
- Speak up for students.
- Provide correct language usage.
- Your tone shows emotion and passion.
- Take care of your voice—try not to yell.

Hands
- Teachers are natural givers.
- Give a handshake or a pat on the back to your students every day.
- Give students positive learning experiences.
- Learn through your hands (kinesthetic learning).

Posture and Balance
- Stand up straight.
- Be proud and positive that you are changing lives and making a difference in the world you love!
- Show strength and a zest for living.
- Serve as a role model.
- Balance work and play (lots of play will keep you happy in the classroom!).

Legs
- Make things happen (movin' 'n' shakin').
- Circulate, be constantly moving.
- Provide extra support for those with special needs.
- This is the base of your strength, a good base is essential.

Brain
- Keep your mind as healthy as your body.
- Read for enjoyment.
- Know your standards.
- Keep current on educational trends and research.
- Plan great instruction.
- Take breaks from thinking; do things away from work that are fun and relaxing!

Ears
- Lend an ear and hear others out; have compassion.
- Listen to your students.
- Listen to your colleagues.
- Listen to the parents/guardians.
- Listen to music!

Heart
- Provide a loving, nurturing environment.
- Exercise daily.
- Give and receive lots of love.
- Believe in yourself.
- Believe in your students.
- Love what you do.
- Give your all.
- Love your family.

Stomach
- Eat healthy foods.
- Provide good nutritional values for your students.
- Trust your gut (instincts).

Teachers sometimes lose sight of the fact that *we* are the most important element in the classroom. Without us, learning does not happen. Always monitor yourself and do not overextend your energies. Get lots of rest and leave as much work at work as you can. Remember, you and your health are vital to the success of all of your students!

Student Overview

Students vary in personality and maturity at each grade level. The following is an overview of students at each grade level. This is just a general overview; your students will vary depending on each individual.

Kindergarteners

- Can describe their needs
- Are myopic or selfish
- Have short attention spans
- Are learning to adjust to group work
- Are acquiring fine motor skills
- Need step-by-step instruction
- Are mostly familiar with personal experiences
- Enjoy singing, dancing, and pretending

First Graders

- Are not able to multitask
- Can function productively in groups
- Are conscious of others around them
- Enjoy learning through activities, games, creative stories, dancing, and singing
- Have the ability to get absorbed in tasks
- Are self-reflective in their work and seek validation
- Are most comfortable with what they already know rather than with what can actually be seen
- Have ability levels different from one another

Second Graders

- Are independent and self-sufficient but still seek validation
- Are beginning to identify details in their environment and surroundings
- Are conscious of nature and creatures
- Are risk takers, becoming confident in their abilities
- Enjoy understanding how and why things work the way they do
- Are aware of new things, such as television, the radio, movies, clothes, or toys

Third Graders

- Are enthusiastic and excited to learn new things
- Are self-reflective
- Are aware of moods
- Are aware of one another's differences
- Have a fear of not being accepted
- Are gender biased during play but cooperate in the classroom
- Test boundaries
- Are conscious of reality versus fantasy
- Are creative in writing and art

Fourth Graders

- Can distinguish seriousness versus humor
- Are aware of ability levels
- Compare work with others
- Are aware of similarities and differences
- Are conscious of popularity, music, movies, television
- Push the limits on rules
- Are specific about likes and dislikes, including subject areas
- Are responsible for their own actions
- Are introspective

Fifth Graders

- Enjoy being original in their ideas and assignments
- Take on responsibilities that might be challenging
- Are becoming problem solvers
- Work cooperatively with peers and/or in groups
- Enjoy working with their hands and producing tangible items
- Begin to be frustrated when classmates are better in subject areas such as art, math, sports, etc.
- Tend to be gender biased and separate based on interests
- Can work independently for longer periods of time
- Have their strengths and weaknesses—academically, athletically, and creatively—becoming more apparent

Sixth Graders

- Are sure of their knowledge and like to be right
- Are still open to new experiences
- Begin to form steadfast opinions
- Look for peer approval
- Realize that their physical changes and emotional changes cause mood swings
- Can get distracted easily at times
- Show greater interest in the media and entertainment
- Like to spend time alone, away from adults
- React positively to praised work

Seventh Graders

- Show interest in opposite sex
- Are more conscious of their physical appearance
- Are more independent and want to be treated like grown-ups
- Still show signs of childish behavior
- Are developing their identity
- Feel it is important to be accepted by peers by identifying with a group
- Are willing to engage in exciting experiences

Eighth Graders

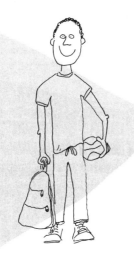

- Are conscious about what others think of them
- Are self-conscious
- Test their roles and identities
- Have fluctuating hormones
- Are conscious of environmental responsibilities
- Wonder how their academics relate to their real-life circumstances
- Take criticism of their work personally
- Like to work with others on projects
- Are interested in abstract ideas

Anatomy of a Student

Eyes
- Students need their eyes checked annually.
- Students with vision issues need to sit in the front.
- Check for students who wear glasses.
- Leave glasses in at recess to avoid serious injury.
- Students need to learn observation as a part of the scientific process.
- Teach students to see needs of others.
- Visual learners learn by seeing.
- Students watch the example you set.

Voice
- Students have a voice and should express themselves.
- Speaking slowly or modeling can be effective in correct pronunciation.
- Indoor vs. outdoor voices
- Use their words not fists.
- Speech/pronunciation issues are referred to speech pathologist.

Hands
- Kinesthetic learners learn through active engagement, by doing.
- Students need to learn to keep their hands to themselves.
- Students need to learn the satisfaction of a helping hand through assigned jobs and responsibilities.
- Students learn to raise their hands, not shout out.

Posture/Balance
- Students need to sit properly in their seats for good blood flow and efficient learning.
- Students need balance throughout their day. Mixing up activities, adding in movement, and avoiding only seat-work gives them the variety they crave.
- Students hold their stature with pride and confidence.
- Students are all simply trying to figure out who they are and what their place in this world is. Every student has a story.

Brain
- Cognitive development varies from student to student and from grade to grade.
- Each student is uniquely different.
- Students can be auditory, kinesthetic, or visual learners.
- Creativity and multiple opportunities to create are essential.
- Students learn they have a choice in how they conduct themselves.
- Students learn focus with age.

Ears
- Rich language experiences across the curriculum help build vocabulary.
- Being read to is essential and creates a love for reading.
- A kind word is heard and can go a long way.
- Classical music can be a great calming force.
- Students respond better to a low, calming voice rather than shouting.

Heart
- Every student wants to feel good.
- Students need to be shown love and respect.
- Students love structure and consistency.

Stomach
- Students need proper nutrition to effectively learn.
- A hungry student will be too distracted to focus.

Legs
- Students need to run and exercise.
- When leaving the classroom, always send students in pairs with a pass.
- Think about what it would be like to walk in their shoes for a day.

The Organized Teacher's Guide to

Setting Up a Terrific Classroom

First-Day Checklists

First-Day Room Checklist

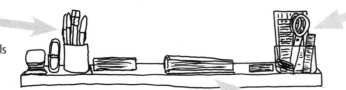

☐ **Desk Arrangement** (equal access to front of room)

☐ **Teacher's Station/Desk** (where you keep all your materials/paperwork)

☐ Stapler
☐ Tape
☐ Pens, pencils
☐ Markers
☐ Notepad

☐ Referrals
☐ Supply requests
☐ Staples
☐ Paper clips
☐ Tacks

☐ **School Binder** (provided or create your own)
   ☐ Class roster, calendar
   ☐ Schedules, emergency plan, teacher/class list
   ☐ School plan/policies, discipline plan

☐ **Hall Passes** (office, nurse, boys' and girls' restroom passes)
   • Make from word cards and cord.
   • Label with room number (and art, if desired).
   • Laminate (see template).

☐ **Welcome Sign**
   • You may need a class sign to pick up class on first few days. Then attach it to the door.

☐ **Bulletin Boards**
   • Blank canvasses with borders in first days
   • Create them the first few weeks, then approximately every six weeks.
   • Content areas: Math, Writing, Language Arts
   • Social Science or Science (alternate if needed)

☐ **Calendar**
   • An excellent learning tool
   • Use what works for you.
   • You can also purchase pocket chart version.
   • Students can create or color numbers each month to match themes.

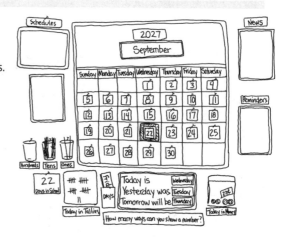

2

☐ Teacher Station

- Stapler, staples, scissors
- Masking and scotch tape, and tissues or paper towels
- Markers, pencils, pens, dry eraser and dry erase board, or chart paper
- Paper clips, sticky notes, and note paper
- Word cards or flash cards
- Student-lined paper and plain paper
- Extra pens, pencils, markers

☐ Closet (for coats and backpacks)

☐ Centers (Listening, Math, Writing, Science, Art)

- Introduce one at a time (one per week).
- Introduced and practiced by the whole class
- Establish center rules.
- Select independent activities.

☐ Library

- Group books by genre or theme.
- Place in bins or use laminated paper dividers.

☐ Game Shelf

- Organize games in one location.
- Introduce games one at a time (one per week).
- Establish rules and times.

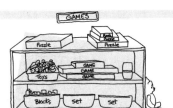

☐ Computers

- Establish computer rules.
- Introduce to small group.
- Pair up computer buddies.

☐ Manipulatives Shelf

- Organize manipulatives in one location.

☐ Table Kits

- Crayons (in resealable bags), books, manipulatives, flash cards

☐ Board

- Teacher's name
- Aide's name
- Student count (boys, girls, total)
- Markers or chalk
- Eraser (chalk or dry)
- Dry erase spray
- Date
- Room number

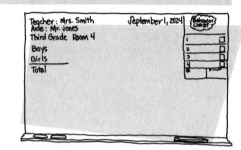

☐ Classroom Conduct

- The whole class establishes three to five rules.
- You guide through questioning.
- Rules should be clear, concise, and comprehensive.
- Emphasize the positive (avoid "do not").

☐ Schedule

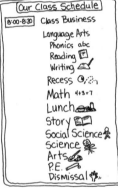

- Check for district- or state-mandated time frames (e.g., ninety minutes of P.E. per week).
- Reference other grade-level schedules.
- Use word cards/attach times = flexibility.
- Laminate.
- You may need to post daily on the board (with objectives)—check with your school.

☐ "We're Out" Sign

- Place on outside of classroom door.
- Change locations when out of room.
- Important for parents, office, and other teachers (see template)

☐ Behavior Chart

- Students collaborate on table names.
- Emphasize the positive.
- Tally points for good behavior.
- Reward winning table(s) at the end of the day.
- Note good behavior.
- Remind student(s) with incomplete work.

First-Day Student Checklist

Student Start-Up Items

☐ **Student Name Tags (K–1)**

(student's name, teacher's name, room number)

☐ **Desk Name Tags**

(student's first and last names)

☐ **Writing Tools**

Pencils

K–2

Colored Pencils/Pens

2–5

Highlighters

Crayons

☐ **Paper**

Lined paper

Story paper (K–2)

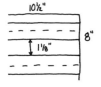

Kindergarten

First

Second–third

Fourth–fifth

☐ **Student Texts or Workbooks**

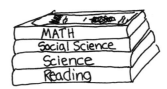

☐ **Journal**

(school supplied or teacher made)

☐ **Homework Folder**

Inside

Outside

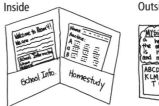

Kindergarten and first-grade folders can have:

- ABCs, numbers
- sight words
- colors
- shapes

Third- through fifth-grade folders vary (see template).

☐ **Student Information and Emergency Card**

☐ **Welcome Letter**

- Welcome/summaries
- Schedule
- Year overview
- Home study
- Attendance
- Discipline
- Curriculum

First-Day Teacher Checklist

☐ Referral File
- File is for all documented referrals.
- Establish a new file for each year.
- Save for three years (legal documents).

☐ Note File
- File is for all correspondence from home.
- Establish a new file for each year
- Note excuses on attendance record.
- Save for three years (legal documents).

☐ Parental Consent File
- File is for all formal consent forms. (SSTs, testing, field trips, etc.)
- Establish a new file for each year.
- Save for three years (legal documents), unless requested by office.

☐ Referrals
- Office and nurse referral forms
- Legal documents, save in the file marked referrals.

☐ Role Sheet or Attendance Cards
- Inquire about school attendance policy.
- Enter student the first day physically present.
- Record all absences.
- If excused, record and file excuse (check school policy).

☐ Personal Information or Emergency Card
- In office
- Check school or district policy.

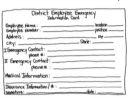

☐ Pens
- Black is good for official documentation.
- * Purple/red for grading

☐ Pencils
- No. 2 is for official forms.
- A good eraser is important!

☐ Assorted Markers
- Water-based for posters and cards
- Dry erase for board
- * Highlighters

☐ Sharpie Markers
- Permanent marker
- Excellent for illustrations
- Excellent for outlining

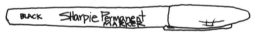

☐ Overhead Markers
- Wipes clean with water and paper towel.
- Use for overheads or laminated surface (e.g., behavior chart).

☐ **Tape**

Scotch™ Tape
- General taping

Masking Tape
- Heavier taping

Book-Binding Tape
- Binding and portfolios

Clear Packing Tape
- Mounting art and charts
- Portfolio binding

☐ **Sticky Putty**

☐ **Stapler and Staples**

☐ **Paper Clips**
- Both small and large are useful.

☐ **Sticky Notes**
- Very useful
- Notes, book marking, student postings, teacher's comments

☐ **Note Paper**
- Notepads are handy for writing notes to other teachers, home, etc.

☐ **Scissors**

☐ **Lined Tag**
- Tag board (lined or unlined)
- Posters, charts, portfolios (folded and bound)

☐ **Sentence Strips**
- Sentence strips
- Bulletin boards, pocket
- Charts, sequencing, labeling, etc.

☐ **Word Cards**
- Word cards (flash or word walls)
- Vocabulary, spelling, sight words, name plates, etc.

☐ **Pointer**
- Great tool for tracking and reading
- Students love to use—good reward.

☐ **Yardstick**

YARDSTKK

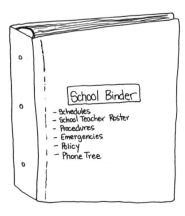

☐ School Teacher/Room List
- Useful to have
- Contact list of other teachers

☐ School Procedures
- Know your school.
- Getting a sub, discipline plan
- Schedules: rain or snow, early releases
- Dismissals: regular, early
- Yard and lunch procedures

☐ Emergency Policy
- Know the protocols for your school.
- Emergency traffic patterns and exits
- Emergency kits

☐ School Policies
- Every school is different.
- Know your school and the law.
- Classroom visitors, weapons, etc.

☐ Staff Phone Tree
- Very helpful
- Subs, questions, confirmations, etc.

☐ Teacher Guidebooks
- An excellent resource
- Spend time and get to know your guides and curriculum.
- Ask other teachers how they use them.

☐ Lesson Plans
- Planning is important! Be Prepared!
- Keep up weekly—they can be part of an evaluation.
- May use objective, motivation, activity, follow-up, standard(s), evaluation (check school or district requirements)
- Tailor your plans to meet requirements, your style, and your comfort level.

☐ Grade Book
- Recording scores and assessments is important.
- It is your evidence of a student's progress.
- It is necessary for report cards, evaluations, retentions, and parent conferences.
- Get in the habit of recording each week.

Sample Room Setups

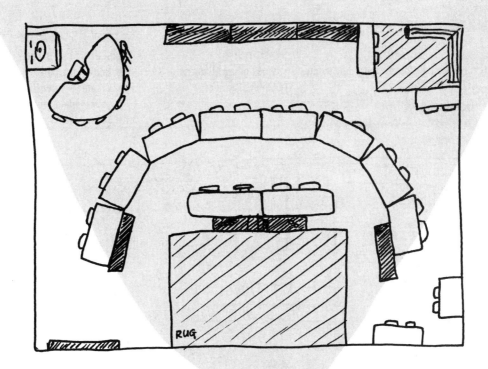

There are many ways to go about setting up a classroom. Many teachers like clustering desks together in lower grades, while others prefer a U-shape or rows for upper grades or secondary classrooms. It all depends on what you are trying to accomplish with your students. And just because you begin the year/semester with one setup doesn't mean you can't change it if it's not working. In this section, you will see a variety of elementary classroom setups. You will also want to consider setting up secondary classrooms in the form of two sides of the room facing one another or a U-shape design to engage all students if most of your teaching comes from the front of the room.

Primary Classroom Examples
Kindergarten

The kindergarten classroom is a room filled with organized activity, and it is arranged to facilitate that activity. The rug is the center of students' learning and its position is very important. Students often work in small groups facilitated by the teacher, an aide, or a parent volunteer. The flow of traffic and setup of these group stations is important for smooth transitions and minimal distractions. Establishing a routine and sticking to it will help facilitate a kindergarten classroom. Visit and observe other classrooms to see what works and why it works. Networking builds relationships and saves time! Set up your room to work for you, your students, and your program.

Do I have . . .
- a sink area?
- soap, paper towels, cleanser?

Library
- Books arranged by theme

Station II
- Small-group instruction
- Materials station

Listening Center
- Books on tape
- Create your own books on tape with stories from your reading series.
- Dictate letters on tape to go with your lessons.

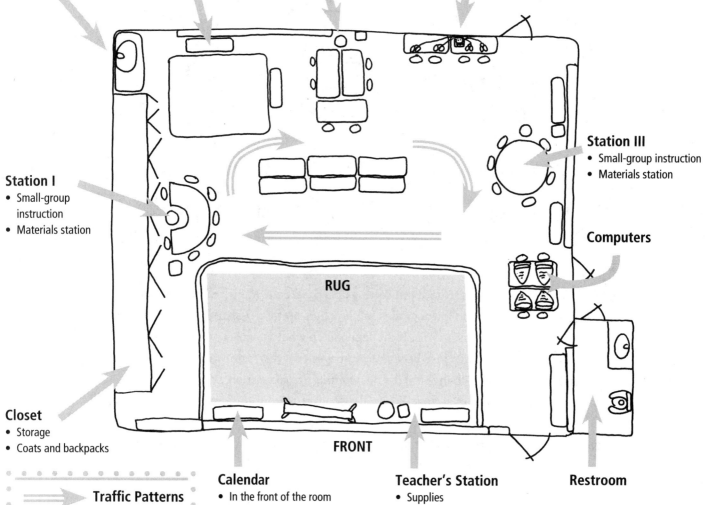

Station III
- Small-group instruction
- Materials station

Station I
- Small-group instruction
- Materials station

Computers

Closet
- Storage
- Coats and backpacks

RUG

FRONT

Calendar
- In the front of the room
- Resource tool

Teacher's Station
- Supplies
- Instructional materials
- Rewards

Restroom

➡ **Traffic Patterns**

➡ **Components**

10

First and Second Grades

The primary classroom is a place of activity. You need to consider equal access to the board and areas of instruction, traffic patterns, and your personal comfort and ease of instructional delivery. You may change the room several times throughout the year until you settle into what works for you. You may also change students' seats as you become more familiar with their personalities and work habits. Reorganization can offer a refreshing change for both you and your students.

Do I have . . .

- equal access for all students?
- a teacher's station?

→ Traffic Patterns

→ Components

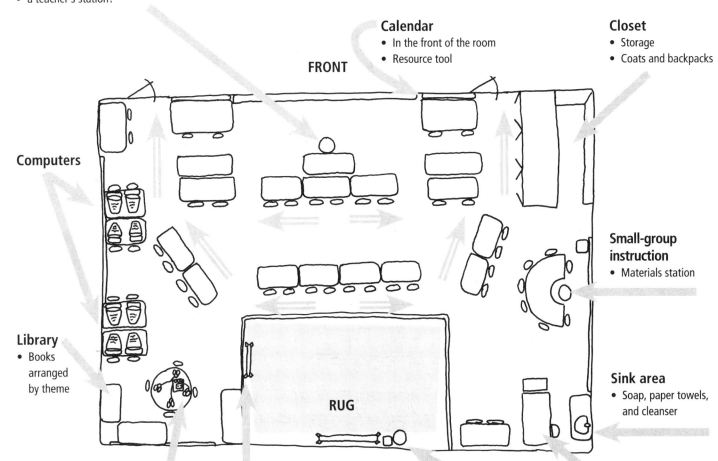

Calendar
- In the front of the room
- Resource tool

FRONT

Closet
- Storage
- Coats and backpacks

Computers

Small-group instruction
- Materials station

Library
- Books arranged by theme

RUG

Sink area
- Soap, paper towels, and cleanser

Listening Center
- Books on tape
- Create your own books on tape with stories from your reading series and your own questions.
- Create dictations on tape to go with your lessons.

Math Station
- Numbers chart
- Chart paper
- Manipulatives

Teacher's Station
- Supplies
- Instructional materials
- Rewards

Teacher's Desk
- Teacher's filing cabinet
- Resource files
- Monthly files for holidays, events, history
- Reading and math support files
- Agendas and trainings (save for possible credential renewal hours)

First and Second Grades

This is yet another example of a first- or second-grade classroom setup. Again, you need to consider equal access to the board and areas of instruction, traffic patterns, and your personal comfort and ease of instructional delivery. In this example, the rug is in the front of the room. The rug, especially in kindergarten and first grade, is an area of primary instruction, and its location is important.

Try an arrangement for a while and see if it works for you; if it doesn't work, change it. These examples are only suggestions, and your room may be different in its setup. Visit other classrooms at your grade level, too. They are an excellent resource for discovering what works.

Do I have . . .
- equal access for all students?
- a teacher's station?

Teacher's Station
- Supplies
- Instructional materials
- Rewards

Calendar
- In the front of the room
- Resource tool

Traffic Patterns

Components

Computers

Closet
- Storage
- Coats and backpacks

Library
- Books arranged by theme

Small-group instruction
- Materials station

Sink area
- Soap, paper towels, and cleanser

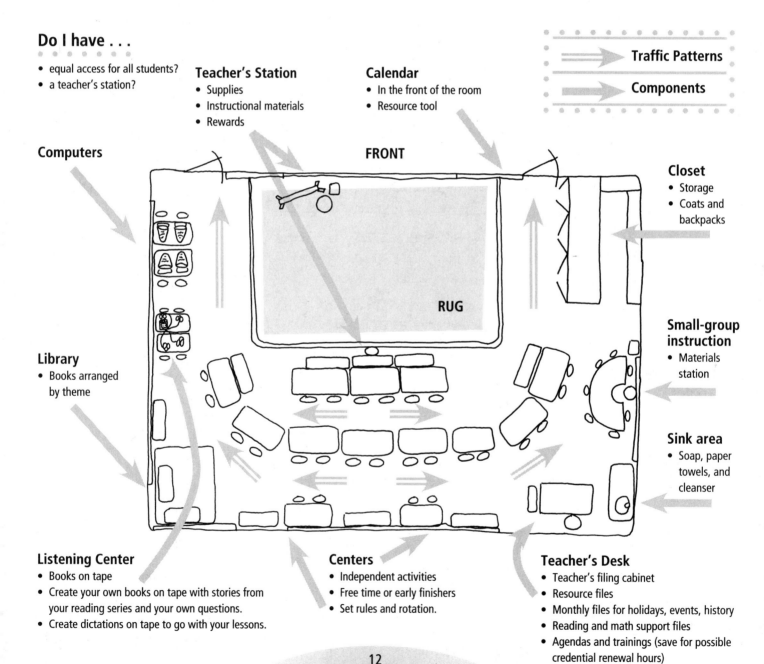

FRONT

RUG

Listening Center
- Books on tape
- Create your own books on tape with stories from your reading series and your own questions.
- Create dictations on tape to go with your lessons.

Centers
- Independent activities
- Free time or early finishers
- Set rules and rotation.

Teacher's Desk
- Teacher's filing cabinet
- Resource files
- Monthly files for holidays, events, history
- Reading and math support files
- Agendas and trainings (save for possible credential renewal hours)

Third Grade

Third-grade classrooms don't always have rugs, but if there is space, a rug is nice to have as a meeting spot. Typically, instruction is done with students in their seats. As with any grade, you need to consider equal access to the board and areas of instruction, traffic patterns, and your personal comfort and ease of instructional delivery. You may change your room as you find what works for you.

This is an example of a working classroom. Your room may be different in proportion and layout, and you may have more, less, or different furniture to arrange. This example, along with your personal creativity, can help you organize your room. It is also important to visit other classrooms at this grade level to see what is working or is standard for your school. Networking is very important and saves time.

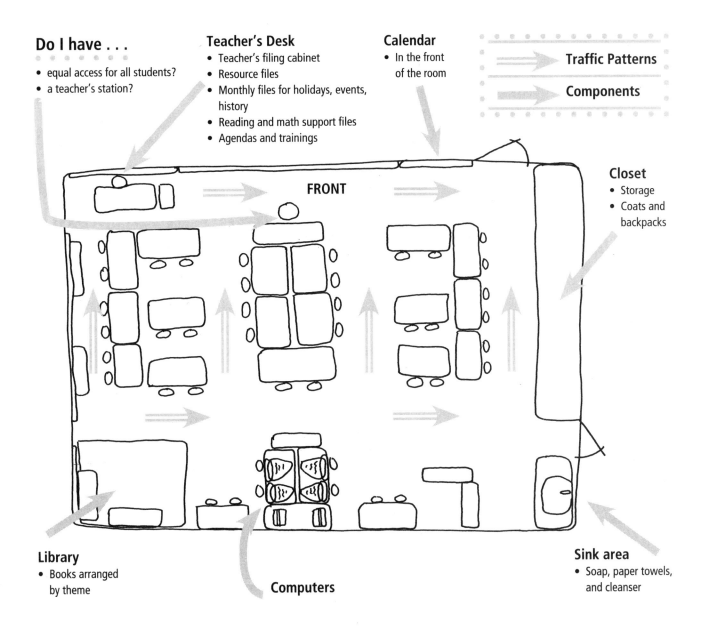

Do I have . . .
- equal access for all students?
- a teacher's station?

Teacher's Desk
- Teacher's filing cabinet
- Resource files
- Monthly files for holidays, events, history
- Reading and math support files
- Agendas and trainings

Calendar
- In the front of the room

Traffic Patterns

Components

FRONT

Closet
- Storage
- Coats and backpacks

Library
- Books arranged by theme

Computers

Sink area
- Soap, paper towels, and cleanser

Fourth Through Sixth Grades

In fourth through sixth grades, instruction is done with students sitting in their seats. A good chair/stool is important to have when delivering instruction. (The majority of the time is spent moving around the room, but this will offer an occasional break.) You need to consider equal access to the board/areas of instruction, traffic patterns, and your personal comfort and ease of instructional delivery. This example, along with your personal creativity, can help you organize your room. It is important to visit other classrooms to see what is working or is standard for your school.

Do I Have . . .

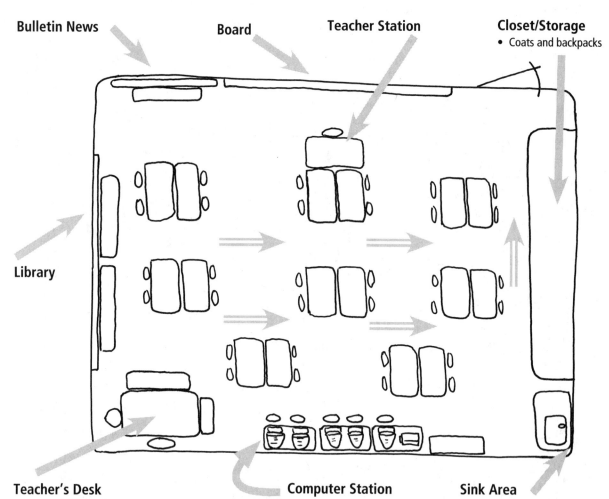

Traffic Patterns

Components

Bulletin News

Board

Teacher Station

Closet/Storage
• Coats and backpacks

Library

Teacher's Desk
• Teacher's filing cabinet
• Resource files
• Monthly files for holidays, events, history
• Reading and math support files
• Agendas and trainings

Computer Station

Sink Area
• Soap, paper towels, cleanser

Classroom Management

This section will help you consider how you have setup the classroom environment to keep things throughout the day flowing with ease. Think about how you can best meet your student's needs, their interests, their access to you, and all classroom materials.

Calendar

Calendars are an integral part of the classroom. They not only teach about time in days, months, and years, but they can also be a powerful tool to reinforce important math skills on a daily basis. Lower grades can use the calendar to review counting, place value, and money. Upper grades can use the calender to reinforce math skills as well as learn about weather and temperature.

Remember to make your calendar come alive. Start with what you can handle then expand as you feel more comfortable. Choose a student daily or weekly to set up and lead the class in a daily calendar review.

Weather and Temperature

- You can use a calendar to teach past, present, and future.
- Sunny, cloudy, foggy, windy, rainy, snowy
- Hot, warm, cool, cold, freezing
- Upper grades can deal with temperature, wind speeds, barometer readings, etc.
- Weather kits can be purchased at a teacher supply store or toy store.

Postings

- Easy references and reminders
- Schedules
- School bulletins and news
- Schedule reminders

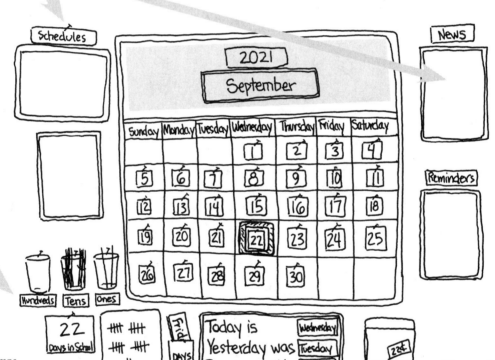

Place Value

- Ones
- Tens
- Hundreds
- Group daily.
- Move to next cup.
- Record number.
- You can record in columns.

H	T	O
	2	2

Tallies

- Record the date in tallies.
- Count by fives or ones.
- Use a heavy laminated surface and overhead markers or scrap paper.

Past, Present, Future, or Days

- Practice verb tense.
- Practice days of the week.
- Expand into daily journals.
- "Write a sentence for each."
  - Today, I am . . .
  - Yesterday, I was . . .
  - Tomorrow, I will be . . .

Money Tool

- Count the date in money.
- "How many ways can we show twenty-two cents?"
  - Choose an example.
  - Show in coins.
  - Write on paper.
- Have several baggies of change.
- Use a money pocket chart.

16

Helper Chart

Assigning class jobs to students teaches responsibility, assists you in the management of your classroom, and gives students a sense of ownership over their learning environment. Students enjoy helping out and can be rotated weekly to give everyone a chance to fill each job position. One easy way to manage this is with a helper chart. This example is easy to facilitate, and you can ask other teachers how they manage this. Initially, students—especially those in the primary grades—will need to be trained to establish a routine.

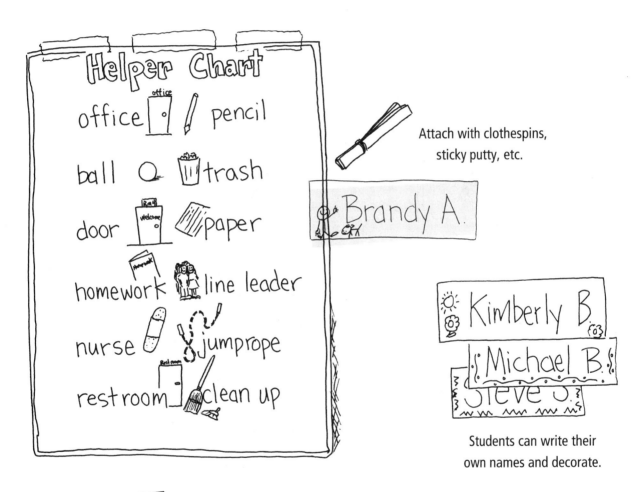

Attach with clothespins, sticky putty, etc.

Students can write their own names and decorate.

A pocket chart and word cards can be used.

- Select appropriate jobs.
- Have clear expectations.
- Pair students if necessary or if they need to leave the room (office monitor).
- Students can write why they would be good for a job.
- Create a job application.

Daily Class Schedule

A class schedule needs to be posted in the classroom, giving the breakdown of your daily schedule. It should reflect a well-balanced program that includes all curricular areas. Each district or state has its own mandated minutes of instruction required for each subject area. Check with your school for a breakdown of these minutes and look at other teachers' schedules on your grade level. Adapt a schedule that meets the requirements. Some teachers leave this posted and/or write a daily schedule on the board to follow that is specific to each particular day. Schedules can change with assemblies, performances, and such, and staying flexible is important.

Do I have:

- ☐ all subject areas or activities listed?
- ☐ word cards?
- ☐ district- or state-mandated subject time blocks?
- ☐ lined tag?
- ☐ tape (clear packing)?
- ☐ sticky putty?
- ☐ markers?

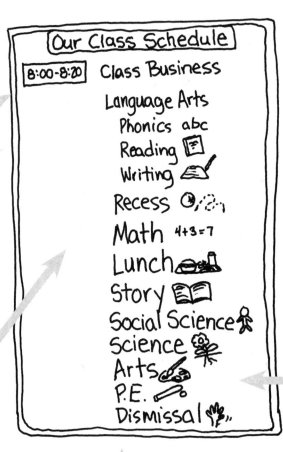

- Use word cards/attach times. This gives you flexibility. You can change your schedule times as needed.

- Place time intervals on word cards and attach to the left.
- Rearrange as the schedule changes.

- Illustrate or let students illustrate.
- Cut and paste selected illustrations.

- Write the subjects on the right.

- Reference other grade-level schedules.
- Some schools may have you also post a daily schedule on board (with objectives).
- Check for district- or state-mandated time frames (e.g., ninety minutes of P.E. per week).

Door Signs

A door sign is very important. Your school needs to be aware of you and your class's whereabouts in case of an emergency or if a parent/guardian needs his or her child, and a sign lets the school staff know where to find you. It is unprofessional if the school has to track you and your class down. It is easy to create a door sign that always lets others know where you are. You can use this template, and you can even choose to cut and paste it to a paper plate to create a spinner sign.

Sorry we missed you!

We are ___ in the computer lab.

Room: 35
Grade: 5
Teacher: Mr. Smith

Attach labels with double-sided tape, sticky putty, or a paper clip.

Color, laminate, and clearly label your door sign.

Keep labels near the door in an envelope attached to the wall.

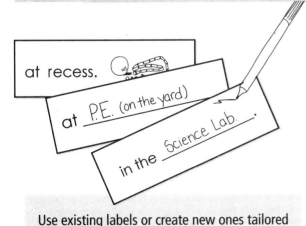

at recess.

at P.E. (on the yard)

in the Science Lab.

Use existing labels or create new ones tailored to your school's situation. Color and laminate.

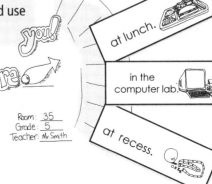

Attach labels to a paper plate and use a spinner.

at lunch.

in the computer lab.

at recess.

Room: 35
Grade: 5
Teacher: Mr. Smith

Door Sign
Master

Sorry we missed you!

We are

Room: _____ Grade: _____

Teacher: _____

Door Sign

Color and cut out sign and location tags. Glue to card stock. Laminate.

Post sign on door so administrators, parents, and other teachers will know where you are when not in the classroom.

Keep tags in an envelope mounted on inside wall of classroom.

Use sticky putty or tape to attach the tag denoting your class location when not in the room.

This is a great job for a monitor! Even younger students can read labels with visual clues.

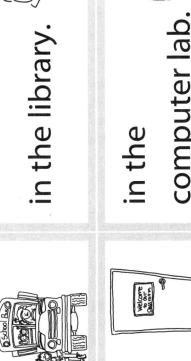

at lunch.

in the library.

in the
computer lab.

in the auditorium.

on a field trip.

in Room _____.

in the _____

in the _____

at _____

at recess.

in the _____

at _____

Boy Pass

Room: _____ Grade: _____ Teacher: _____

Girl Pass

Room: _____ Grade: _____ Teacher: _____

Hall Passes

Office Pass

Room: _____ Grade: _____ Teacher: _____

Nurse Pass

Room: _____ Grade: _____ Teacher: _____

School Binder

Having school information and policies at your quick disposal can be very important in facilitating an organized classroom. Many schools provide you with a binder containing their policies and procedures. Some schools provide you with bulletins that contain this information. You will refer to them throughout the year, and establishing and maintaining a binder is an excellent way to manage this paperwork. Always update binder with any new material you receive. These are suggestions for what to include.

Teacher/Room List
- Useful to have
- Can contact other teachers

School Procedures
- Know your school.
- Getting a sub
- Discipline plan
- Schedules: rain or snow early releases
- Dismissals: regular, early
- Yard and lunch procedures

Emergency Policy
- Know protocols for your school.
- Know emergency traffic patterns and exits.
- Emergency kits

School Information
- Very helpful for grant writing
- School population and makeup
- Services
- Resources

Staff Phone Tree
- Very helpful
- Subs, questions, confirmations, etc.

School Policies
- Every school is different.
- Know your school and the law.
- Classroom visitors
- Retention
- Releasing a student
- Attendance and absences
- Support referrals and testing

Schedules
- Daily school hours
- Current school calendar
- Holidays
- Vacations
- Minimum, shortened days
- Teacher workdays
- Conferences
- Reporting periods
- Duty schedule

Classroom Information
- Class roster
- Student phone list
- Special or pull-out student programs
- Reporting grade sheets

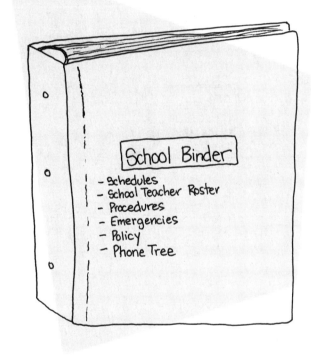

- Three-ring binder (about a two-inch one)
- Plastic sheet protectors

Student Table Kits

Student table kits are a great way to organize student materials. Some teachers use bins, baskets, or small containers. Visit other classrooms to see how other teachers manage student materials, books, etc. Tabletop bins are helpful because they can hold a variety of materials, and students can even share bins. Having students maintain their materials can be incorporated into the table point reward system—it is an excellent opportunity to teach responsibility and sharing.

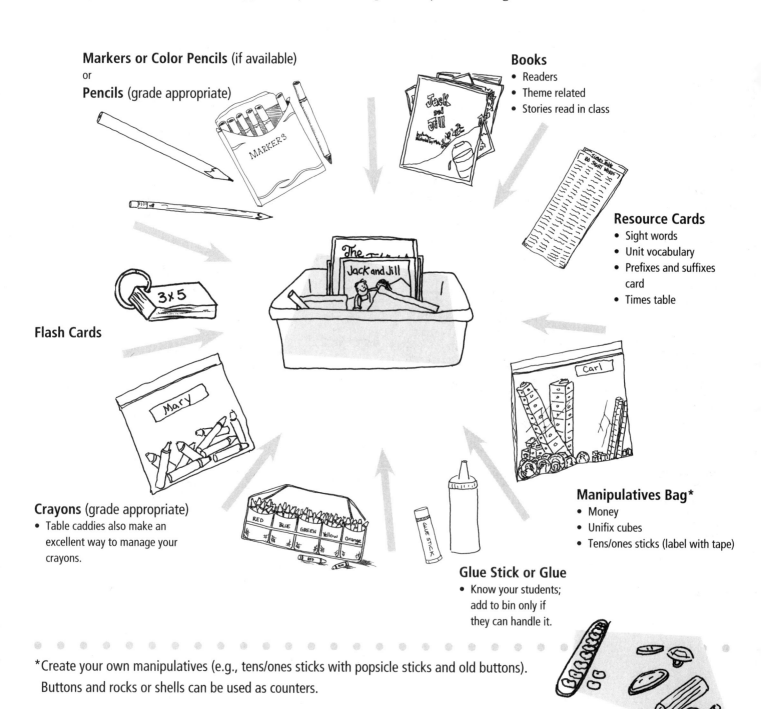

Markers or Color Pencils (if available)
or
Pencils (grade appropriate)

Books
- Readers
- Theme related
- Stories read in class

Resource Cards
- Sight words
- Unit vocabulary
- Prefixes and suffixes card
- Times table

Flash Cards

Crayons (grade appropriate)
- Table caddies also make an excellent way to manage your crayons.

Glue Stick or Glue
- Know your students; add to bin only if they can handle it.

Manipulatives Bag*
- Money
- Unifix cubes
- Tens/ones sticks (label with tape)

*Create your own manipulatives (e.g., tens/ones sticks with popsicle sticks and old buttons). Buttons and rocks or shells can be used as counters.

Classroom Rules and Behavior Management

Classroom Rules

Classroom rules are a necessity. Keeping them clear, concise, and comprehensive is important. As a great first-day activity, have students work together in small groups to collectively establish reasonable classroom rules, which will get them more invested than they would be if you had created the rules on your own. For secondary students, you may even want to approve different rules for different periods. Depending on what you teach and the grade levels you teach, these might need to vary based on subject and maturity level. This in turn creates an understanding of what is expected and clear expectations. Students are more likely to follow what they have established than what they are told. You, as the teacher, can guide your students to establish a set of fundamental rules that work for you and them. Three is a good number of rules for the lower grades and five for the upper grades. Keep in mind that they need to be specific. State the rule with positive wording—emphasize the "Dos" and avoid the "Don'ts."

Too Specific

Better

Suggestions for Creating Your Classroom Rules

1. Take suggestions from the whole class in group discussion and record on the board.
2. Challenge proposed rules: "If that is a rule, what happens if . . . ?" "How could we say that differently?"
3. Vote on five rules that everyone agrees on (as many as necessary for upper grades and secondary classrooms).
4. Create a poster that you can laminate and post on a classroom wall.
5. Add a drawing to make it more appealing. Students can color and even do the drawing.
6. Laminating it will help it hold up better.
7. Review with the class and display it in the front of the room where all can see.

Activities

Students can record rules and illustrate them to take home and share with their parents.

Students can create consequences for not following the rules.

Students can write stories about a student who doesn't follow the rules.

Classroom Behavior

It always helps to use some type of behavior system in your classroom. Students like structure. This behavior system can be designed specifically for your classroom. The different methods used to promote excellent behavior will make your job easier. The type of behavior method—how it works and the rules that are applied—can be left up to your imagination. These are some ideas to help you get started or to give you fresh ideas.

- Make your behavior program as positive as possible. Intrinsic rewards should always be the goal—even if the reward is good grades, a note home, or free time on the computer.

- Let the students control the chart, the more in charge the children are, the more powerful this tool will be for you.

- Share your behavior plan with students' parents so they know what to expect from your class and what they should expect of their child.

- Keep your reward or behavior system or chart in an open, visible place. Having students see it will help reinforce the message.

- Be consistent. Whatever your program may be, consistency works best!

- Evaluate your behavior modification program frequently and make changes if necessary.

- *Upper grades* (6–12)—Other behavior methods can be used that are more appropriate for the age of students you are teaching. For upper grades, try charts or graphs for no tardies, completed assignments, and finished homework.

- Make this system work for you! If your method is too difficult, too time consuming, or not working, try something new. What has worked for one year may not work for the next. Change is good!

Classroom Behavior Ideas

These ideas may help you set up a system for managing student behavior within your classroom. Remember to try new things, make modifications, and rotate ideas throughout the year. Students respond best to positive feedback and praise!

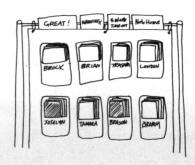

1. Behavior Chart

This is a chart where every student has a pocket with color-coded cards that are pulled as warnings. Each color has its own consequence or reward.

2. Name Cards

You can make cards for all of your students and give out stickers or stamps if they perform well or have good behavior. You can create a reward per number of stars earned.

3. Names on Chalkboard

Create a chart or list on the chalkboard where names can be written. For every good action, the student receives a check mark. This should only be used as a positive reward type of list.

4. Individual Behavior Cards

These cards can be used for individual students as you see fit. Again, these can have a student's name with a place to receive a star or a smiley face for good behavior.

Classroom Behavior Management Chart

Behavior management is vital to your success and the success of your students. Consistency is the key. Teams (four to six students) work well to teach cooperation and accountability. It is important to mix the students so that the teams are fair. Occasionally, a student has difficulty with the team effort; when this happens, see the progress and growth that has been made and award points based on that. If a student continues to affect the team, discuss the situation with the student and the team. If it continues, that student is making a choice not to reap the rewards of the team.

Do I have:

☐ Fair teams (mixed behavior levels)?
☐ Tables assigned to teams?
☐ Team-selected names?
☐ Understanding of rewards and consequences?

- Tallies are given throughout the day. The teacher is ultimately in control and can "catch" a table doing well, hence students can make it work to their advantage.

- Laminate and use overhead markers or mount team names to board and use chalk.

- Winning table(s) receive(s) reward (extra play, candy, early release to lunch or recess, etc.). Depending on needs, this can be at recess, at lunch, or at the end of the day (wean to longer stretches of time).

- Teams can collaboratively select their own names and sit at the same table(s).

- Can post names of students who need to complete assignment.
  - No recess
  - No free time

- Reserved for excellent behavior

Note poor behavior.

Warning system:
1. Name on teacher clipboard ✓
2. Time-out (five minutes) ✓✓
3. Office referral ✓✓✓
4. Note home ✓✓✓✓

Erase letter by letter as behavior improves

Circle Talks

Circle Talks are just what the name says, a gathering of students in a large circle to discuss and share on designated topics. These discussions can be used from kindergarten to twelfth grade. All students can benefit, regardless of their age. Often our students have no other means of sharing. A Circle Talk is a purposeful model to use in the classroom for encouraging dialogue, respect, and sharing ideas. It's an opportunity to develop a sense of community and for developing a way of communicating in the classroom. When everyone has a turn to be heard in a respectful and attentive way, the learning environment becomes more inclusive, accessible, and enjoyable.

    Talking Circles date back to First Nations leaders and their tribal councils. It was a process they developed to provide everyone with an opportunity to speak and be heard in a respectful manner. (http://www.firstnationspedagogy.ca/circletalks.html#)

Circle Talk Process

Why Circle Talks?
Circle Talks provide a safe platform for all students to share and be heard.

What does it look like?
Students sit in a large circle or pull their desks or seats into a circle so that everyone can be seen. Someone shares a topic or a question is asked. A designated object or a "talking stick" is passed from one student to the next. When a student possesses the object, he or she has the floor to respectfully comment on what has been said or share his or her perspective.

What do you need?
Historically a "talking stick" was used, but a variety of objects could be used, keeping in mind not to use something that could be potentially distracting. A small stuffed animal, a stone, a ball, a pine cone, and a shell are just a few examples of objects to consider.

What else?
✓ The discussion is passed along the circle, in a designated direction, from person to person.
✓ Only the person who has the designated object speaks.
✓ A student doesn't have to respond and can take a pass.
✓ Students are encouraged to speak from the heart, openly and honestly.
✓ Everything discussed in the circle stays in the circle.
✓ If time permits, a second round around the circle can take place.

Circle Talk Steps

1. **Remind.** Remind students that they should listen when others are speaking, they should be respectful, they speak from the heart, and what is discussed in the circle stays in the circle.

2. **Introduce.** A student or the teacher can introduce the topic or question that will be shared to the whole group before responding.

For example: How would you describe …? How do you feel about …? What is your idea of …? I feel sad when …. Be mindful that sometimes students can become emotional as they share.

3. **Begin.** The talking object is passed to the next person to share, comment, or pass. Remind students to share but be mindful of the time so that everyone gets a chance.

4. **Share.** Each student with the talking object responds to the prompt with a comment or can respectively share his or her perspective on what has been shared.

5. **Close.** Once everyone has had a turn, everyone is thanked and reminded that this was a safe space and what was shared stays in the circle.

Circle Talk Seating Chart

Class: _____   **Date:** _____

Classroom Incentives

Classroom incentives give students goals to achieve. These can serve as a motivation for the entire class or individual students. For incentive goals to work, you need to provide clear expectations and follow through on them. Incentive goals encourage teamwork and cooperation within the class. Individually, these goals can keep a student focused on a behavior or an academic goal. It is important to make each goal realistic and obtainable. Younger students will need a shorter wait time or reward/consequence time than older students. It is important to know your students and when they need to be encouraged or possibly rewarded. Be flexible, and allow them to know success. They can be weaned into longer intervals once a pattern is established.

Desired behavior goals can range from paying attention and participating during a lesson to staying on task and completing assignments. Desired academic goals can range from applying a grammar skill appropriately to achieving individual reading goals. Keep in mind that academic achievements will vary, so individual achievement must always be considered first, and then collective growth across all levels can be rewarded.

Whole-Class Incentives

Fill the Jar

- Students collectively fill a jar with marbles, rocks, or shells, etc.
- Each time students demonstrate desired behavior as a collective group or in small groups, a marble or selected object is added to the jar, and the jar is slowly filled.
- Once the jar is filled, the class is rewarded with a designated prize.

Note: Keep the goal obtainable. Start with a smaller jar to establish a pattern.

Stars

- Set up a chart to record a designated number of stars.
- Class receives stars for desired behavior.
- Once star count reaches the established number, a reward is given.

Note: Keep number obtainable; start with a lower number and then increase.

Fill the Fish Tank

- A fish tank, if permissible in your district, can be set up with no fish.
- Students can earn points to use toward adding fish to the tank.

Note: Always check district policy regarding animals in the classroom.

Fishbowl

- Students can keep fishbowl or class pet at their table for the day.
- Students can earn points to use toward keeping the pet for a day.

Note: Always check district policy regarding animals in the classroom.

Table Points

- Table teams are established and given names.
- Tally points are given for desired table behaviors throughout the day.
- Winning tables are rewarded daily at dismissal.
- Rewards can include stickers, pencils, snacks, etc.

Note: Table groups can be renamed according to themes (animals, modes of transportation, etc.).

Cushion Reward

- Students whose table group collectively wins the most points or achieves a set goal win the use of seat cushions for the week.

Note: Use the cushions that tie on to avoid slipping.

Individual Student Incentives

Popcorn Party

- Plan a popcorn or snack party prior to dismissal on Fridays
- Students who have received points for good behavior (an established number, e.g., three checks) can participate.
- This is very powerful.

Note: If permissible in your district, you can use a hot air popper, as the smell adds to the excitement. Always check first.

Sticker or Stamp Cards

- Index cards can be taped to each student's desk.
- Stickers or stamps are given for desired behavior.
- A set number is rewarded.
- Good for homework, class work, participation, etc.

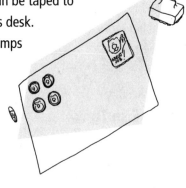

Individual Student Contract

- This is a personalized contract of behavior modifications. Teacher and student establish contract. Each student's input is important and helpful on his or her own contract (establishes meaning and purpose).

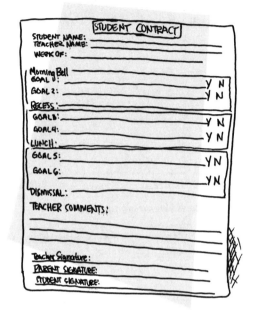

- Goals are explicit and concise.
- Student is observed throughout day and checked off on behavior.
- The contract is sent home daily or weekly for the parent/guardian to sign.

Citizen of the Week

- Students who have a good week (demonstrate good school citizenship) receive a weekly Good Citizenship Award.
- Can be as simple as an index card with a sticker labeled "Good Citizen."

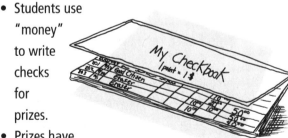

- Establish clear expectations, as with any reward.
- Notify parents to expect this weekly reward.
- Students are warned with name on board and further with checks beside name.
- Establish a set number of checks that would prevent students from getting their award and how they can work to remove checks and name.

Tickets

- Students earn tickets throughout the day.
- Students visit a prize chest on Fridays and exchange tickets for prizes.
- Prizes have established values.

Note: To avoid conflicts, always have students put their name on their tickets and keep them in a resealable bag with their name on it.

Student Checkbooks

- Students earn "money" for good behavior throughout the day or week.
- Students deposit and balance their checkbooks.
- Students use "money" to write checks for prizes.
- Prizes have designated values.

Behavior Contracts

These behavior contracts are meant to help you with particular students who have a hard time following rules. Of course, you can always make your own behavior contracts that pertain directly to the student you are working with. These contracts are helpful when you are dealing with a student who just can't stay on task, is unable to raise his or her hand, or does not complete in-class assignments. These contracts help modify a student's learning and provide one more layer of structure for them to be successful within the classroom.

- Circle the face depending on the student's performance on the particular goal.
- This behavior contract is more for daily behavior modification. Choose three specific desired behaviors.
- Send this card home each day to have the parent/guardian sign it.

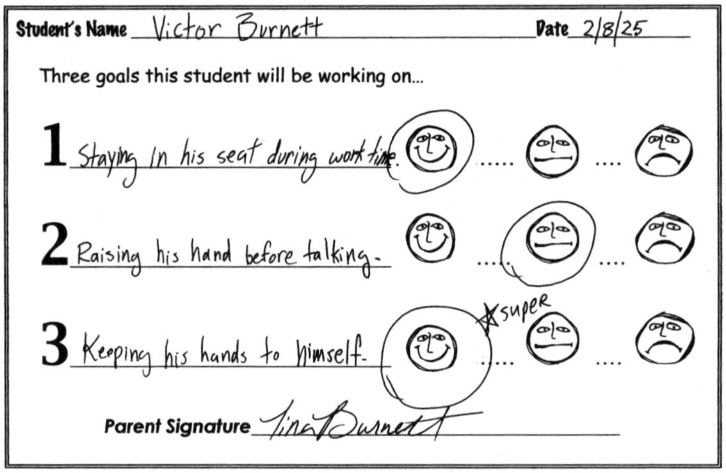
Student's Name Victor Burnett Date 2/8/25

Three goals this student will be working on...

1 Staying in his seat during work time.

2 Raising his hand before talking.

3 Keeping his hands to himself. *super

Parent Signature Tina Burnett

- This contract is a weekly behavior contract. The card can be sent home at the end of the five days.
- Each time the student demonstrates the desired behavior, a positive mark is given (try using star stickers, stamps, or a Bingo inker).
- Both contracts work well with the student receiving some type of reward for getting all positives or mostly positives.

Name Julie Hartmane Daily Behavior for the week of Feb 5

Parent signature Carol Hartmane

	Early Morning	Late Morning	After Lunch	Late Afternoon	Dismissal
Monday	★	★	—	★	★
Tuesday	★	★	★	★	★
Wednesday	★	★	★	—	★
Thursday	★	★	★	★	—
Friday	★	★	★	★	★

Behavior
Contract
(Faces)

Behavior
Contract
(Weekly)

Student's Name: _____ Date: _____

Three goals this student will be working on:

1. _____

2. _____

3. _____

Parent's Signature: _____

Name: _____ Daily Behavior for the Week of: _____

	Early Morning	Late Morning	After Lunch	Late Afternoon	Dismissal
Monday					
Tuesday					
Wednesday					
Thursday					
Friday					

Parent's Signature: _____

Student Contract

| Student Name: _____ | Grade: _____ |
| Teacher Name: _____ | Class: _____ |

WEEK: _____	GOALS	YES/NO
Morning _____ _____	Goal/s:	
Nutrition/Recess	Goal/s:	
Mid-Morning _____ _____	Goal/s:	
Lunch	Goal/s:	
Afternoon _____ _____	Goal/s:	
Dismissal	Goal/s:	

Comments: _____

_____

_____

Student Signature: _____ Teacher Signature: _____

Parent Signature: _____ Principal Signature: _____

Acknowledge students' good behavior by putting stickers or stamps on their card. Completed cards receive a designated award.

Good Job Cards
and Stamps

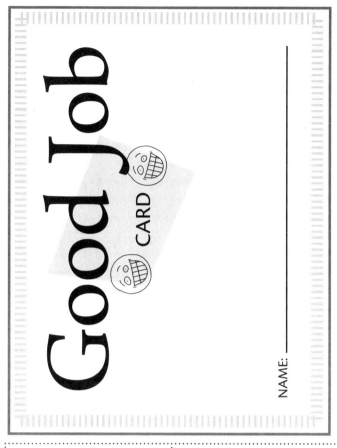

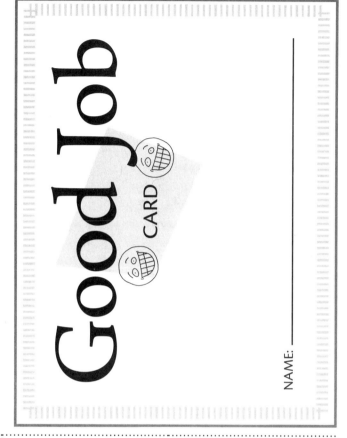

Good Job!	Good Job!	Good Job!	Good Job!
Good Job!	**Good Job!**	**Good Job!**	**Good Job!**
Good Job!	Good Job!	Good Job!	Good Job!
Good Job!	***Good Job!***	***Good Job!***	***Good Job!***
Good Job!	Good Job!	Good Job!	Good Job!
Good Job!	**Good Job!**	**Good Job!**	**Good Job!**
Good Job!	Good Job!	Good Job!	Good Job!
Good Job!	**Good Job!**	**Good Job!**	**Good Job!**
Good Job!	Good Job!	Good Job!	Good Job!

Awards Certificates

Award certificates are an easy and excellent way to motivate and recognize student performance. Planning out what and when you will present awards is important, not only for consistency but so you don't get overwhelmed. Making them a part of your program will give parents and guardians something to motivate their child to work towards. The following pages have a variety of certificates that can be tailored for your needs.

When to give:

- Weekly*
- Monthly
- Quarterly
- Every trimester
- Annually

*Be sure you can commit to this each week; consistency is the key. Otherwise, give out awards at various benchmarks throughout the year.

What to reward:

- Academics: language arts, reading, grammar, composition, math, science, social science
- The Arts: visual, music, dance, theatre/performing arts
- Health/P.E.
- Attendance
- Behavior
- Citizenship
- Other: book reports, math facts, books read, spelling, memorized poems/speeches

Perfect
Attendance
Award (Students)

Perfect
Attendance
Award

PERFECT ATTENDANCE
AWARD

This award certifies that

_____

has perfect attendance for

_____

_____   _____
Administrative Signature   Teacher Signature

Perfect Attendance Award

THIS AWARD CERTIFIES THAT

_____

HAS PERFECT ATTENDANCE FOR

_____

_____   _____
ADMINISTRATIVE SIGNATURE   TEACHER SIGNATURE

Student of
the Week
Award

Student of
the Month
Award

STUDENT OF THE WEEK AWARD

This award is given to

_____

for

_____

_____   _____
Administrative Signature   **Teacher Signature**

Student of the Month Award

This award is given to

_____

for

_____

_____   _____
Administrative Signature   Teacher Signature

STUDENT

RECOGNITION

THIS CERTIFICATE RECOGNIZES

FOR

TEACHER SIGNATURE

ADMINISTRATIVE SIGNATURE

Adademic

ACHIEVEMENT

This certificate recognizes

FOR OUTSTANDING ACADEMIC ACHIEVEMENT IN

FOR

DATE

ADMINISTRATIVE SIGNATURE

TEACHER SIGNATURE

Attendance Award

This certificate certifies that

has perfect attendance for

Teacher Signature

Administrative Signature

Growth Mindset

We now recognize how important a mistake can be. Every mistake shows us how not to do something and should be embraced as importantly as every success. We need to nurture this in our students and foster the growth mindset. This is the mindset of perseverance; it embraces the "not yet." With such a mindset, students have permission to keep trying, to embrace the struggle, and to know that they can improve.

The brain is like a muscle and can be strengthened. A **growth mindset** is always trying and reaching to do better. The opposite of a growth mindset is a **fixed mindset**. A fixed mindset is set in its ways, never believing that things can be improved. Our students need to be able to think outside the box, to take on challenges and persist through them. Those with the tenacity of a growth mindset will excel.

Students sometimes arrive with a fixed mindset; they are easily frustrated and quick to give up. We change that by modeling and nurturing the growth mindset.

Fixed Mindset

- Avoids a challenge
- Gives up too soon
- Doesn't seek or take advice or feedback very well
- Says things are *too hard*
- Makes *mistakes*
- Is threatened by the successes of others

You may hear comments like: *This is too hard. I can't do this. I quit. I am not good at this. I can't do any better. It's good enough.*

Growth Mindset

- Embraces a challenge
- Keeps trying and does his/her best
- Welcomes the advice and feedback of others
- Says, *This is difficult, but I will keep trying until I get it*
- Makes *opportunities* for how not to do something
- Praises and is inspired by the successes of others

You may hear comments like: *This is hard, but I will keep trying. Mistakes show me ways not to do it. Is this my best? What else can I add? I am on the right track. I will use another strategy. I am going to try what he/she did. I will train my brain to get better. I want a more difficult challenge.*

Consider your *own* mindset. Do you have a growth mindset? Do you model a growth mindset for your students?

Growth Mindset versus Fixed Mindset Brain Cards

Use these cards creatively to demonstrate growth versus fixed mindset. Students can color and glue them back-to-back to use as responses in a discussion. They could also write quotes that represent a growth versus fixed mindset, demonstrating each mindset.

Growth

Fixed

Growth

Fixed

Growth

Fixed

Classroom Organization

Parent Letter

Communication home is critical to the success of your classroom and the students. A welcoming opening letter to parents/guardians can set the tone for the year. This is a great way to introduce yourself, your classroom management plan, and your take on timeliness and absences. It's also a good place for you to share the curriculum and your homework policy. Ask other teachers what they do.

Create a letter that is personal and outlines your goals and policies. Here are some tips and ideas about what you may want to include in your letter home.

Policies and Procedures:
- Daily agenda
- Home-study policy and expectations
- Classroom rules
- Attendance policy
- School calendar
- Emergency contact form
- Sign and return portion
- Field-trip procedure
- Suggested materials needed

Home Support Suggestions:
- Read twenty minutes a day.
- Ask questions about what students read.
- Practice counting (primary).
- Practice multiplication facts.
- Practice spelling words orally.
- Go to the library.

Teacher:
- Be positive!
- Be concise and to the point.
- Tell a little bit about yourself.
- Give school your contact information.

School Information (check for):
- School contract or rules
- School calendar
- Testing calendar
- Emergency cards
- Lunch forms
- Student release forms

Goals and Expectations:
- Standards covered at grade level
- Goals you have established
- Behavior expectations
- Home support expectations

Weekly Parent Newsletter
Welcome to
Room 209
Date_____

Homework

Monday:

Tuesday:

Wednesday:

Thursday:

Friday:

Quote of the Month

Monthly Character Trait

Community Volunteer Opportunities

Standards of the Week

Monthly Curricular Topics

Classroom Organization

Organizing your classroom can keep it running smoothly throughout the day. Training your students in organizational procedures is important, and the first few weeks of school are critical in laying the foundations for your classroom. Organizing class work in a specific location makes for easy access. Having a designated home-study basket helps with its distribution. An office basket by the door is a convenient drop-off for anything from the office and limits interruptions. A designated home-study folder box keeps folders organized and makes for easy preparation when going home. A work template file box allows you to organize and file extras of your favorite resource templates and access them easily. Label these baskets to avoid confusion.

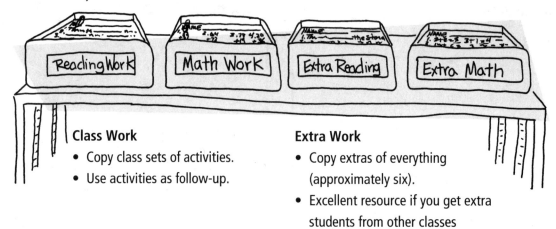

Class Work

- Copy class sets of activities.
- Use activities as follow-up.

Extra Work

- Copy extras of everything (approximately six).
- Excellent resource if you get extra students from other classes
- Provides work for early finishers

Home-Study Basket

- Holds daily home study
- Easy to distribute

Office Basket

- Paperwork from office
- Easy to access or distribute
- Keep near door.

Work Templates

- Organize resource templates.
- Copy extras so they are always available.
- Story papers, spelling forms, writing templates, etc.

Home-Study Folders

- Classroom monitor collects daily.
- Classroom monitor fills with new work each day.
- Easy access if student leaves early

Math

Reading

To Go Home

Office

Seat Work

Lined Paper

Math

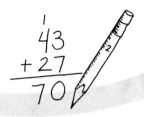

Reading

Paper

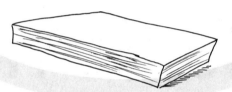

Science

Social Studies

To Be Graded

Writing Table

Organizing your writing table can make the writing process easier to facilitate. Having extra templates for each stage really helps. Consistency and repetition are the keys to successful writing. It is helpful to designate one location where students' ongoing writing folders and writing portfolios (completed work) are easily accessible. Making overheads of your writing templates or paper can be helpful to model whole-class writing. They are also helpful in singling out a particular skill (e.g., write a piece void of adjectives or capitals and then have the class model the editing on the overhead). It is best to focus on one skill and then apply it to students' writing.

Writing Process Templates

Writing-in-Progress Folders

Writing Portfolios

Writing Table

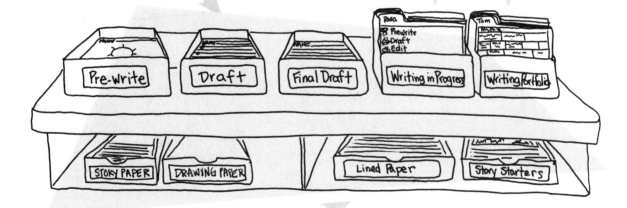

Pre-Write   Draft   Final Draft   Writing in Progress   Writing Portfolio

STORY PAPER   DRAWING PAPER   Lined Paper   Story Starters

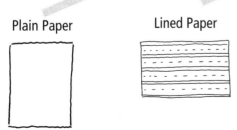

Plain Paper   Lined Paper

Possible Writing Templates or Paper

- Story starters (first sentence given, students complete)
- Letter template
- Theme paper (theme-related shape or border, e.g., bunny shape)
- Story paper (lines and illustration space)
- Minibook template pages
- Book-report forms

Portfolios

Student portfolios are a place for students to keep their best work. As with any portfolio, they should be reviewed periodically to update the work. Students can add or dictate why they have chosen a particular piece of work. A handful of work (up to ten pieces) can be kept in the portfolio. Portfolios can be used at parent conferences, with students sharing their best work and reflections. You may have separate folders for work samples that you choose to keep (work folders). Students can be easily trained to maintain their own portfolios. Younger students may need to be reminded or asked, "Do you want to put this in your portfolio?" It is easy to add items and then periodically review the portfolios as a whole, selecting approximately the best ten items to stay.

Front

- Leave room for name.

- Students can draw quarterly self-portraits to show growth.

- Book-binding tape or clear packing tape

Back

- Tag (full or half sheet)
- Folded and taped
- Large size is great for art assignments that are selected.

Work Folder
- Your selections
- Evidence of work progress

Assessment and writing portfolios can also be maintained. Check with your school's requirements for record keeping. Writing portfolios house students' writing assignments throughout the year. Assessment portfolios hold all formal assessments given throughout the year. Both have cover pages (found in the "Portfolios" section of this book) that attach to the outside of the folder and can be used to record results.

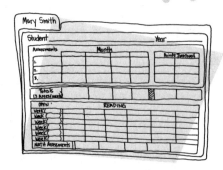

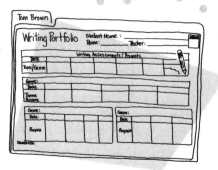

Assessment Boxes

Assessment boxes are an important tool for teaching. These boxes, composed of students' work, can provide you with important feedback on a student's progress within your class. These various boxes can also be useful during parent conferences or meetings with an administrator. Although you may currently have a system in place, these are just a few ideas as to how you could add to your already successful program or simply begin a few of these boxes.

For a colorful box, try going to a local office supply store and get colored folders.

Folders are easy to locate with good labels. Try creating a sheet that goes on the front of each folder that tells the contents of that particular folder. Some folder covers are included in this book (see "Portfolios") if you do not want to make your own.

Your students' portfolios can contribute to your grading as well as to filling out report cards.

There should be a current folder for each student in each box.

Three assessment boxes we recommend are Writing, Math, and Assessments.

Your portfolio boxes should be in a visible place in your room so that anyone walking in can see where they are. Easy access to these is always a good idea!

Easy-to-read labels can save you a lot of time when you are trying to locate a particular box or a student's folder.

Filing Cabinet Ideas

Filing cabinets are a great source for organization within any classroom. Even in a technology-oriented world, teachers often become inundated with thousands of papers, assessments, notes, and worksheets! Using files can save you the headache of a messy room, lost thematic units, and lost papers of great importance. Below are a few different types of files you may wish to keep or add to your system. Remember that these are just to get you started—try thinking of other titles you can use for folders.

Holidays

- Halloween
- Thanksgiving
- Christmas
- Valentine's Day
- St. Patrick's Day
- Easter
- Fourth of July

Class Subjects

- Math
- Science
- Art
- Language Arts
- Social Studies
- Physical Education
- Literature
- Health/Nutrition

Themes

- Pirates
- Plants
- Dinosaurs
- Ancient Egypt
- Solar system
- Sea life
- Birds
- Animals
- Native American civilizations
- Continents
- Family
- Games
- Homes
- Life cycles
- Transportation
- The market
- Community helpers
- Farms

Types of Writing

- Poetry
- Short stories
- Letters
- Descriptive
- Recipes
- Informative
- Procedures

Months

- September
- October
- November
- December
- January
- February
- March
- April
- May
- June
- July
- August

Movement Within the Classroom

No matter what grade level or subject you teach, you can establish some patterns and rules for how students move throughout the classroom. Traffic patterns help establish safe and smooth movement throughout the room so that students can get from one destination to the next without having their space impeded with overflowing backpacks, unnecessary chairs, and materials not in their place.

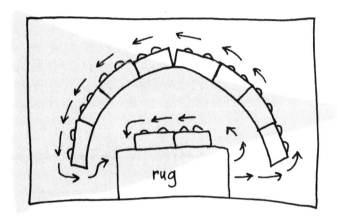

Remember to:

- keep these patterns simple!
- establish a rhythm.
- streamline transitions.
- review daily.

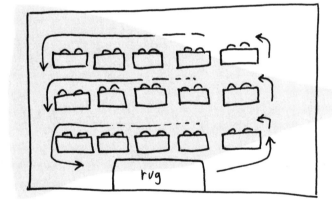

Reasons for Use:

- Getting and putting away backpacks
- Lining up for recess and dismissal
- Going to and from the rug
- Emergencies

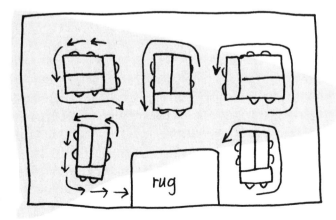

Try:

- different patterns.
- asking other teachers for advice and about what they do to succeed.
- using a signal to get students moving in the right direction.

Classroom Centers

Classroom Centers

Classroom centers are an important part of self-learning and exploration. They can range from an organized station on a desktop to a designated area in the room for an activity. A rotation can be established so that students move from center to center and everyone gets a turn. Centers do not have to be complex or involved. Set up centers that support your themes or units. Earlier finishers can go to their favorite center, but watch out for students who rush to get through early just to go to centers. Train your students so that early finishers understand that they must still present quality work before they can move on to centers is important. Liken their work to their "ticket" to a center. Establish an order: first, assigned seat work (tasks 1, 2, and 3); second, a choice from the extra work basket; third, a center. Have students check each other's work for quality and accuracy, sign each other off, and then proceed to centers. It is nice to have enough thought-out center activities, from established centers to a simple game, so that your entire class can participate if need be.

Always introduce a center to the class and establish center rules. Students can work in pairs.

Center Ideas

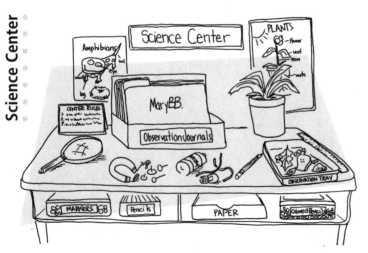

Math Center

Ten Activity Ideas

1. Counting or sorting
2. Weighing (scale)
3. Measuring (ruler), e.g., string
4. Story problems
5. Flash cards
6. Tangrams (geometric patterns)
7. Practicing fact sheets or timers
8. Calculators
9. Measurement in volumes
10. Problem of the day

Science Center

Ten Activity Ideas

1. Growing beans in baggies
2. Magnifying glass (observations)
3. Electricity (battery or lightbulb)
4. Magnets (metal vs. nonmetal)
5. Animal or dinosaur models
6. Simple machines
7. Life cycle (butterflies, tadpoles)
8. Sink or float
9. Reactions (simple)
10. Classroom pet (approved)

Note: General activity is observing, recording observations, and illustrating.

Publishing Center

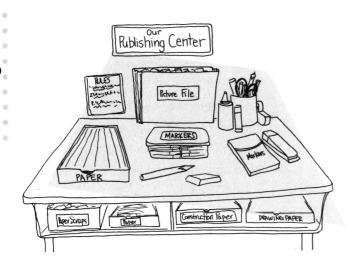

Ten Activity Ideas

1. Writing about a magazine or calendar picture
2. Creating a minibook
3. Creating a comic strip
4. Finishing a story starter
5. Creating a bound book
6. Writing a poem
7. Writing a letter (to a friend or a character)
8. Creating a greeting card
9. Writing a story on a theme template
10. Writing directions or instructions to a prompt

Note: Desks make great centers and provide extra storage. Students can keep ongoing activities in a folder.

Clay Table

Clay Table Hints

- Cover desk with tag and tape down edges.
- Do not place the desk in the sun.
- Clay colors will mix together.
- Students need to wash hands—clay can be messy.
- Excellent for increased dexterity.
- Students of all ages love it!

Rug Center (Primary)

Ten Activity Ideas

1. Board games
2. Building sets
3. Puzzles
4. Teacher's station (playing school)
5. Dress-up (trunk)
6. Animal figures
7. Train set
8. Doll house
9. Electronic games (portable)
10. Marbles or jacks

Note: Can have up to about six at the rug

Listening Center

Listening Center Hints

- Train students in using cassette/CD player/tablet/MP3 player.
- Use Books on tape or create your own MP3/digital recording.
- Can be interactive- e.g. Dictation, questions
- Store books in zip-lock plastic bags.
- Number/Color code/ level books.
- Tablet applications for listening to stories.

Computer/Tablet Center

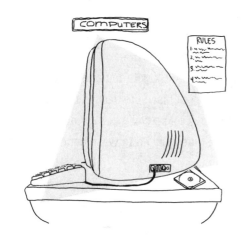

Computer/Tablet Hints

- Always introduce each game to the class.
- Find a dependable student who is good with computers and train him or her to assist.
- Have a computer/tablet sign-in to keep track of visits.
- Have a set of established rules.

Sample Rules

1. Play only the currently set game.
2. Take turns.
3. Only print with permission.
4. Use the computer with care and respect.
5. Leave the computer as you found it.

Tracking Your Students' Computer Time

Tracking Hints

- Establish an order.
- Students can sign in and date their turn.
- Rotate through the whole class.
- A clothespin list is another excellent option.
- Have a student monitor maintain rotation.
- When finished, each student can notify the next student on the list to continue the rotation.

Each time a student is finished, he or she removes the clothespin, places it in cup, and calls the next student (skipping any absent students).

Painting Center

Painting Center Hints

- Cover floor area under easel with butcher paper or plastic and secure with tape.
- Have a smock or large shirt available for painters to wear.
- Use paint containers with lids to avoid drying out paints.
- Establish procedures, especially clean-up.
- Schools usually provide classes with easels.

Art Center

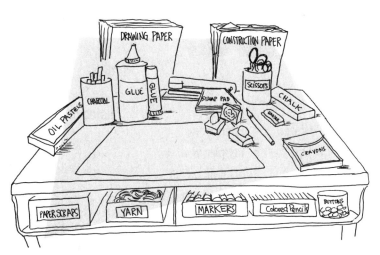

Art Center Hints

- Always introduce and work with a medium several times prior to placing it in the art center.
- Establish rules for the center and for each medium's use.
- Save paper scraps for the center. (A good rule: We save the scrap if it is larger than our hand.)
- Paper towels, wet wipes, etc., should be handy.
- Allow students to explore and create freely.
- A sign-in is a good idea—this is a popular center! Use a clipboard or a chipboard and a clamp to create a sign-in.
- Desks make the best art centers. You can utilize the insides for storage.

Classroom Library

Classroom libraries are an integral part of every classroom. A classroom library is an excellent way to organize your books. This allows for easy access to theme-based collections of books. Students, too, can easily find books related to themes that they are interested in. As your collection of books grows, you can keep them organized by using plastic bins or even laminated colored paper markers. Clearly label both for easy access. Choose an organization that aligns with the themes and subjects you are teaching within your grade level. Again, set it up to work for you. Visit other classrooms to see how they have organized their libraries and how they manage their books.

Science
- Animals
- Plants
- Fish
- Insects
- Physical Science
- Earth Science
- Weather

Literature
- Folktales and fairy tales
- Poetry
- Informative
- Historical
- Trade books
- Core literature chapter books

Social Science
- Community
- Historical figures
- History
- Multicultural
- Wars
- Regions
- Presidents
- Civics

Other
- Holidays
- Sports
- Crafts
- Art

Math
- Place books with math-related topics together.

Stories
- Characters
- Multicultural
- Language
- Ethnicity
- Religion
- Gender related
- Immigration and migration
- Family
- Friendship
- People with disabilities

Helpful Tips:
- Start with general themes, and, as the library grows, subdivide them (e.g., animals into mammals, reptiles, amphibians, and fish).
- Mark, number, level, or color-code the books for easy management.
- Organize books by ability level, maturity level, and/or age range appropriateness.
- Create a library area, a comfortable place to read (e.g., a rug, beanbag chair, pillows for the lower grades, and/or a table and comfortable chairs for older students).

Classroom Tools

School Supplies

Schools will provide most of your supplies. You may have to request them from a designated supply person or you may actually have access to materials in a supply room that you just need to sign out for. Anticipate holiday and project needs early to assure proper supplies. Each school is different. Ask your office staff how this is handled.

- Supply request forms are usually in a designated location—an office or supply room.

- They may have a carbon copy.

- Supplies may be picked up or delivered depending on school policy.

Color Ordering Considerations
(These colors of paper are popular and need to be requested early!)

September, October, November (fall, Halloween, Thanksgiving)
- Orange, yellow, brown, black, white, purple

December, January (Christmas, Hanukkah, Kwanzaa, winter)
- Red, green, white, blue, orange, yellow

February (Valentine's Day, African-American History Month, Presidents' Day)
- Pink, red, white, green, yellow, black

March, April, May, June (Saint Patrick's Day, Easter, spring)
- Green, yellow, white, pink

July, August (Fourth of July, summer)
- Red, white, blue

Paper

Copy Paper

Ream of Paper

Small Construction Paper (9 × 12")

Large Construction Paper (12 × 18")

Graph Paper (Math— upper grades)

Lined Paper	Kindergarten	First	Second–third	Fourth–fifth
	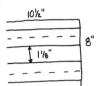			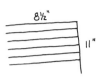

Story Paper	Journals	Word Cards or Sentence Strips (flash cards, vocabulary, name plates, hall passes)	Tag or Poster Board (lined or unlined) (charting, posters)
		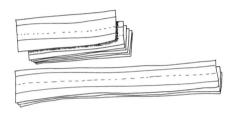	

Chipboard
(good for testing dividers)

Index Cards
(notes, name tags, student input)

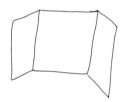

Arts and Crafts

Yarn	Cord (heavy yarn)	Brads (fasteners)
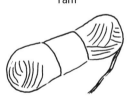		

Glue	Rubber Cement	Glue Stick

Student Scissors

Glue Bottles

Tempera Paint

Watercolor Paint

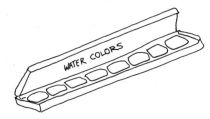

Paint Container
(fill with liquid paint)

Tissue Paper

Round Paintbrush

Flat Paintbrush

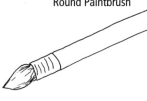

Felt

Pipe Cleaners

Rings (large/medium/small)

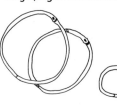

Clothespins

Liquid Starch

Clamps or Clips

Markers

Primary Crayons (K–2)

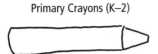

Standard Crayons (2–5)

Primary Pencils (K–2)

Pencils (2–5)

Teacher

Chalk
(yellow or white) (colored)

Eraser

Dry Erase Markers

Scotch™ Tape (individual or dispenser)

Masking Tape (thick and thin)

Clear Packing Tape (mounting, binding)

Book-Binding Tape (book
repairs, portfolio edges)

File Folders

Stapler

Staples

Staple Remover

Water-Based Markers

Overhead Markers

Pens

Pencils

Permanent Markers

Paper Clips

Sticky Notes

Butcher Paper (assorted colors)

Sticky Putty

Scissors

Teacher's Workstation

Teacher's workstations are a great way to organize all your most used materials in one location, making them easily accessible. When strategically located, workstations can save you time and help things run smoothly. Personalize your workstation with items you use in your instruction and facilitation of the classroom. Office supply stores sell inexpensive storage units that you can use, or you can create your own system. Having these materials at your fingertips avoids interruptions while someone searches for the stapler or scissors. You can house instructional materials here as well. Flash cards, learning games, minibooks—whatever you may be using at the time and need readily accessible. Being organized is the key to a well-run classroom.

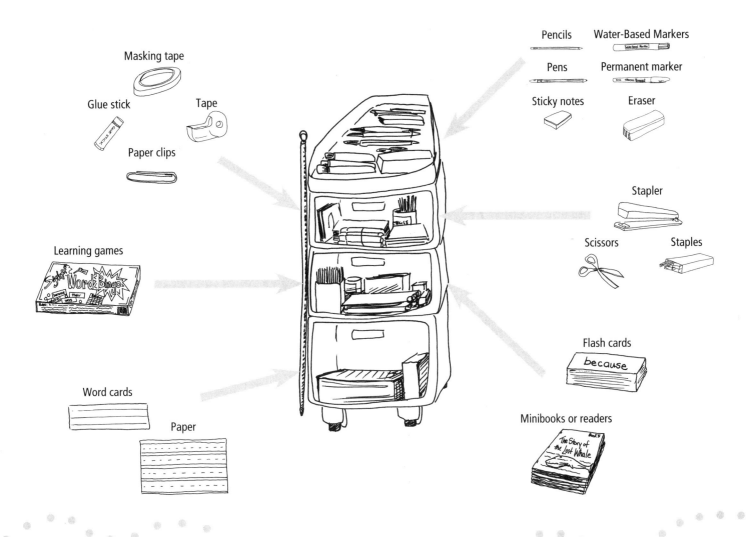

Materials:					Resources:	
☐ Pens	☐ Sticky notes	☐ Staples	☐ Masking tape	☐ Word cards	☐ Flash cards	☐ Learning
☐ Pencils	☐ Eraser	☐ Scissors	☐ Glue stick	☐ Paper	☐ Decodables	games
☐ Markers	☐ Stapler	☐ Tape	☐ Paper clips		or readers	

Teacher's Math Workstation

Math workstations are a helpful way to organize your math instructional materials and manipulatives. If you are teaching a primary grade, you may find it helpful to set up an easel, using the tray to hold your things and the easel as a writing or poster surface. If you are teaching an upper grade, you can organize these items in an area that is easily accessible and near the front of the room or focal point of instruction.

The idea is that you are not scrambling for materials so that your instructional delivery is as smooth as possible. When teachable moments arise throughout the day, you are ready.

Chart Paper
- Math problems
- Class-generated story problems
- Counting
- Number play
- Etc.

Number Chart
- Counting
- More and less
- ±

Flash Cards
(purchased or created)
- Math facts

Money Manipulatives
- Counting money
- ± Money
- Purchasing

Thermometer
(manipulative)

Clock
(manipulative)

Geometric Forms and Shapes

Instructional Posters
(purchased or created)
- Money
- Shapes
- Fractions
- Measurement
- Times table
- Etc.

Manipulatives
- Hundreds, tens, and ones
- Counters
- Unifix cubes
- Etc.

Ruler
- Measurement
- Inches and centimeters

Resources:

- ☐ Number chart
- ☐ Chart paper
- ☐ Instructional posters
- ☐ Manipulatives
- ☐ Ruler
- ☐ Geometric forms and shapes
- ☐ Clock
- ☐ Thermometer
- ☐ Money manipulatives
- ☐ Flash cards

Manipulatives

Manipulatives are tangible items that can be used as instructional math aides. They offer a visual, hands-on approach to learning. Some students need manipulatives to solidify concepts, and all students can benefit from their use. It is important to give students free exploration time with manipulatives as they are introduced. Getting the playing out of the way enables students to focus and use the manipulatives as a tool. With time, they become less and less of a distraction. You may bag up manipulatives for easy distribution and collection. You may even prepare manipulatives bags for each student with a collection of commonly used manipulatives for easy access. These bags can be kept in their table boxes. Manipulatives are more common in lower grades, but are helpful even with upper-grade concepts. You can even create your own manipulatives with common objects such as beans, buttons, bottle caps, etc. Send a letter home and invite students to bring in items.

Container Options

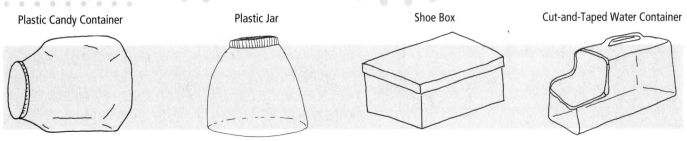

Plastic Candy Container   Plastic Jar   Shoe Box   Cut-and-Taped Water Container

Manipulatives Use Guide

Beans
- Counting
- Sorting
- ±
- Tens/ones sticks
- Graphing

Counters
- ±
- Numbers chart
- Probability

Money
- Counting $
- ± $
- Buying
- Probability

Bears (animals)
- Counting
- Sorting
- ±
- Graphing

Dice
- Probability
- ±

Tangrams
- Shapes
- Geometry
- Puzzles

Blocks or Cubes
- Counting
- Sorting
- ±
- Graphing

Forms
- Geometry
- Volume

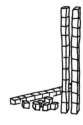

Quisinar Rods (tens/ones)
- Counting hundreds, tens, ones
- Double digit
- ±
- Regrouping

Buttons
- Counting
- Sorting
- ±
- Graphing

Geo Boards
- Geometry
- Shapes
- Angles
- Sides

Unifix Cubes
- Counting
- Sorting
- ±
- Graphing
- Measurement

Clock
- Telling time

Links
- Counting
- Sorting
- ±
- Graphing

Dominoes
- Counting
- ±
- Grouping
- Sorting

Websites for Teachers

The Internet is an excellent resource for both you and your students. The best way to find sites is to surf the Web. Sites have links to other websites, and you can spend hours discovering valuable resources. Find ones you like and bookmark them into a folder. The following is a list of some useful teacher websites. From lesson plans to great art ideas, the Internet is the best overall resource you can use.

Site	Description
www.teacherspayteachers.com	Curriculum resources created by teachers
http://abcteach.com	Core subjects, holidays, clip art, activities
http://echantedlearning.com	Theme-related worksheets, mini-books, vocabulary and more
http://www.billybear4kids.com	Holidays, screen savers, certificates, and more
http://www.orientaltrading.com	Arts and crafts supplies
http://www.edhelper.com	Subject-related lessons, units, worksheets, holidays/graphic organizers, curriculum
http://www.playbasedlearning.com.au	Play-based learning ideas
http://www.teacherplanet.com	Calendar of events/lessons/ideas
http://www.schoolexpress.com	Makes subject-related games, quizzes, worksheets, word walls, etc
http://www.rubistar.4teachers.org	Rubric building
http://www.theteacherscorner.net /printable-worksheets	Printable worksheet makers
http://www.teach-nology.com/worksheets	More than 8,000 free printable K–12 teacher worksheets
http://www.worksheetworks.com	Subject/content-related worksheets
http://www.teacherweb.com	Build your own classroom website
http://www.ixl.com	Math practice K–8
http://www.brainpop.com	Creates animated, curriculum-based content
http://www.quia.com	Game/quiz generator

Websites for Students

The Internet is an excellent resource for your students. Always preview sites prior to allowing students to use them. Most schools/districts will have a firewall (a barrier that is set up to block inappropriate sites), but it is your responsibility to know what your students are looking at. The following is a list of websites that students can utilize. Inquire about any district/school approved website lists.

Site	Description
http://www.cybersleuth-kids.com	Internet search guide for kids
http://www.kidzone.ws	Learning facts for kids
http://www.ajkids.com	Question search
http://www.yahooligans.yahoo.com	Web guide for kids
http://www.theartgallery.com.au	Kid art
http://www.learningupgrade.com	Online experiences featuring songs, videos, and games
http://www.kidsdomain.com	Resource/links
http://www.kidsread.com	Reading resource, books to games
http://www.mrnussbaum.com	Fun curriculum-related games
http://www.science.howstuffworks.com	Science resource
http://www.storylineonline.net	SAG members read children's books aloud
http://www.coolmath4kids.com	Math resource
http://www.funbrain.com/kidscenter.html	Resources/games kids explore, collect, and compete
http://www.pbskids.org	Games to prepare children for school
http://www.kids.yahoo.com	Games, music, movies, sports, jokes
http://www.starfall.com	Teaches children to read with phonics
http://www.explorelearning.com	Interactive online simulations for grades 3–12

Handheld Technology

The twenty-first-century classroom has multiple opportunities to incorporate technology into any instructional program. Computers are the most common form of classroom technology used, but handheld devices are another way to incorporate technology as well.

Many students have access to a handheld device. To the modern student, it is second nature for them, and they are often more capable with than most adults. Even for those who don't own their own devices, they are still usually able to navigate them.

Considerations:

- Technology grants are available and might be a nice resource for purchasing a class set of tablets or the like.
- Many students already own a Smartphone or iPod, or the like. If not, this is another option for earmarked district technology money and/or grant money. iTunes or Amazon gift cards, or the like can be purchased for buying games and applications (apps).
- Depending on the app, you may or may not need wireless connectivity via a WiFi network.
- If you do use a class set with all students engaged at once on the Internet, be aware that a surge in activity can occur and slow the network down.

Management:

- Be careful to adhere to your school policy on handheld devices. They should only be out when in use.
- Keep your handhelds charged.
- If you do not have a class set, establish a checkout system with a rotation so all the students get a turn.
- Purchase inexpensive headsets to use with each device.
- Have a sign-in and sign-out sheet to track the devices.
- If using students' personal devices, write a letter home explaining why the student can bring their technology to school and what they will be used for.
- Send a disclaimer/release of liability form home for parents to sign clearing you of any broken, stolen, etc., handheld devices.
- Establish clear rules for usage, care, and storage:
  - Handle with care
  - Share
  - Use only designated apps
  - Use for allotted time period
  - Return to charger when finished

Applications

There are thousands of applications, or "apps" as they are commonly referred to, that can be used in the classroom. These can be purchased through iTunes and range in price from free on up. The following are some suggested apps that have potential to be incorporated into your curriculum. New apps are added daily and should always be researched prior to their use. Note that tablet and Smartphone apps can be used across devices though varied devices have their own way of browsing for and acquiring apps.

Reading

Word Wall (word families)
K12 Timed Reading Practice
Sammy Squirrel (letter recognition)
Read Me Stories
Dr. Seuss Stories

ESL

Sentence Builder
Story Builder
Language Builder
Food Cards
Animal Cards
Insects

Social Studies

Brainpop
Stack the States
U.S. States
Civil War Today
Constitution
America Dreams
Canada Facts
World Explorer

Writing

Comic Touch
Mad Libs

Story Buddy
Story Kit
Key Note
Pages

Science

Star Walk
PBS for Kids
Google Earth
NASA
Solar Walk
The Elements
Beautiful Planet
Zoo Sounds
Farm Sounds

Music

Piano Man
Bongos
Bebot
Virtuoso Keyboard
Maracas
Tambourine

Art

Art Authority
Sketch Book Pro
Draw
Art Puzzles

MoMA
Kid Art

Math

Everyday Math
Sammy Squirrel (Math)
Coin Math
Mathaliens
Sudoku
Piggy HD Math
Pizza Fractions
Number Line Frog
Math Ninja
Math Tutor
Math Test Prep
Math Bingo
Math Board
Mad Math
Numbers

Games

Ultimate Hangman
Word Search
Scrabble

The School

Ten Teacher Reminders

Teachers are faced with many challenges today, especially with legalities that can be easily avoided. This suggested list of reminders is very important to consider in this profession to avoid potential problems. Know your school or district policies, and always ask other teachers and/or your union representative. In many instances, just using common sense will go a long way.

1. *Never* stay alone with a student behind closed doors. Always have the doors open and, better yet, have other students around.

2. *Never* photograph or digitally record your students for use outside of the classroom without a signed legal consent form from the parent/guardian. Your school or district should have a standard release form. Ask how others handle this.

3. Be very careful with any snacks you have in the classroom. Students may have allergies. Peanuts, dairy products, and so on can all cause reactions. Know your students!

4. *Never* strike or aggressively grab a student. Any contact, depending on your rapport and the student, can be misconstrued into something it is not.

5. *Never* leave your school site with any student without a signed permission slip and the emergency contact information. Your school should have a standard trip slip form. Ask.

6. *Never* release a student to anyone without an official school release from the office. The office has a list of approved individuals that students can be released to.

7. Always document student referrals to the office for behavior or health issues. Cover yourself. Save all such documentation.

8. *Never* solicit funds or donations without first checking your school or district policy and protocol. Always ask first to cover yourself.

9. Get to know your union representative and union rights. Union reps can be helpful in answering contract questions and are an excellent resource. You may need their support one day.

10. *Never* let your credentials expire. Stay on top of what you need to do to stay current. This is your job! It is your responsibility and can easily be neglected. Don't get caught—be proactive.

Procedures for Bathroom, Nurse, and Office

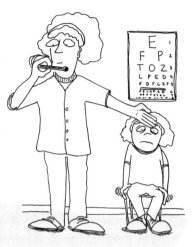

Here is a list of reminders about sending students out of the room throughout the day. These ideas apply to every grade level. Remember to check your school's guidelines in case there are other requirements for students leaving the room.

Reminders

1. In the lower grades (K–2) always send children in pairs. (for the restroom, boys with boys and girls with girls)

2. Always send students with a hall pass. If students are going to the nurse or the office, a note may also be required.

3. If students are going to the restroom, remind them to wash their hands. Even students in the upper grades can use this reminder.

Library Visits

School libraries are a fantastic resource. Many schools have a librarian and/or library aide trained to facilitate your visits and book checkouts and computer use. These visits not only provide you with a break from the classroom routine but lay the foundation for your students to make hard copy and electronic books a consistent part of their lives as well. These visits also help them learn valuable research skills whether through hard copy books or Internet use.

You need to find out:

If the library is available.

what the sign-up policy is.

whether there are scheduled days or times.

what the librarian's or aide's name is.

Library Hints and Considerations:

- Review library rules (obtain from the library or use generic rules listed).

  - No food or drink in the library
  - Use inside voices.
  - Follow directions.
  - Preview one book at a time.

  - Use a marker to save book's location.
  - Shelve books with the spine facing out.
  - If you are unsure of a book's location, leave for the librarian or teacher to reshelve.

- Review the parts of a book.

Front cover

Spine

Author
Illustrator

Table of contents

Copyright
Publisher

Back cover

Book synopsis

Author's bio

- Review types of books and their uses.

  - Fiction
  - Nonfiction

  - Expository
  - Historical

- Create student book markers.

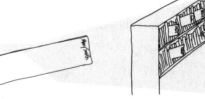

- Review library policy and procedure.

  - Checkout-card information (name, class, date, title, due date)

  - Checkout time limit
  - Lost or damaged book policy

Computer Lab Visits

Many schools have computer labs that classrooms visit on a rotating schedule. There may be a full-time computer teacher and/or lab aide with a set curriculum of lessons that they follow. This is a critical part of any student's education and should be fully taken advantage of.

You need to find out:

- if a computer lab is operational
- what grades utilize the lab
- whether the lab is on a sign-up basis
- what the scheduled days or times are
- what students will do in the lab
- what your role is in the lab
- what software is available on the computers (e.g., iMovie, Garage Band, etc.)

Computer Lab Hints and Considerations:

- Review computer lab rules (lab rules or generic rules listed).
  - No food or drink in the lab
  - Do not operate computer until instructed to do so.
  - Follow directions.
  - Stay only on assigned task.

- Review computer etiquette and usage.
  - Use with care.
  - Shut down properly.
  - Never disassemble or insert foreign objects.
  - Never disconnect cables or any external hardware.

- Establish lab buddy partners.
  - Group high to medium and medium to low.
  - Keep in mind that computer skills don't directly correlate to academic performance.

- Surf the Internet for websites that your students can browse related to current theme.
  - Always be prepared to go it alone in case there is no assigned teacher and/or aide.
  - Always have a list of approved websites for students to visit.

Fire Drills, Earthquakes, and Emergencies

Any time there is an emergency, you should have some type of plan established with your class. When you are in charge of a group of students, it's important to have this emergency plan well rehearsed. Your school and school district should have developed plans for emergencies already in place. However, if you are not sure about what to do in an emergency, check with your administration for procedures. Being prepared for an emergency is essential when moving students to safety, and it can save lives. Along with your school plan, you should have an established plan within your classroom as well. These are a few ideas to help in your preparation.

- Have an emergency kit in your classroom. This kit should be in plain sight and easy to grab in an emergency. The contents should be checked and updated every six months. Check the following page for items your emergency kit should contain.

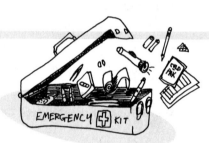

- Develop an emergency signal or a code word that your class will respond to immediately. This signal can be specific to your class—a clap, a bell, and a word phrase.

- Develop an ordered plan of actions your class will follow in response to the emergency signal. For example, when the emergency signal is given, they should put their hands on their head, turn their eyes on you, and listen for directions.

- Establish a partnership with another teacher next door or across the hall. If one of you were not able to respond in an emergency, your partner could get students to safety.

- Be safe, and practice once a month.

Classroom Emergency Supplies

Item	Quantity
Adhesive Tape	1 roll
Ammonia Inhalants	5
Backpack/Duffel Bag	1
Bandages	1 box
Batteries	4
Cold Packs	2 packs
First-Aid Handbook	1
Flashlight	1
Gum	2 packages
Hydrogen Peroxide	1 bottle
Ibuprofen/Tylenol®	1 bottle
Latex Gloves	10 pairs
Life Savers® (candy)	2 packages
Light Stick	2
Pad of Paper	1 pad
Paper Cups	1 bag
Pen	1
Pencil	1
Premoistened Towelettes	1 package
Resealable Bags	1 box
Roller Bandage—3"	1
Safety Pins	1 package
Saline Solution	1
Sanitary Napkins	1 box
Scissors	1 pair
Sewing Kit	1
Solar Blanket	1
Toilet Paper	2 rolls
Trash Bags	1 box
Tums®	1 pack
Tweezers	1 pair
Water	1 bottle
Waterproof Matches	1 box
Whistle	1

Temporary
Student
Displacement
Form

Use this form to document the change in location of a student to another classroom. This might occur if a student is left behind from a field trip because he or she has no consent form or if a student needs to complete missed work while the rest of the class is at recess or nutrition.

Temporary Student Displacement Form

Date: _____ Grade: _____ Room: _____ Teacher: _____

Reason for Displacement:

☐ Field trip—student has no written consent.

☐ Activity exclusion due to: _____ health _____ religion _____ other (_____)

Student's Name	Room Number	Teacher	Additional Information
1.			
2.			
3.			
4.			
5.			
6.			

Temporary Student Displacement Form

Date: _____ Grade: _____ Room: _____ Teacher: _____

Reason for Displacement:

☐ Field trip—student has no written consent.

☐ Activity exclusion due to: _____ health _____ religion _____ other (_____)

Student's Name	Room Number	Teacher	Additional Information
1.			
2.			
3.			
4.			
5.			
6.			

Record Keeping

There are a variety of reasons you will need to keep records from keeping inventory of classroom materials and equipment, as well as personal records and student records. These ideas will help you manage your classroom and records.

EQUIPMENT INVENTORY

Teacher: _____ Room: _____ Grade: _____ Date: _____

Equipment	Make	Model	Serial Number

Professional Records

You should always maintain evidence of your personal professional growth records, trainings, and classes. These not only create a portfolio but also may serve as necessary documentation for credential renewal, depending on your state's credentialing guidelines and renewal policy. Maintaining a professional file of all such documentation is highly recommended and saves time if and when you need such documentation.

You should save:

Current Professional Résumé

Letters of Recommendation

Certificates
- Course completions
- Recognitions

Agendas
- Professional developments
- All trainings

Professional Trainings

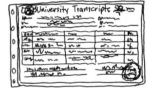

University Transcripts

Records and Documentation

Photographs of:
- Classroom
- Bulletin boards
- Centers
- Student projects

Performance Evaluations

Observations of Yourself

Sample Lesson Plans
- Weekly
- Long term or annual
- Unit or theme

School-Year Inventory

The following is an overview of possible paperwork, record keeping, and assessments that your school or district may require. Half the battle is staying up to date on this.

Beginning of the Year

☐ **Enrollment** _____ Boys _____ Girls

☐ **Emergency Contact Information Cards** (Check about school procedures—usually kept in office.)

☐ **Open Formal Records** (Check with school for format and procedures.)

☐ **School Paperwork** (Check with school for release paperwork, compacts, government-funded forms, etc.)

☐ **Evaluation Paperwork** (Some schools may have you submit professional goals and long-term plans prior to a formal evaluation. Check for sign-up procedures, available dates, person evaluating you, subject observed.)

☐ **Substitute Folder** (Some schools require general information turned in for subs or emergency plans for up to three days.)

☐ **Initial Assessments** (personal assessments, schoolwide assessments, e.g., assessments for funding programs)

☐ **Portfolios and Assessment Folders** (Establish and have initial samples in first few days of school.)

Middle of the Year

☐ **Assessments** (Check school for district assessment schedule. Conduct personal midyear evaluation. Some districts conduct six-week assessments in Math and Reading.)

☐ **Ongoing Record Keeping** (Some districts have you complete and submit a monthly attendance evaluation or register.)

☐ **Formal Evaluations** (Check to see if you are being evaluated, on what subject, with what expectations. Set up dates for formal evaluation(s) and check how many informal evaluations will be conducted.)

End of the Year

☐ **Close formal records or retentions.** (Check with school for procedures and due dates.)

☐ **Reorganize class for placement.** (Some schools have reorganizations, where each teacher divides his or her class into boys and girls, ability levels, behavior, and language levels. Classes are created to meet student needs.)

☐ **Inventory room equipment.** (List name and serial numbers for all equipment.)

☐ **Return all textbooks and library books.** (Inventory books against bar code and return.)

☐ **Submit all attendance records.** (Ink in with *black* ink over any pencil.)

End-of-Year Tips

The end of the school year can be exhilarating as your vacation awaits, but it can also be stressful, with so much to do as you close down your classroom and wrap up all your final paperwork. This is the time to reflect and close down your classroom with intention, so that the start of the school year will be efficient and stress-free as you return from your long summer break.

As you look back at the previous school year, think about what worked well and what might need improvement. Don't forget the following:

✓ **Remember.** Remember why you became a teacher. Be mindful and present. You have finished another year of service and witnessed the miracle of the development of your students' young minds as they have learned from your guidance and instruction. What a gift! Finish the race strong with no regrets. If nothing else, it will help you more fully enjoy your summer break.

✓ **Have fun!** This can be the best time of the year if you relax and truly enjoy your students. You have spent the year getting to know them and no one knows them better. These are the last days of your influence on them. How do you want to be remembered? Explore, investigate, play, and apply all that has been learned throughout the year. Consider the following end-of-the-year activities:

- **Culminating Projects.** There are plenty of projects out there that can showcase student learning and take-a-ways. They can be individual or group projects that allow students to apply what they have learned in meaningful ways. Explore Teachers Pay Teachers, Pinterest, educational resources like this one, YouTube, and so on, for ideas that are age-appropriate and will inspire your students.

- **Portfolios.** These can be digital or hard-copy collections of student work that students can assemble and reflect on. Student reflection is important. What did they learn from the activity? What could they do differently next time? How does this inspire you to dive deeper into this and how would that look?

- **Year-at-a-glance Poster.** Brainstorm ideas and concepts and list them on the board. Students can then create a poster of their favorite take-a-ways from the year. This can be across the curriculum or can be subject-specific. You could even assign chapters or concepts to groups of students. Then you could display the posters in a timeline of what was learned.

- **Letter to next year's incoming students.** This is a powerful way for students to reflect on their school year and give advice to incoming students.

- **Letter of introduction to their next year's teacher.** This is an excellent tool for self-reflection. Students can describe what type of student they are or aspire to be, personally and academically.

- **Movies/Movie Trailers summarizing the school year.** If you have the technology, students can get very creative with this. Starting with a script, students can create shorts or trailers that highlight aspects of their school year. These can even be shown to incoming students the next year. Consider having an end-of-the-year movie festival.

- **Goal List for the summer.** Students can create a list of goals that they want to accomplish over the summer. The list could include activities they want to participate in, books they want to read, friends they want to see, trips they want to take, and so on.

Note: These activities can also give you some insight into what stood out and what was most meaningful to your students.

✓ **To Do It.** This time of the year can be overwhelming. Take some time to create a to-do list. Keep this list out and add to it as things come your way. Getting it onto paper and out of your head can help alleviate stress. Each time you think of something else, write it down. Check off items as you go. Breaking it down into areas you need to tackle can help; these smaller lists don't seem as overwhelming. Consider the following possible areas:

- School
- Classroom
- Students
- Curriculum
- Assessments
- District
- Communication

✓ **Pace.** You can't do it all in one day. Take a deep breath. You got this. Don't compare yourself to other teachers that may be closer to closing down their classrooms. Just focus on yourself. Decide each day what you want to get done for that day and focus on those items. Set that intention in the morning before your day starts. Highlight three must-do items from your to-do list and accomplish those. If there is time, tackle more. If you don't get something done, then move it to the next day. Be easy on yourself. Don't get so focused that you neglect your last days with your students.

✓ **Communicate.** This is your final opportunity to share your thoughts and leave a final impression on others, from your students and parents to the faculty and staff. Something as small as a thank-you note or card or a list of suggested tips to support a student over the summer can have an impact and show that you care. Also, recognizing your students with a certificate of achievement or a card sharing why you enjoyed having them in your class can have a lasting impact. Keep it simple.

✓ **Prep.** Think ahead to next year and determine what worked and what didn't, so you can strategically organize for next year. Are there supplies you need or can organize now to save time upon your return? Make notes to yourself and attach sticky notes to materials, charts, etc., if you know of any suggestions or things you would do differently. Strategize and organize in a way that allows you to access what you need to start your new school year first. Order materials from front to back in a sequential order based on how you will use them as you move through the curriculum, with beginning-of-the-year items in front. Labeled containers, organized by month or topic, can be handy to house all the items you need for a topic or time period.

✓ **Reflect.** This can be done after your students have left and you can quietly reflect. Think about your year. Flip back through your plans, and ask yourself about what worked, what didn't work, what could be changed or done differently, and in what ways you could stretch your instruction. Just like we ask our students to do, now is the time for you to identify your "grows" and "glows." Unpack your year and add notes to your plans as reminders. This is probably the last thing you want to do, but if you can, it will make a difference. Additionally, think about where you see yourself next year and what involvement you want to have. Everything is fresh, so taking the time now can be helpful.

✓ **Plan for you.** Think ahead and plan out what your summer will look like. Summers can fly by. Setting goals can help you to maximize your time for fun and personal/professional growth. Consider any professional developments you may want to attend, books you want to read, podcasts you want to listen to, and trips you want to take. Heading into summer with goals in mind will assure that you get to everything, keep you organized, and allow for some well-deserved rest and relaxation.

Attendance

Good attendance is essential to learning. Depending on where you teach, attendance may be consistent, or it could be varied. Wherever you are, having a class with great attendance makes your job easier and the students learn better. While students are required by state laws to be at school, this isn't an "end all, cure all." You will always have students who never miss a day, but what can be done about those few students who just aren't getting to school? If you are looking for some ideas to improve your attendance, the following will be helpful.

☐ Be diligent with your record keeping! Take attendance every day. Attendance cards are legal documents that require your attention and accuracy.

☐ Establish a system of rewards or incentives for perfect attendance

- Give a weekly award.
- Give a monthly award.
- Give an end-of-the-year award.

☐ If an absence occurs, try to call home, text, or e-mail on the day missed. Although this is usually not required, getting in touch at home is a great way to get students back to school and lets the parents know you care!

☐ Get acquainted with your district and school attendance policies.

☐ Report outstanding absences. If a student is absent for more than a few days, it's a good idea to bring this to the attention of an administrator or your school counselor.

Class Roster
(with Contact Info)

Teacher: _____ Room Number: _____ Year: _____

Student's Name	Address	Phone Number	E-mail Address

Class Roster
(with Birthdays)

Teacher: _____ **Room Number:** _____ **Year:** _____

Student's Name NAMES	Birthday HAPPY BIRTHDAY	Phone Number
1.		
2.		
3.		
4.		
5.		
6.		
7.		
8.		
9.		
10.		
11.		
12.		
13.		
14.		
15.		
16.		
17.		
18.		
19.		
20.		
21.		
22.		
23.		
24.		
25.		
26.		
27.		
28.		
29.		
30.		

Cumulative Records

Most school districts have some sort of cumulative record that follows a student from traditional kindergarten through the twelfth grade. These records are legal documents that contain a student's scholastic history. Depending on your district, this information may be in a hard-copy file format or may be input into a computer. Information may vary, and it is important to familiarize yourself with what information is recorded. The beginning of the school year is an excellent time to open these records, inputting students' most recent information. It is also an opportunity for you to get to know your students, their scholastic history, and any special services and/or needs they may have.

You need to find out:

- **if the school or district has cumulative student records.**

- **if records are hard-copy files. How are they accessed?**
  (location, available times, contact person, school checkout policy)

- **if the records are electronic computer files. How are they accessed?**
  (URL/website, computers [school or home, necessary passwords])

- **what the school or district policies and dates are.**

- **what the opening date is.** (opening information/procedure)

- **what the closing date is.** (closing information, procedure, deadline)

- **what is housed in these records.**
  - Special services documentation
  - Health records
  - Intervention records
  - Report cards
  - Student study team records
  - Language records
  - Standardized test scores
  - State/federally funded program information
  - Evaluations and testing results
  - Annual photographs

Possible Student Information:

- Student's ID number
- Student's date of birth
- Current address and phone number
- Dates of enrollment—entered and exited (e.g., "E")
- Special codes for entrances and exits (e.g., "E-2")
- Attendance (present, absent, tardies)
- Teacher
- Picture

Possible Curricular Information:

- Text series, publisher, edition
- Reading, Science, Social Science

Possible Scholastic Information:
- Teacher's initials and grade
- Teacher's comments
- Conference or meeting dates and attendees
- Standardized test scores

Possible Additional Records:
- Special services
- Interventions
- Language
- Health records

Student Inventory

Teacher: _____

Grade: _____ Room: _____ Date: _____

Track information and observations that could be helpful in conferences, retentions, and referrals. Keep with any work samples and/or observation logs. Use back of sheet for additional comments and observations.

Student Name		I.D.	
D.O.B.	Age	Home Language	ELD Level
Year	Days Present	Absent	Tardy

Previous Attendance

Suspensions (date/reason)

CONCERN ☐ Academic ☐ Behavioral ☐ Emotional ☐ Physical

Description:

Notified	Notified	Notified
Date	Date	Date
How	How	How

ACADEMIC ☐ Reading ☐ Writing ☐ Spelling ☐ Math ☐ Science ☐ Social Studies

Description

HEALTH ☐ Glasses ☐ Medications ☐ Allergies ☐ Asthma ☐ Other

Description

General Observations

☐ Interventions	Outcomes
☐ Modifications	
☐ Accommodations	
☐ Resources	
☐ Referrals	

102

Report-Card Checklist

Several times a year, teachers will formally record the progress of their students. This is an excellent opportunity to focus on each student and his or her progress. It is very important for your students, too. It is important that you be well prepared with evidence to support your scores. Ongoing work sample collections from a portfolio and a work folder can be helpful. Additionally, it is nice to use a quick one-on-one assessment inventory in Math and Reading to confirm each student's progress and to clarify your observations.

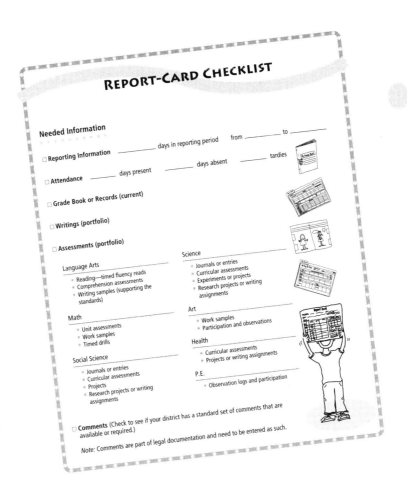

Comment Considerations:

- Brief
- Professional
- Positive (Try to always find the positive, nice way to end your comments.)
- Nondiagnostic (ADD, ADHD, etc., can only be diagnosed by a doctor or a licensed psychologist.)
- Nonaccusatory (Avoid direct accusations, e.g., "Sam hits children in the yard" is better stated as "Sam has a hard time maintaining his hands and feet to himself when in the yard.")

REPORT-CARD CHECKLIST

Needed Information

☐ **Reporting Information** _____ days in reporting period   from _____ to _____

☐ **Attendance** _____ days present   _____ days absent   _____ tardies

☐ **Grade Book or Records (current)**

☐ **Writings (portfolio)**

☐ **Assessments (portfolio)**

Language Arts

* Reading—timed fluency reads
* Comprehension assessments
* Writing samples (supporting the standards)

Math

* Unit assessments
* Work samples
* Timed drills

Social Science

* Journals or entries
* Curricular assessments
* Projects
* Research projects or writing assignments

Science

* Journals or entries
* Curricular assessments
* Experiments or projects
* Research projects or writing assignments

Art

* Work samples
* Participation and observations

Health

* Curricular assessments
* Projects or writing assignments

P.E.

* Observation logs and participation

☐ **Comments** (Check to see if your district has a standard set of comments that are available or required.)

Note: Comments are part of legal documentation and need to be entered as such.

Student Referrals

Sometimes it is necessary to seek additional assistance for a student who has special circumstances beyond your capabilities. It is important to exhaust your resources first and to document every intervention. This documentation of behavior will greatly assist any professional handling the student's case. *Never* diagnose a student's issue, even if it seems obvious. A professional needs to conduct a formal evaluation, and it must go through the proper channels. Only report what you see and what you have tried to do to assist your student in need. Always check with your school or district about referral procedures and your responsibilities in the process. Some schools may have a team of professionals that handles the referrals.

You need to be prepared, and the information you need depends on your school or district.

Needed information:

☐ **Student's Information**
- Name/student ID (where applicable)
- Date of birth/current age
- Current address
- Parent/guardian's name and home environment (foster care, guardianship, etc.)
- Primary language (if applicable) ELD level: _____

☐ **Attendance**
- Current year's: absences: _____ tardies: _____
- Previous years' (down to kindergarten) attendance
- Suspensions _____

☐ **Description of Concern**
- Academic
- Attendance
- Emotional/behavioral
- Speech
- Other

In a paragraph, describe your concerns. Do so in an objective manner. Simply state the facts—facts that you can support with documentation and attempted interventions.

☐ **Parental/Guardian Notification**
- Notified/conferenced with parent/guardian on several occasions about concern(s)
- Notified parent/guardian about referral and referral procedures

☐ **Academic Information**
- Current assessments in Math and Reading
- Other assessments or inventories

☐ **Health Information**
- List of any known health issues (eyeglasses, diagnosed conditions, etc.)
- List of any current known medications child is receiving at school

☐ **Observations**
- Academic—work habits, motivation, subject difficulties, understanding, attention, focus
- Medical—hygiene, energy level, physical complaints, restroom visits (frequency), asthma, eyeglasses, etc.
- Behavioral—withdrawn, violent, depressed or sad, temperamental, aggressive, disruptive, immature

☐ **Interventions**
- Teaching Modifications—positive feedback, visual aids, peer or cross-age tutoring, reteaching, small-group instruction, individual instruction, goals, contracts
- Teaching Accommodations—seating adjustments, changing classes
- Teaching Materials—remedial work or less work, manipulatives, books on tape, graphic organizers, blocking text or color coding

Anecdotal Behavior Tracker

Anecdotal
Behavior
Tracker

Student's Name: _____

Grade: _____   Room: _____   Teacher: _____

TIME AND DATE	BEHAVIOR

Retention Checklist

Retention is a critical decision that has a tremendous impact on a student's life. It is a last resort only after all other options have not yielded the results necessary to bring him or her academically to grade level. The goal of a retention is for the student to have an opportunity to mature and grow academically to grade level and even beyond. In the right situation, the student can flourish and gain confidence. It can be harder on older students, who tend to be more aware of how a retention can be perceived. The teacher plays a critical role in such a transition, and needs to be positive and sensitive. This is not a quick fix but a calculated move. A retention can be a lost year if a student is not qualified, and it should never be taken lightly. Because of this, a number of criteria need to be considered prior to making a retention. Start by checking with your school or district for specific qualifications and age cut-offs. Ask other teachers when a student should be considered for retention. Keep in mind that the student's parent/guardian always has the final approval. The information you need depends on your school or district.

Needed information:

☐ **Student's Information**
- Name/student ID (where applicable)
- Date of birth, current age, and age entering sixth grade if retained
- Current address
- Parent/guardian's name and home environment (foster care, guardianship, etc.)
- Primary language (if applicable) ELD level: _____
- Attendance
- Current grade: _____ days absent (_____ excused/_____ unexcused)
  Previous:
  _____ Grade: _____ days absent (_____ excused/_____ unexcused)
  _____ Grade: _____ days absent (_____ excused/_____ unexcused)
  _____ Grade: _____ days absent (_____ excused/_____ unexcused)
- ELD level: 1 ☐   2 ☐   3 ☐   4 ☐   5 ☐

☐ **Reason for Retention**
- Write a statement that specifically states why you feel student needs to be retained. This statement should not be diagnostic, but be based on your observations.

☐ **Parental/Guardian Notification or Request**
- Notification on report card (Some districts have a warning notification check-off.)
- Notification/discussion of potential at conferences (Note dates of each conference and participants.)
- Notification specifically for submission and request ("May be retained.")
- Parent/guardian request for retention: _____ Written _____ Oral _____ Date(s)

☐ Consultation with Previous Teacher/Student's Cumulative Record

- Discuss observations and academic performance.
- Check for documented support and possible explanations.

☐ Health Status

- Check with school nurse.
- Consult records for any health issues or medications that should be considered.
- Physical size in present grade: Small   Medium   Large

☐ Academic Records

- Standardized test scores: _____ Reading _____ Math _____ Language

☐ Referral Services

- Special services received
- Reading resource
- Speech
- Adaptive P.E.
- Other

☐ Agency Support

- Outside agency support

☐ Referral for Evaluation

- Reason (if different from retention)
- Evaluation committee
  _____ Administrator _____ Teacher _____ Parent/Guardian _____ Student _____ Psychologist _____ Counselor
  _____ Outreach Consultant _____ Social Worker _____ Speech Therapist _____ Reading Resource
- Date
- Recommendation

Follow-up may include:

- school administrator approval/"OK" = "will be retained."
- school or district letter to parent/guardian.
- notation in student's cumulative record. (Check for documentation procedure.)
- notation on final report card.

Student Information Card

School Year: _____

Student Name: _____ D.O.B. _____

Student ID Number: _____ Age: _____

Siblings: _____ Grade: _____ Siblings: _____ Grade: _____

Emergency Contact: _____ Relation: _____

Cell: _____ Other: _____

Parent/Guardian: _____ Cell: _____

E-mail: _____ Work: _____

Allergies/Medications: _____

Special Needs: _____

Please write any pertinent information
on the back of this card.   Parent/Guardian Signature: _____

Student Information Card

School Year: _____

Student Name: _____ D.O.B. _____

Student ID Number: _____ Age: _____

Siblings: _____ Grade: _____ Siblings: _____ Grade: _____

Emergency Contact: _____ Relation: _____

Cell: _____ Other: _____

Parent/Guardian: _____ Cell: _____

E-mail: _____ Work: _____

Allergies/Medications: _____

Special Needs: _____

Please write any pertinent information
on the back of this card.   Parent/Guardian Signature: _____

Curriculum

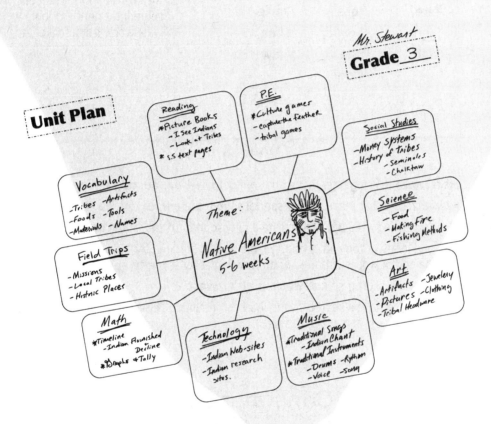

Unit Plan

Mr. Stewart
Grade 3

Reading
*Picture Books
  - I See Indians
  - Look at Tribes
* S.S text pages

P.E.
*Culture games
  - Capture the feather
  - tribal games

Social Studies
- Money systems
- History of Tribes
  - Seminoles
  - Chalktaw

Vocabulary
- Tribes - Artifacts
- Foods - Tools
- Materials - Names

Science
- Food
- Making Fire
- Fishing Methods

Field Trips
- Missions
- Local Tribes
- Histric Places

Theme:
Native Americans
5-6 weeks

Art
- Artifacts - Jewelery
- Pictures - Clothing
- Tribal Headware

Math
*Timeline
  - Indian Flourished
    Decline
*Graphs & Tally

Technology
- Indian Web-sites
- Indian research
  sites.

Music
*Traditional Songs
  - Indian Chant
*Traditional Instruments
  - Drums - Rythan
  - Voice - Song

Language-Arts Overview

Spelling Patterns

Consonants: b, c, d, f, g, h, . . .

Vowels: a, e, i, o, u

Short Vowels: **a**pple, **e**gg, **i**gloo, **o**ctopus, **u**mbrella

Long Vowels: **a**pe, **e**normous, **i**ce, **o**at, **u**nicorn

Long A	Long E	Long I	Long O	Long U
b**a**ke	m**e**	K**i**nd	n**o**	**u**nicorn
p**ai**l	P**e**te	b**i**ke	j**o**ke	m**u**le
acorn	f**ee**t	cr**y**	b**oa**t	h**u**e
d**ay**	S**ea**t	h**igh**	t**oe**	f**ew**
	Ch**ie**f	t**ie**	sh**ow**	
	Cit**y**			

C = consonant

V = vowel

VC word = at

CV word = go

CVC word = cat

CVCC word = back

Sight Words = high-frequency words, sometimes nondecodable words: I, me, was, were, from, make, etc.

Vowels

Vowel Digraphs: Two letters (vowels) that together make one sound: **ai, ay, oa, oe, ow, ee, ey, ea, ie, ei**.

Vowel Dipthongs: Two vowels that together make a new, special sound: **au, aw, oi, oy, oo, eu, ue, ew, ui, ou, ow**.

R-Controlled Vowel Sounds: Vowels followed by *r* that create a new sound: **ar, er, ir, ur, or**.

The Letter Y: *Y* has the sound of a long *i* at the end of one-syllable words: cr**y**, m**y**, fl**y**; *y* has the sound of long *e* at the end of words with two or more syllables: cit**y**, prett**y**, rub**y**.

The Letter W: *W* can make an *a* have a short *o* sound: **wa**sh, **wa**tch, s**wa**t.

The Letters QU: *Qu* can also make an *a* have a short *o* sound (*qu* is pronounced "kwah," like it has a *w*): s**qua**t, **qua**drant.

Consonants

Two-Sounded Consonants: (1) *G* and *c* can be hard or soft.
soft *c* = **c**ent, **c**ircle, **c**ytoplasm; hard *c* = **c**at, magi**c**, s**c**an
soft *g* = **g**entle, **g**iraffe, **g**ym; hard *g* = **g**um, ba**g**, **g**rape
(2) *S* can make an *s* and *z* sound.
s = **s**: **s**ee, pa**ss**
s = **z**: bee**s**, lo**s**e

The Letters X and Q: These consonants have the sounds of two consonants combined: *x* = "ks"; *q* = "kw."

Silent Consonants: These are two consonants with one silent letter: **kn**ight, **wr**ite, **rh**yme, co**mb**, autu**mn**, ni**gh**t.

Consonant Blends: These are two consonants blended in which you hear a little of each consonant.
L blends: **bl, cl, fl, gl, pl, sl**.
S blends: **sm, sn, sk, sc, st, sp, sw, str, spr, spl, scr**.
R blends: **br, cr, dr, fr, gr, pr, tr**.

Consonant Digraphs: Two consonants come together to make one new sound: **sh**ip, **ch**in, ba**ck**, **ph**oto, **th**in, **wh**ip, lau**gh**.

The Writing Process and Stages

The Writing Process

Prewrite
- Ideas on paper
- Graphic organizers

Draft
- Write it all down.
- Notes to main idea/details
- "No Worry" writing

Edit and Revise
- Check for clarity and content.
- Add or change information.

Proofread
- Check grammar and spelling.
- Check mechanics.

Publish
- Create final draft.
- "My best"

Share and Reflect
- Display
- Share
- Discuss

Writing Stages

Precommunicative
- Pictures, attempts, letters

Semiphonetic
- Initial consonants to initial and final

I sau detm
W pla n d prk

Phonetic
- Vowels and syllables represented

I lik to swim n d osun

The elafant ran in the jungul.

Transitional
- Sentences with correct spelling emerging

I went to the park to play
Wit mi frend. We playd on
the slide and we playd ball.
It wuz fun to play.

Conventional Spelling
- Standard spelling and writing

Types of Writing

Independent Writing: Independent, variety of forms and purposes (journals, labeling, student books, etc.)

Interactive Writing: With teacher or class, students plan or write together as a group; take turns, models, supports phonics (whole-class story).

Shared Writing: Teacher writes and students compose, copy, or transcribe.

Guided Writing (writer's workshop): Teacher or small group write together; a community of writers.

Basic Grammar and Punctuation

Grammar

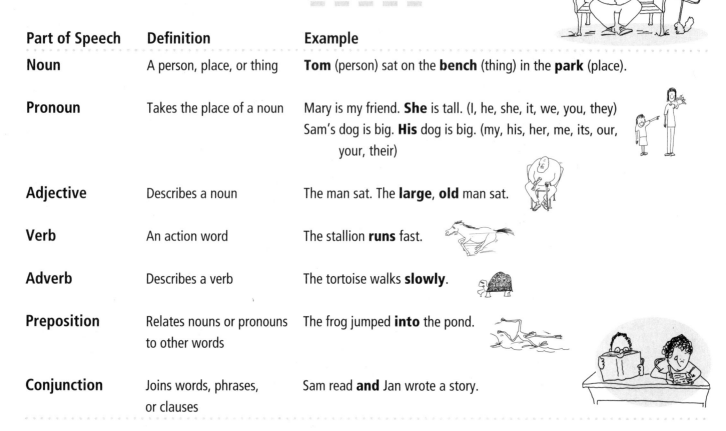

Part of Speech	Definition	Example
Noun	A person, place, or thing	**Tom** (person) sat on the **bench** (thing) in the **park** (place).
Pronoun	Takes the place of a noun	Mary is my friend. **She** is tall. (I, he, she, it, we, you, they) Sam's dog is big. **His** dog is big. (my, his, her, me, its, our, your, their)
Adjective	Describes a noun	The man sat. The **large**, **old** man sat.
Verb	An action word	The stallion **runs** fast.
Adverb	Describes a verb	The tortoise walks **slowly**.
Preposition	Relates nouns or pronouns to other words	The frog jumped **into** the pond.
Conjunction	Joins words, phrases, or clauses	Sam read **and** Jan wrote a story.

Punctuation

Period (.): Ends a telling sentence: *The horse eats hay.*

Question Mark (?): Ends a question: *What color is the horse?*

Exclamation Mark (!): Ends an exclamation: *The barn is on fire!*

Quotation Marks ("/"): Around a quote: *He said, "The horse is white."*

Comma (,): Gives pause or is used in a series: *"Next time, use . . ."; red, blue, green.*

Semicolon (;): Separates two sentences that are closely related: *My family is Jewish; we celebrate Passover but not Easter.*

Colon (:): Precedes a list or greeting part of a business letter or indicates dialogue: *You need: a bag, . . .; Dear sir:*

Hyphen (-): Unifies words, prefixes, numbers: *city-state, half-asleep, twenty-two*

Apostrophe ('): Possessives, contractions: *Sarah's cat, don't*

Writing Genres

Narrative Writing

- Tells a story
- Gives an account

Uses: imagination, personal accounts

Written in first or third person (I, we/he, she, it, they)

Expository Writing

- Explains or defines
- Gives information

Uses: facts, statistical information, cause and effect, examples

Written in third person (he, she it, they)

Descriptive Writing

- Describes
- Is useful in all writing

Uses: descriptive language, adjectives

Written in first or third person; shows, doesn't tell

Summary Writing

- Summarizes
- Maintains integrity of original document

Uses: main ideas, events, concepts

Written in first or third person

Response to Literature

- Reaction or response to literature
- Personal connection to writer's ideas or experiences

Use: meaning

Written by retelling, summarizing, analyzing, and/or generalizing

Poetry Writing

- Arranged composition

Uses: sound and rhythm

Written types: haiku, cinquain, limericks, concrete, closed verse, lyric, nonsense verse, narrative, jump rope

Report Writing

- Explains and informs
- Gives information and facts

Uses: to educate, report facts, predict based on data

Letter Writing

- Friendly, formal, or business
- Conveys or shares information

Friendly Letter Parts

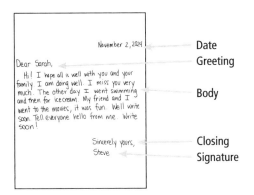

- Date
- Greeting
- Body
- Closing
- Signature

Business Letter Parts

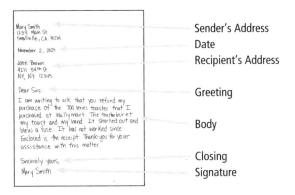

- Sender's Address
- Date
- Recipient's Address
- Greeting
- Body
- Closing
- Signature

Ways to Write

First Person: **I**   Second Person: **you**   Third Person: **he, she, they**

Proofreading Marks

Correction	Symbol	Example
Capitalize.	≡	a̲ dog ran in the park.
Add punctuation marks.	⊙	Where are you going⊙
Add word(s).	∧	My ∧is red. _(bike)_
Delete word(s).	ℓ	Her mother is ~~so~~ nice.
Check spelling.	◯	When did you ⟨leaf⟩?
Indent paragraph.	¶	¶ The morning I woke with a cold...
Change to lowercase.	/	My family I̸s going to the park.
Reverse.	∼	The ⟨shorts blue⟩ are dirty.

Annotation of Text

As students move into middle school and beyond, knowing how to annotate text is an important skill. It helps students with analysis of texts from literature to science. Annotating texts gives students clues to return to when they are asked to interpret or formulate an opinion about what they have read. The physical act of annotation not only helps them to remember what they have read but also helps them dive deeply into an understanding of what they have read. Learning how to focus on only key elements of the text without underlining every word is the goal of good, effective annotation.

Teachers should introduce basic symbols for students to use while annotating text. In the beginning, it is a good idea to give examples of them. Thinking out loud with the students and using annotation symbols on real text is a great way to help students understand their use. Here are a few suggested symbols that can be used in conjunction with notes and words to help the reader dissect text for its meaning. Whichever symbol you are demonstrating, it is important that the class understands how you are using annotation.

- A circle calls attention to words or an idea that is unfamiliar, or perhaps an important concept.
- Underlining can be used to emphasize a key word or idea/detail.
- A star can be used to stress an important concept or idea/detail.
- An infinity symbol or "C" can be used to stress a connection to the text.
- An exclamation can indicate an "aha!" or something important.
- A question mark indicates text that is unclear to the reader or that he or she questions.
- A check can indicate an idea or concept that the reader understands.
- An "X," like the question mark, can be something that is not understood.

Here is an example of how an annotated text can look like with the symbols above. As students become more comfortable with annotating text, allow them to do it in the way that makes the most sense to their individual selves, to personalize it. Note that words and comments can further clarify any symbol. Students will carry this skill through life. It is more than simply marking up a page; it is an intentional road map for students to use as they look back at the text.

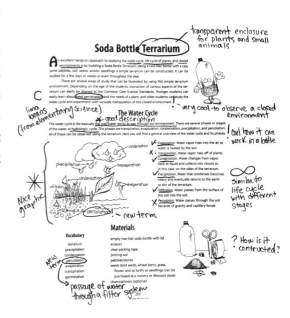

Writing Workshop

What is it?

Writer's Workshop allows students to learn through their own experience of writing and gives them the opportunity to build their own understanding. Similar to Reader's Workshop, Writer's Workshop sees the students as capable writers who can communicate and tell stories through writing. The role of the teacher is to model writing techniques and meet with students as they move through the writing process on their own.

How is it structured?

Writer's Workshop follows a structure similar to that of Reader's Workshop. There is a mini-lesson with a specific aim or target skill, followed by an independent writing time with conferencing, and concludes with a time for sharing. Teachers are able to address both the whole group's needs as well as differentiating the needs of small groups and individuals. In this way, all students can have their needs met and learn the skills of writing that they are ready to learn. Writer's Workshop typically is done 5 days a week for 45–60 minutes a day. An ongoing list of ideas can be helpful, it might include topics such as what they like to do and know about, adventures they have had, a trip they took, and a special person in their life or their pet.

What is the intention?

Writer's Workshop focuses on writing skills and the writer's craft. Writing skills include writing mechanics (spelling, punctuation, capitalization, and paragraphs), editing, and publishing. Writer's craft focuses on leads, endings, figurative language (metaphor, simile, personification, and hyperbole), genres, topics, point of view, and the six traits of writing (ideas, organization, voice, word choice, sentence fluency, conventions, and presentation).

Mini-Lesson (5–10 minutes)

Teachers introduce a skill or aim for the day based on student needs. This is direct instruction and modeling, using the teacher's own on-going writing piece as an example. Mini-lessons are short, focused and direct. Students watch an actual writer use the skills that have been targeted for that lesson. Students then have a quick opportunity to practice the skills, in the same writing genre, with the teacher before they are asked to write on their own. It is important for them to think about what they are writing about—pairing up students with another student to share their intentions is an excellent strategy. Graphic organizers can be used to also help brainstorm.

Independent Writing (35–45 minutes)

Students start writing independently armed with the skill they just learned. This involves sustained writing time about topics that they've chosen and offers an opportunity to apply that skill or skills from their goal card. They are drafting, planning, rereading, editing, revising, proofreading, and talking with other writers about their pieces—doing the real work of writing. While they write, the teacher circulates and conferences with students, meeting them where they are in their writing. Conferencing is done one-on-one or in a small group, depending on the needs of the students. In this way, the teacher can differentiate the strengths and weaknesses of students' writing and support them in the process. Assessment information can easily be informally gathered at this time as well: notice areas across the class that need work, introduction, or review. Independent Writing is the key to a successful Writer's Workshop. In time, students become more independent, not relying solely on the teacher. Although this may take a while, being independent is a necessary part of becoming a writer.

Share Time (10–15 minutes)

The teacher strategically selects students to share their writing with the class. The selection can intentionally highlight that day's skill or a skill that they have worked on previously. These writings are good examples of that day's aim—or simply good writing examples. These do not have to be completed pieces of writing; the example might be a draft. Students can receive feedback and support from the class. This also serves as an inspiration for the other students as they continue to edit and revise their own writing. Giving feedback and receiving it in a public setting can foster a young writer's confidence and growth.

Writer's Workshop is a powerful approach. Students become truly independent writers. They own their writing and consequently become more excited about their writing—and in turn are more motivated. Students aren't the only ones who are motivated: teachers too can be enthused to watch their students grow into writers and own their teaching of writing as they drive their instruction according to their students' needs.

Reading Genres

Realistic Fiction
- Takes place in modern time
- Here and now
- Realistic events

Mystery
- Mysterious event(s)
- Explained or revealed at the end of the book
- Suspenseful

Poetry
- Verse
- Creates thoughts or feelings
- Rhythm and rhyme

Historical Fiction
- Made-up
- Pertains to time in past
- Setting real, characters fictional

Folktale
- No known author
- Passed from generation to generation

Nonfiction
- True facts
- Any subject
- About people = biography

Drama
- Written to act out
- Audience

Biography
- Story of a person's life
- Told by another person

Myth
- Explains something
- Gods or superhumans

Autobiography
- Story of a person's life
- Told by that person

Science Fiction
- Blends scientific fact and fiction
- Futuristic technology

Writing Goal Cards

Students record writing goals and strategies. Students can make notes on their progress.

Name: _____

Goal#1: _____

_____

Strategy: _____

Goal #2: _____

Strategy: _____

Notes:

Name: _____

Goal #1: _____

_____

Strategy: _____

Goal #2: _____

Strategy: _____

Notes:

Writing Goal Cards

Students use these cards to help them achieve their goals. Date or Check as practiced.

_____'s Writing Goal Card

I am working on _____

_____

My strategies are _____

_____

_____

Check off: ☐ ☐ ☐

_____'s Writing Goal Card

I am working on _____

_____

My strategies are _____

_____

_____

Check off: ☐ ☐ ☐

Ways to Read

Choral Reading

- "Unison reading"
- Many opportunities for repeated readings of a selected piece
- Practice in oral reading
- Excellent for poetry or rhymes
- Repeated readings of big books

Shared Reading

- Teacher reads a big book or text.
- Students view or follow.
- Early reading strategies
- Phonemic awareness
- Model reading strategies
- Predicting
- Use of contextual clues

Read Aloud

- Teacher reads to class.
- Class discussion and dialogue
- Follow-up activity: journals, art, etc.
- Pure enjoyment (Teacher doesn't stop to summarize or ask questions.)

Popcorn Reading

- Teacher asks students to begin reading aloud.
- Any willing student can start.
- When student stops, another student continues (without teacher's direction).
- Continues until all have read
- Builds responsibility to participate and gives a choice of when to do so
- Lower-grade students can pick next reader who has not read yet.

Timed Reading

- Designated number of minutes
- Student reads twice.
- Attempts to read further the second time
- Number of words/minute
- Builds fluency

Buddy Reading

- Students pair up.
- Lower-grade student pairs with upper-grade student.
- Students read and discuss the story.
- Students take turns reading aloud.
- Older student serves as coach or reading mentor.

Partner Reading

- Students in a class pair up.
- Take turns and assist one another
- Showcases their skills
- Select special spot to read in the room
- Can pair high/medium and medium/low or allow students to select

Independent Reading

- Students read independently.
- Practice learned strategies
- Builds fluency
- Problem-solving application

Sustained Silent Reading (SSR)

- Students read.
- Independent and silent
- Individual instructional levels
- Provides practice
- Encourages reading
- Uninterrupted sustained silent reading (USSR)
- Drop everything and read (DEAR)

Guided Reading

- Teacher and student read text together.
- Teacher and student read, think, and talk through text.
- Supports intervention
- Teaches problem solving
- Can also "echo read" (teacher reads and students reread)

Comprehension

Author Considerations

Author's Point of View

- Who is telling the story?
- First person: I, me, my
- Third person: he/she, him/her, they/them

Author's Purpose

- To entertain
- To explain
- To inform
- To persuade

Good Reader Considerations

Main Ideas and Details

- What is the primary focus of the story?

Compare and Contrast

- Find similarities and differences.

Cause and Effect

- What took place (problem)?
- What were the outcomes (solution)?

Classify or Categorize

- Sort story elements into similar groups.

Opinion and Fact

- Feeling vs. real

Shared Reading

- Predict, infer, make assumptions, and discover author's meaning.

Make Connections

- Relate to a personal experience.

Guided Reading

Guided Reading gives students the opportunity for modeled instruction using the same text. This approach can be executed from K–12. Typically, it is done with a small group of readers based on their reading levels and needed skill sets. Such groupings allow teachers to meet the students where they are in their reading ability and plan accordingly to help them improve. This can build stamina and strengthen students' ability to comprehend and read more fluently. It also gives teachers the opportunity to support students with instructional level texts as they introduce new strategies of good reading. The ultimate goal is independent reading and, for older students, text analysis. It's also a useful strategy in working with struggling readers at any age.

What does it look like?

The teacher makes flexible small groups of students based on reading levels and skill sets. Students in each group read the same text (which is slightly harder than what they can read without support).

How is it structured?

Re-reading/Warming Up   Students re-read familiar texts to build fluency and warm up.

Introduction   The teacher introduces the text. Students examine the book itself: covers, illustrations and pictures, vocabulary and concepts, and any connections to the text. The lesson goal for the day, consisting of skills or strategies that good readers use, is clearly stated.

Reading   Students group read the same text together—silently or in low voices—in its entirety while the teacher coaches individuals. The teacher can discuss the lesson's aim and dive deeper into individual student goals as they coach.

Discussing   The group discusses what was read. What was noticed?

Teaching   The teacher discusses the goal for that day based on student needs, as well as individual student goals.

Guided Reading can complement Reader's Workshop. There are numerous resources that go into depth and the theory of both of these models. You know your students best and can tailor your instruction to meet their needs. The most important aspect of any good reading instruction is to plan intentionally to address the skills your students lack. Above all, reading should be enjoyable for your students and for you.

Reader's Workshop

Why Use Reader's Workshop?

Reader's Workshop is a differentiated instructional practice that fosters students' individual needs and strengths as they mature into fluent readers who can comprehend text. Reader's Workshop also develops students' speaking skills as they read aloud and share ideas and helps them become independent thinkers as they interact with other readers and the text.

The Reader's Workshop incorporates modeling of a set aim or target reading skill/strategy, followed by a guided practice reading with an emphasis on that skill/strategy and, finally, having students practice reading books of interest individually at their own pace and appropriate reading level. The goal of Reader's Workshop is to use explicit instruction to empower students to better comprehend whatever text that they read.

In Reader's Workshop, students have a choice in what they read at their level. It may involve a specific genre that the student chooses, although the teacher assures time is spent in both fiction and non-fiction genres. This serves as a powerful intrinsic motivator and naturally builds an appetite for reading. With the support of the teacher, students can become confident readers. This support incorporates techniques of what good readers use to comprehend what they have read. Mini-lessons, conferences, and interactions with the students on what they are reading foster their development as readers.

Reading instruction includes:

- Direct instruction of good reading habits
- Nurturing individual reading interests within a student's given level
- Book Talks to nurture response to text and articulation of what has been read

Reader's Workshop Breakdown

Step 1: **Instruction** Direct and explicit instruction in all areas of reading as a daily practice

Looks like: The teacher leads a 10 to 15 whole-group mini-lesson that target a specific aim or objective of a specific reading skill/strategy that the teacher wants to focus on for that day. This is laid out systematically in the following manner:

✓ **Hook 'em.** Remind students of what was taught in the previous lesson.

✓ **Establish the aim.** Introduce a new reading skill, strategy, or behavior that all good readers use. The aim is what the reader is trying to accomplish. Readers use skills and strategies to achieve this. These skills and strategies are systematic and target the needs of the reader one skill or strategy at a time.

✓ **Model.** Students need to see what fluent reading looks like. The teacher reads a text aloud to the entire group. While reading, the teacher can strategically pause periodically to model higher-level thinking, demonstrating for the whole group the targeted skill (sitting up straight, tracking with your finger, jotting down notes, etc.) or the targeted strategy (wondering, making connections, predicting, etc.).

✓ **Engage.** Students "turn and talk" about the skill/strategy being presented. The students see the skill/strategy in action and gain understanding of it prior to reading on their own.

Step 2: ***Independent Reading Time*** Students read independently.

Looks like: Students read books at their level and interest individually for a sustained period.

Students should have set goals (goal cards that evolve and change) that list skills, strategies, or behaviors that they are working on. Students can apply the practice they have learned from the day's mini-lesson or focus on a previously introduced skill/strategy that's been set as an individual goal. This should be the largest chunk of Reader's Workshop: just let them read, uninterrupted, for a set time. Students actively participate in their process of reading. During this time the teacher can circulate and check in or ***conference*** with their readers, asking how they are using the targeted skill/strategy or a skill/strategy from their goal card. It is also an excellent time to work with a student or group of students (at the same instructional level) that need more support. Opportunities are provided to learn strategies and skills to read increasingly more difficult texts on their own. Students can also use this time to reflect, think and confer about what they have read by sharing with other students, journaling, using a graphic organizer, or tracking their reading with small sticky notes.

Step 3: ***Sharing Time*** Students share with whole group what they used in that day's workshop. This could be the specific skill/strategy they applied from their goal card. It also could be their take away from that day, what they noticed when using that skill/strategy.

Looks like: Students in a whole group take turns sharing what they used in their Reader's Workshop that day.

This is an important aspect of Reader's Workshop. Sharing can be in a whole group setting to reinforce the mini-lesson. This creates a collective culture of reading in the classroom. You might have good readers articulate what they have read, sharing skills/strategies that they have used while reading to gain better comprehension. Other students can give feedback. While Sharing Time is the smallest allotted period in your lesson, it should add closure to reading instruction and reiterate the day's aim. Teachers can also informally assess students as they listen to discussions and even highlight a good use of a skill or strategy for further reinforcement. This encourages students to engage and interact with books on a consistent basis in a climate where reading is valued. Students can have rich conversations about their reading and take pride in being capable, independent readers.

Step 4: **Assessment/Running Records** Teachers make on-going records and observations about students throughout independent reading and sharing.

Looks like: The teacher observes individual student performance during workshop and speaks with each student over the course of several workshops.

Assessment records are important to keep on students so their progress can be tracked and necessary skills that need support can be reinforced. Teachers can also observe student comprehension, fluency, and accuracy: these records help to ensure that students are reading at their appropriate reading level.

Leveled Classroom Library

Students need access to a rich library of reading materials. Reading levels can be assessed by using systems like Lexile leveling, Reading Recovery, or Fountas and Pinnell (F & P). When students read books at their level, they can access the text, have better comprehension, and become confident readers. The F & P levels use the letters of the alphabet to indicate the approximate grade-level range, Lexile leveling uses numbers up to 1300 and Reading Recovery uses numbers as well, 1–34. There are sites and apps that will give you the level of any selected title, which will assist you in determining the levels in your classroom library.

F & P		Lexile Levels	Reading Recovery
A–D	Kindergarten	25	1–4
E–J	Grade 1	50–325	5–17
K–M	Grade 2	325–525	18–20
N–P	Grade 3	525–675	20–24
Q–S	Grade 4	675–775	25–26
T–V	Grade 5	775–875	27–28
W–Y	Grade 6	875–950	29–30
Z	Grades 7–8	950–1075	31–34
Z+	High School/Adult	1075–1300	

> http://www.fountasandpinnell.com/
> https://lexile.com/
> https://readingrecovery.org/

Why is leveled library of high-interest text or books so important?

When students spend time reading texts that are accessible or at their level, they can read with success. Decoding, reading fluently, and comprehending what is being read allow each student to become a successful reader. Coupling this with books chosen by interest and genre increases motivation to make sense of text. The foundation of Reader's Workshop is a leveled reading library and an environment where text choices are valued.

Levels are determined by:

- **Accuracy** Observing the accuracy with which a student can read a text; an appropriate level would be able to be read with about 95% or greater accuracy
- **Retelling** The ability for a student to retell and answer questions about a text
- **Fluency** The pace and flow of a student's reading aloud of a text

Considerations

- To learn to read, students need to read. Reading high-interest text at their level can motivate students to read along with an environment that fosters the love of reading. To be successful readers, students will need scheduled time to read independently on a daily basis.
- Targeted skills and practices of good readers that you can present in your mini-lessons include:
  - Previewing
  - Predicting
  - Visualizing
  - Summarizing
  - Connecting
  - Inferring
  - Responding
  - Decoding
- A leveled classroom library to meet your student's needs and interests, a variety of genres
- Guided Reading should be at the student's "instructional level" (in which the student is still working on fluency and comprehension) rather than his or her "independent level" (where the student has a greater than 95% accuracy and is a fluent reader who is understanding what they read and can dive deeper into the text). In the case of Fountas and Pinnell, if a reader was independent at level L, their instructional level would be at level M.
- Running records to keep track of your students' progress
- Community of readers: books are shared and discussed
- Students can write recommendations for books they enjoyed.
- Students can create individual goal cards, targeting specific goals to work on. They revisit and update the cards as they achieve their reader goals.

Building your craft

Don't reinvent the wheel. You and your students need to feel good about the learning environment to be inspired to read. Research what other teachers are doing and use the ideas that work for you and your students. There are a vast number of professional books and resources found online (Teachers Pay Teachers, Pinterest, YouTube videos, and teacher blogs, for example) that you can use as inspiration. Many will help you avoid trial and error and help in your establishment of the perfect Reader's Workshop.

Track the strategies that you introduce and use, and the ones students share. These can be displayed in the classroom as evidence of your work and serve as teaching tools. They can be revisited with frequency and provide students with ideas and reminders of what good readers do.

Just like athletes, young readers need time to develop their craft. Start with small chunks of time and increase it as they build up their stamina. You don't want to discourage students. They should look forward to Reader's Workshop.

You will have great success if you make reading the foundation of your classroom. Consider showing the students a video of what Reader's Workshop looks like. If they understand the routine and you are consistent with it, you'll have an easier time implementing it. Build excitement and lead them to books. Share what you are reading, and allow students to share their favorite books. Visit your school or community library and encourage students to use these resources. Consider school magazines that students might keep and take home. You want to normalize reading as something that is enjoyable, informational, and what we all do.

Connect reading to the lives of the students. Provide opportunities in other curricular areas for reading. Let students discover how reading can help their understanding of the world around them. Let them use reading to create reports, posters, movies, and art. Make a display of these in the classroom to nurture the environment of reading.

Map your year and days to systematically cover essential reader skills, strategies, and practices. Be intentional: prepare and carefully plan to cover the lessons you'll teach as you move through the year. Be flexible: you might need to adjust your lessons depending on your students' needs and abilities. Be consistent: have your workshop during a time of day in which there are minimal interruptions.

Reading Goal Cards

Students use these cards to help them achieve their goals. Date or check as practiced.

_____'s Reading Goal Card

I am working on _____

_____

_____

My strategies are _____

_____

_____

_____

Check off: ☐   ☐   ☐

GOAL

_____'s Reading Goal Card

I am working on _____

_____

_____

My strategies are _____

_____

_____

_____

Check off: ☐   ☐   ☐

GOAL

Reading
Goal Cards

Reading Goal Cards

Students record reading goals and strategies. Students can make notes on their progress.

Name: _____

Goal#1: _____

_____

Strategy: _____

_____

Goal #2: _____

_____

Strategy: _____

_____

Notes:

Name: _____

Goal #1: _____

_____

Strategy: _____

_____

Goal #2: _____

_____

Strategy: _____

_____

Notes:

Math Overview

Mathematics is a core subject to be taught every day. It is taught sequentially, aligning to the developmentally age-appropriate skills and concepts. In other words, students are introduced to skills that they are ready for and that lay the foundation for consecutive higher-level skills to be introduced in subsequent grade levels. The following is an overview or breakdown of the basic math strands taught for each grade level. This is just a glimpse of what each grade level looks like at each strand, which can vary from state to state. As with all curricular areas, consult your state standards and your state's or district's adopted curriculum. The major strands are as follows.

Number Sense

Number sense is gaining an understanding of numbers, their relationships, and what they represent.

Teaching Tips:

- Manipulatives are excellent for building number sense.
- Hundreds chart and number line are excellent tools.
  - Counting and counting patterns—one more/one less, ten more/ten less, etc.
  - Counting on and counting back to ±

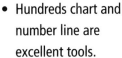

Measurement/Geometry

Measurement involves length, volume, and weight. Geometry deals with shapes and solids, their characteristics, and their area/perimeter.

Teaching Tips:

- Solids or shape manipulatives are excellent tools.
- Measure something every day; repetition builds mastery.
- Set up a center for measurement and volumes.

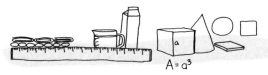

$A = a^3$

Algebra

Algebra involves solving mathematical problems through interpretations and properties.

Teaching Tips:

- "Problem a day" with the whole class

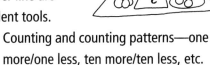

$$3 + \_ = 7 \qquad 3n + 2 = 14$$
$$3n = 12$$
$$n = 4$$

Statistics, Data Analysis, and Probability

Involves analyzing, comparing, and interpreting data; prediction and probability.

Teaching Tips:

- Manipulatives with graphing grids or mats
- Coin tossing or dice rolling

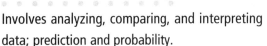

Mathematical Reasoning

Explaining approach and solution, application to other problems

Teaching Tips:

- "Problem a day" with whole class
- Math journals

Number Sense

Kindergarten

Numbers 1 to 30 ······ 0, 1, 2, 3, 4, 5, 6 . . . 30

Patterns ······ △ ○ △ ○ △ ○ △ . . .

± ······   3 + 1 = 4   5 − 1 = 4

Fact families ······ 1 + 3 = 4   4 − 1 = 3
3 + 1 = 4   4 − 3 = 1

Fractions ······ □ 1   □□ ½ ½

Place value ······
T	O
3	5	= 35

Money ······ 1¢ 5¢ 10¢ 25¢ $1.00

First Grade

Counting by 1s, 2s, 5s, 10s to 100 ······
1, 2, 3, 4, 5, 6, 7 . . . 100
2, 4, 6, 8, 10, 12 . . . 100
5, 10, 15, 20, 25 . . . 100
10, 20, 30, 40 . . . 100

Patterns ······ △ ○ ▭   △ ○ ▭   △ ○ ▭ . . .

± ······ 11 + 3 = 14 $\begin{array}{r}64\\+23\\\hline87\end{array}$ $\begin{array}{r}38\\-12\\\hline26\end{array}$ $\begin{array}{r}3\\5\\+2\\\hline10\end{array}$
14 − 6 = 8

Fact Families ······ 4 + 3 = 7   7 − 4 = 3
3 + 4 = 7   7 − 3 = 4

Comparison ······ 7 > 3   16 < 23   25 = 25

Place value ······
H	T	O
3	4	7	= 347

Fractions ······ ◯ 1   ½   ⅓   ¼   ⅛

Money ······ 1¢ 5¢ 10¢ 25¢ 50¢ $5   10¢ 1¢ 1¢ = 5¢ 5¢ 1¢ 1¢

Second Grade

Counting by 1s, 2s, 5s, 10s to 1,000

1, 2, 3, 4, 5, 6 ... 1,000
2, 4, 6, 8, 10 ... 1,000
5, 10, 15, 20, 25 ... 1,000
10, 20, 30, 40, 50 ... 1,000

±

$8 + 7 = 15$ $19 - 4 = 15$

Regrouping

$$\begin{array}{r} \overset{1}{2}3 \\ +\ 7 \\ \hline 30 \end{array} \qquad \begin{array}{r} \overset{1}{\cancel{2}}3 \\ -\ 7 \\ \hline 16 \end{array}$$

Fact families

$12 + 3 = 15$ $15 - 3 = 12$
$3 + 12 = 15$ $15 - 12 = 3$

Comparison

$352 > 248$ $672 = 672$
$173 < 183$

Fractions

1   ½   ⅓   ¼   ⅛

Place value

Th	H	T	O
3	4	2	7

= 3,427

Money

1¢ 5¢ 10¢ 25¢ 50¢ $1, $5, $10, $20

$$\begin{array}{r} \$\ 5.42 \\ +\ \$\ 3.27 \\ \hline \$\ 8.69 \end{array}$$

Third Grade

Counting to 10,000

1, 2, 3, 4, 5, 6 ... 10,000

Place value

TTh	Th	H	T	O
3	1	2	6	5

= 31,265
Thirty-one thousand two hundred and sixty-five

Expanded form

$30,000 + 1,000 + 200 + 60 + 5 = 31,265$

Decimals

32.7
(tenths)

Rounding

$9,986 \sim 10,000$

+/−/×/÷

$37 + 29 = 66$ $41 \times 3 = 123$
$264 - 77 = 187$ $9\overline{)81}$

$$\begin{array}{r} 16 \ \text{R1} \\ 2\overline{)33} \\ -2 \\ \hline 13 \\ -2 \\ \hline 1 \end{array}$$

Multiplication

$6 \times 7 = 42$
$6 \times 8 = 48$
$6 \times 9 = 54$

Fact families

$6 \times 9 = 54$ $54 \div 9 = 6$
$9 \times 6 = 54$ $54 \div 6 = 9$

Fractions

1   ½   ⅓   ¼   ⅛ $2/4 = ½$ $¼ + 2/4 = ¾$
                          $½ = .5$

Money

1¢ 5¢ 10¢ 25¢ 50¢ $1, $5, $10, $20

$$\begin{array}{r} \$20.37 \\ +\$13.23 \\ \hline \$33.60 \end{array}$$

Fourth Grade

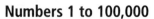

Numbers 1 to 100,000	1, 2, 3, 4, 5, 6 ... 100,000
Standard form	$\begin{array}{c|c|c|c|c|c} \text{HTh} & \text{TTh} & \text{Th} & \text{H} & \text{T} & \text{O} \\ \hline 8 & 9 & 3 & 2 & 1 & 7 \end{array}$ = 893,217
Expanded form	800,000 + 90,000 + 3,000 + 200 + 10 + 7
Word form	eight hundred ninety-three thousand two hundred and seventeen
Place value	
Decimals	8.73 (tenths / hundredths)
Rounding	7,789 ~ 8,000
Negative numbers	←—┼——┼——┼——┼——┼——┼——┼——┼——→ -4 -3 -2 -1 0 1 2 3 4
Prime numbers	1, 3, 5, 7, 11, 13 ...
+/−/×/÷	$\begin{array}{r} 637 \\ \times\ 24 \end{array}$ $6\overline{)426}$ $6\overline{)247}^{41\ R1}$
Multiplication facts to 10	4 × 4 = 16 4 × 5 = 20 4 × 6 = 24
Fact families	2 × 8 = 16 16 ÷ 2 = 8 8 × 2 = 16 16 ÷ 8 = 2
Fractions	6/12 = 1/2 6/8 = 3/4 = .75 9/4 = 2 1/4 = 2.25
Money	$\begin{array}{r} \$1.34 \\ +\ \$\ .95 \end{array}$ $\begin{array}{r} \$2.76 \\ -\ \$2.17 \end{array}$

Fifth Grade

Numbers 1 to 1,000,000	1, 2, 3, 4, 5, 6, 7 ... 1,000,000
Place value **Standard form**	$\begin{array}{c|c|c|c|c|c|c} \text{M} & \text{HTh} & \text{TTh} & \text{Th} & \text{H} & \text{T} & \text{O} \\ \hline 2 & 3 & 6 & 1 & 4 & 1 & 5 \end{array}$ = 2,361,415
Expanded form	2,000,000 + 300,000 + 60,000 + 1,000 + 400 + 10 + 5
Word form	two million three hundred sixty-one thousand four hundred and fifteen
Decimals	9.325 (tenths, hundredths, thousandths)
Rounding	6,889 ~ 7,000
Percentage	75% = 3/4 = .75
± Integers	←—┼——┼——┼——┼——┼——┼——┼——┼——┼——┼——→ −4 + 2 = −2 −3 × −4 = −12 −5 × 3 = −15 -5 -4 -3 -2 -1 0 1 2 3 4 5
Mixed numbers	16/3 = 5 1/3
Prime factors **Exponents**	$2^4 \times 3$ (2×2×2×2) × 3
+/−/×/÷	$\begin{array}{r} 734 \\ \times\ 227 \end{array}$ $32\overline{)692}$
Fractions	14/20 = 7/10 4/6 + 2/6 = 6/6 = 1 1/2 × 1/2 = 1/4 3/4 ÷ 1/4 = 3
Money	$\begin{array}{r} \$3.61 \\ \times\ .85 \end{array}$ $\$1.50\overline{)3.50}$

(prime factor tree for 48: 48 → 12, 4 → 3, 4, 2, 2 → 2, 2)

Algebra

Kindergarten

Sorting, classifying, identifying

First Grade

Number sense
+/−/=

Word problems
+/−/=

$3 + \_ = 7$ $8 - \_ = 5$

$4 - 1 = 3$

Second Grade

Communicative and associative rules
Number sentence with symbols
+/−/=
Problems using data from
   charts and graphs ±

$3 + 2 = 5$ so $2 + 3 = 5$

$3 + 2 = 5$

$5 - 3 = 2$ more ☼ than ⛅

137

Third Grade

Numeric equations and inequalities
Communicative and associative properties
Unit conversions
Operational symbols
Functional relationships and patterns

$3 + n = 7$

$2 + n > 1$

$2 \times 3 = 6$ so $3 \times 2 = 6$

$12 \text{ inches} = 1 \text{ foot}$

$4 \_ 3 = 12$

4 legs so $4 \times 4 = 16$ legs
(4)

Fourth Grade

Operational symbols
( ) in math expressions
Formulas
    Properties of equality

$n \times 3 = 12$

$25 \div \square = 5$

$3 \_ 6 = 18$

$4 + (2 \times 3) =$
$4 + 6 = 10$

$y = 4x + 2$
$x = 2$
$y = 4(2) + 2$
$y = 10$

$A = lw$

$2(6 + 2) = (8) \times 2$

$8 + (2 + 3) = 5 + 8$

Fifth Grade

Identifying and graphing ordered pairs
Using graphs or equation data to solve problem situations
Using letters to represent unknown numbers
    Distributive properties

$\square - \Diamond = \_ \text{ more } \square$
$5 - 2 = 3 \text{ more } \square$

$(-2, 2)$ $\cdot (2, 2)$

$(-2, -2) \cdot$ $\cdot (2, -2)$ (x, y)

$y = 3x + 5 \qquad x = 2$
$= 3(2) + 5$
$= 6 + 5$
$= 11$

$3 + (6 \times 4) =$
$6 + (3 \times 4) =$

138

Measurement and Geometry

Kindergarten

Time
Units of measure
Calendar: days of the week, months of
the year
Geometric shapes
Planes and solid objects

First Grade

Length (in./cm), weight, and volume
Time: hour, half hour
Identifying and classifying
Planes and solid objects
Proximity and position

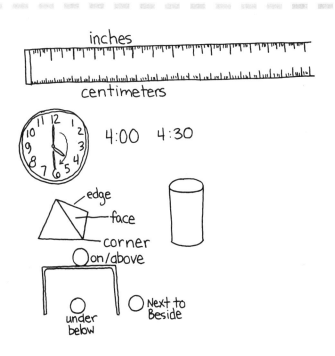

Second Grade

Length (in./cm), weight, and volume
Units of measure: in./cm
Time: hour, half hour, quarter hour
Identifying, classifying, and describing
Planes and solid objects
Time equivalents
Duration of time intervals

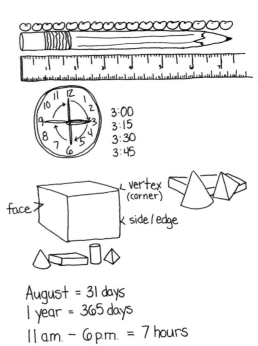

August = 31 days
1 year = 365 days
11 a.m. – 6 p.m. = 7 hours

Third Grade

Length, volume, and mass
Area and volume of a solid
Perimeter
Attributes of triangles
Quadrilaterals
Polygons
Right angles and angles
Identifying, classifying, and describing
Planes and solid objects

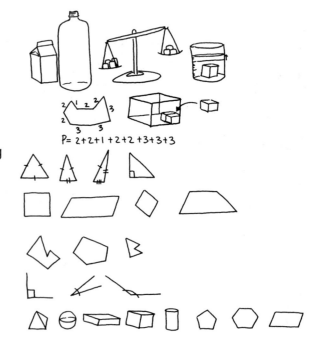

Fourth Grade

Area and volume of a solid

Perimeter

2-D coordinate grids

Parallel and perpendicular lines

Radius and diameter of a circle

Congruent and similar figures

Symmetry

Right, obtuse, and acute angles

Attributes of triangles

Identifying, classifying, and describing

Planes and solid objects

Quadrilaterals

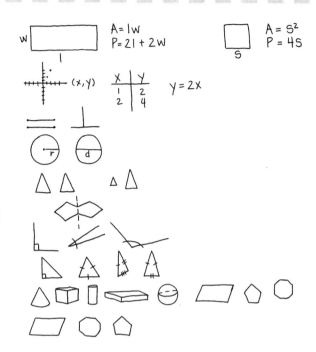

Fifth Grade

Area and perimeter formulas

Sum of angles in a triangle

2-D coordinate grids

Parallel and perpendicular lines

Radius and diameter of a circle

Congruent and similar figures

Right, obtuse, and acute angles

Geometric solids

Defining triangles and quadrilaterals

Constructing 2-D patterns

Volume

2-D vs. 3-D objects

Measuring, identifying, and drawing
angles: protractor and compass

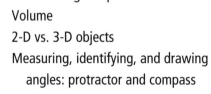

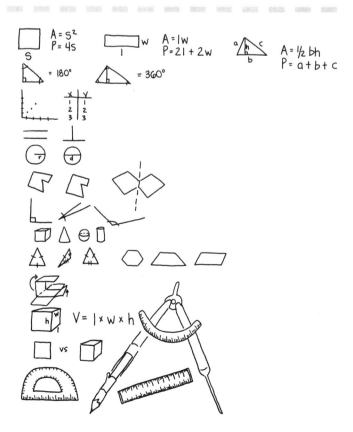

Statistics, Data Analysis, and Probability

Kindergarten

Sorting by common attributes
Data collection
Recording with pictograph
Simple patterns

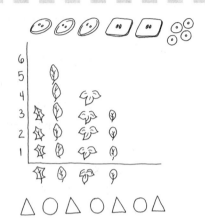

First Grade

Sorting objects, data by common attributes
Bar graph and pictograph
Tally charts
Simple repeating patterns

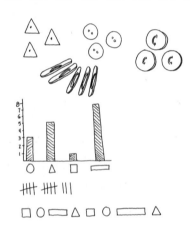

Second Grade

Recording number data
Graphs and charts
Mode and range
Extended patterns
Tally charts

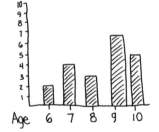

range = 6 - 10   (10 - 6 = 4)
mode = 9

3, 6, 9, □, □, □

卌 卌 |||

Third Grade

- Certain, likely, unlikely, improbabl
- Outcomes and probability
- Bar graph
- Line plots, coordinate points
- Predicting future events
- Mean, mode, and range

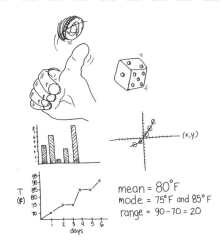

mean = 80°F
mode = 75°F and 85°F
range = 90 - 70 = 20

Fourth Grade

- Formulating survey questions for data collection
- Graphs, tables, and charts
- Mode, median, and range
- Representing outcomes
- Tables, grids, and tree diagrams
- Outcomes and probability

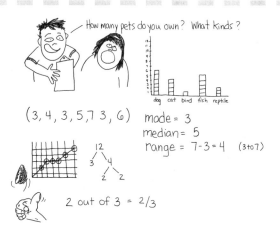

How many pets do you own? What kinds?

(3, 4, 3, 5, 7 3, 6)

mode = 3
median = 5
range = 7 - 3 = 4   (3 to 7)

2 out of 3 = 2/3

Fifth Grade

- Mean, median, and mode
- Organizing and displaying data
- Pie graphs
- Bar graphs
- Histographs
- Line graphs
- Comparing data sets
  - Fractions and percents
  - Identifying and writing ordered pairs

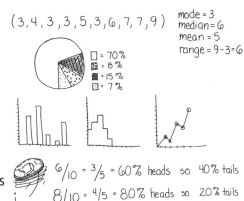

(3, 4, 3, 3, 5, 3, 6, 7, 7, 9)

mode = 3
median = 6
mean = 5
range = 9 - 3 = 6

☐ = 70%
▦ = 8%
▨ = 15%
▢ = 7%

6/10 = 3/5 = 60% heads so 40% tails
8/10 = 4/5 = 80% heads so 20% tails

(2,3) (3,8) (4,1)

Mathematical Reasoning

Kindergarten

Using tools, strategies, and manipulatives
    to model problems

Explaining reasoning

First Grade

Using tools, strategies, and manipulatives
    to model problems

Determining approach

Explaining reasoning

Making exact calculations

Making connections between

Second Grade

Using tools, strategies, and manipulatives
    to model problems

Defending reasoning

Third Grade

Breaking problems down to simpler parts

Estimating

Explaining reasoning

Supporting solutions with evidence

Making exact calculations

Developing generalizations

Fourth Grade

Sequencing and prioritizing information

How and when to break down a problem

Variety of methodologies

Expressing solutions clearly and logically
    (math notation)

Exact and proximate solutions

Making exact calculations

Developing generalizations

Fifth Grade

Sequencing and prioritizing information

How and when to break down a problem

Variety of methodologies

Expressing solutions clearly and logically
    (math notation)

Exact and proximate solutions

Making exact calculations

Developing generalizations

Math Strategies

Students can use multiple approaches to solve any math problem. They can innately see and tackle any math problem from their own perspective. For years, teachers have not capitalized on this. To allow each student the space to solve and make sense of mathematical problems for himself or herself is a powerful way to facilitate your math lesson. Sharing student strategies and even naming them after the student used them can bring about a broader understanding of number sense and empower your mathematicians.

Here are a few strategies of varying difficulties that students use. They will come up with their own as well—again, seeing the solution through their eyes. Remember that you need to give students the time and space to solve problems. It is not about you necessarily teaching the strategies but rather helping the students as they come up with their strategies. You can introduce a strategy in a mini-lesson, but then allow them to work on their own or in groups to solve a given problem with the demonstrated strategy and then a different strategy of their own.

Adding Strategies

Branching

$12 + 14$

10 2   10 4

$20 + 6 = 26$

Decompose/Partial Sum

$47 + 24$

$47 + 20 + 4$

$67 + 4$

71

Break Apart Addend

253
$+ 123$

$100 + 200 = 300$
$50 + 20 = 70$
$3 + 3 = + 6$
376

Number Line

+10 +10 +10 +7

24   34   44   54   61

$24 + 37 = 61$

Subtracting Strategies

Compensation

$67 - 18$

$67 - 20 = 47$

$47 + 2 = 49$

Bar Model

$36 - 14 =$

| 14 | ? |

$14 + \_\_ = 36$

$14 + 22 = 36$

Counting Back

$47 - 23 = 24$

-3 -10 -10

24 27   37   47

Decompose

$63 - 12 =$

$60 + 3$
$- 10 + 2$
$50 + 1 = 51$

Multiplication Strategies

Area Model

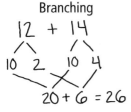

36
$\times 42$
$1,512$

Partial Products

36×42

$(30 + 6)(40 + 2)$

1200
240
60
+ 12
1512

First 30×40 1200
Inside 6×40 240
Outside 30×2 60
Last 6×2 + 12
1,512

Distributive Method

$3 \times 27 =$

$(3 \times 20) + (3 \times 7) =$

$60 + 21 = 81$

Strip Diagram

4×7

| 7 | 7 | 7 | 7 |
?

4

Array

4×7

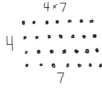

7

Division Strategies

Number Line

$12 \div 3 = 4$

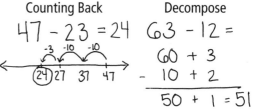

0   3   6   9   12

Inverse Operation

$12 \div 3 = 4$

$3 \times \square = 12$

$3 \times 4 = 12$

Array

$12 \div 3 = 4$

x x x x
x x x x
x x x x
① ② ③ ④

Equal Groups

$54 \div 6$

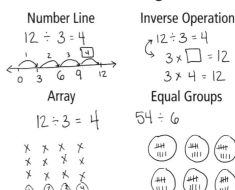

Area Model

$4324 \div 3 =$

$1,000 + 400 + 40 + 1 = 1,441\ R\text{-}1$

	4,324	1,324	124	4
3	-3,000	-1,200	-120	-3
	1,324	124	4	1

Counting Objects

Counting objects is a great way to build number sense, oral counting skills, and grouping strategies. Students can work in pairs or individually to accomplish the counting of a collection of objects. Pair work on such a task can be a powerful learning experience, as students share ideas and responsibilities in accomplishing the task at hand. Not only do they share strategies, but they also learn how to represent what they have counted and record their data in a meaningful way. This simple activity helps build the foundation for the subsequent math operations of addition, subtraction, multiplication, and division. This activity also offers an opportunity for those struggling in math to better hone their skills. The tactile experiences are good for English learners and students with special needs, and for those who have trouble processing math skills via paper and pencil only.

Counting objects can increase in difficulty as students become more accustomed to the practice:

1. **Have students count the total number in a group** (one to one correspondence). Start with a manageable number and increase the quantity as they demonstrate mastery.

   Students typically start counting by ones (1's), then expand to counting by 2's, 5's, 10's, etc. They can group into quantities that they find easier to count.

2. **Have students count packages or set groups of objects.** This can challenge students into counting by multiples of the number in the package, predicting how many will be found in several packages. Students don't open the packages but work with the quantity number given on the packages.

3. **Have students combine groups of objects.** This allows students to count larger collections and combine sets. The whole class can count a large collection of the same item or combine sets of different items.

Objects to Count. You have plenty of items around the classroom to count and each year you can build new collections. Students can bring objects from home and take ownership of this math practice. Some items include beans, bottle caps, corks, paperclips, Q-tips®, cereal (a favorite), rice, buttons, condiment packets, and plastic silverware. Packages come prepackaged (for example, boxes of 100 paperclips or bundles of 12 pencils or can be created using Ziploc® snack bags.

Teacher role: Observe, Ask, Challenge. The teacher becomes a facilitator as students tap in to their own mathematical sensibilities; they innately count the way that makes sense to them. While working in pairs, students often share their strategies and learn from each other. One student may record the information while the other counts, or they both may count. The students are in charge. The teacher can move from group to group and ask questions of the students. This is also a great time to track individual students on their number sensibility.

How do you know…?

How do you know these add up to 125?

How do you know 6 groups of 7 is 42?

How many groups of … do you have?

How many … are in each group?

Why did you group … in those groups?

Why did you count … like that?

Can you explain why you grouped … like this?

How are you grouping …?

How are you representing … in your grouping?

What would you do differently?

Sharing out. This perhaps is the most important part. Students share their counting strategies and results with the whole class. These can be charted out, displayed in the classroom, and even named after the student who shared it. Students learn from each other. The teacher is again the facilitator, asking questions that encourage depth and understanding. This sharing of strategies gives students the opportunity to learn new strategies and ask questions, which build upon their own number sense.

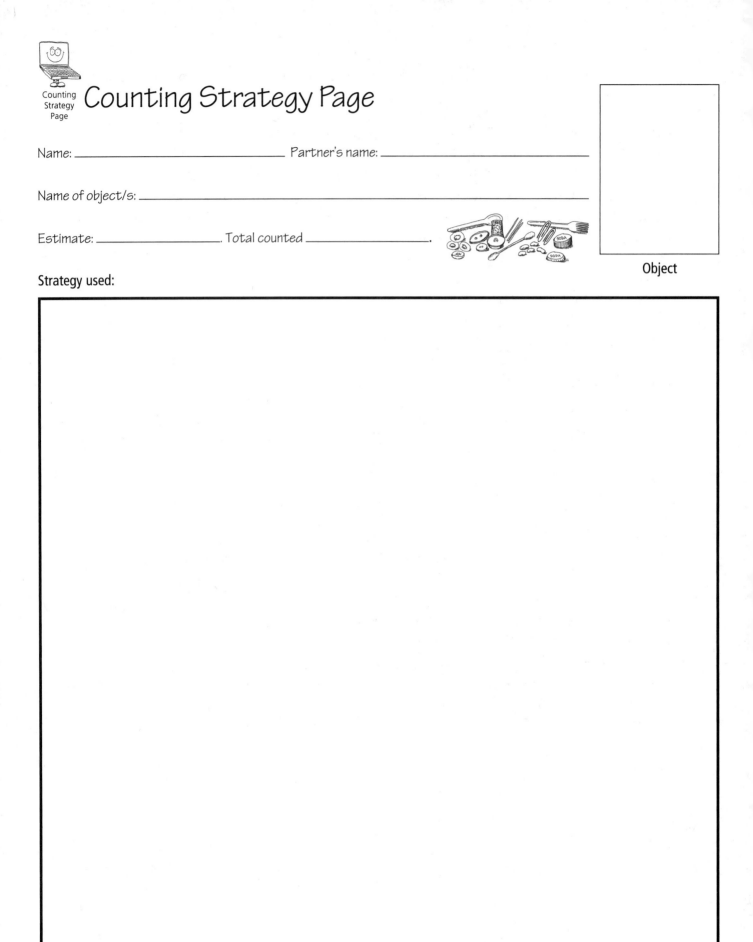

Counting Strategy Page

Counting Strategy Page

Name: _____ Partner's name: _____

Name of object/s: _____

Estimate: _____. Total counted _____.

Object

Strategy used:

My Counting Recording Page

Name: _____ Partner's name: _____

Today we counted (name of object): _____

We estimated _____ objects. We counted _____ objects altogether.

Object

Our strategy looks like:

Social Science Overview

Social Science is the study of our world and its people and their interactions. It brings together connections and relationships that give students an understanding of their place and role in their school, community, state, and country as well as in the world. As with any subject area, strands are introduced at the various grade levels and then continued in subsequent grades. They are introduced at age-appropriate levels of understanding. Always follow your curriculum or standards first to ensure that your students have an understanding of the skills they need to prepare them for subsequent learning. You are sometimes laying a foundation and at other times you are building on a foundation that hopefully is already in place. Once that commitment is fulfilled and if time permits, you can branch out into areas of personal interest. The following is an overview of the various strands that may be covered in your district's curriculum and/or state standards.

Careers

Present vs. Past

National Symbols, Icons, and Traditions

Time Lines

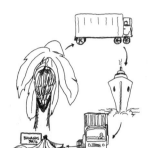

Commerce

Conflict Resolution and Communication

Cultural Diversity

Traditional Holidays

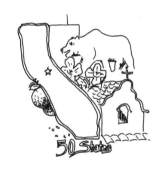

State History (generally fourth grade)

United States History (generally fifth grade)

Ancient History (generally sixth grade)

Folklore

Heroes

Economics

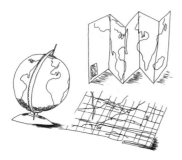

Maps and the Globe

Character

Citizenship

Government

Community

Community Service/Community Service-Learning Project

As our world recognizes the importance of being more mindful and the importance of making a difference, community service and service learning have become an integral part of the school curriculum. **Community service** is a project, usually one opportunity that students can participate in often to fulfill requirements bestowed upon them by their school. These projects can involve volunteering with, or donating to, a group or organization, and are powerful ways to make a difference. Community service learning takes this a step further and incorporates students in the research and development of a project based on a need in the community. This makes for an exceptional, more meaningful, and purposeful project, which is student driven.

    Service learning incorporates what students are learning in the classroom and allows them the opportunity to apply this learning to real-world scenarios in the community that need support. Students gain experience in collaboration, research, and problem solving. Students create an action plan and partner with members of the community to execute their plan. This is a "win-win" situation for everyone involved. Colleges and universities seek out students involved in Community service-learning projects because their involvement demonstrates character, the ability to work with others to accomplish a common goal, and the ability to see a world beyond their own. These are all qualities that make for a successful student.

Steps for a Community Service-learning Project

Have students work together in pairs or small groups to determine the following:

1. Identify the need. **Research**.
   - *Consider a list of ideas that have a need and could be addressed.*
   - What issues are affecting your community? What issues are affecting your environment? Who needs your help or support in your community?
   - How can you make a difference?
2. Connect to student interest. **Connect.**
   - *Consider which project motivates you.* Of these needs, is there one that you feel a connection to? What are you passionate about?

3. Think it through. **Decide.**
   - *Consider the feasibility of the project.*
   - Is this even possible? What would it take to accomplish this?
   - Can the project be done within the given timeframe?
   - What resources would be necessary to execute the project?

4. Gather information. **Investigate.**
   - *Consider all the players that could contribute to the project.*
   - Who could you ask about this? What agencies are involved with this issue?

PLAN OF ACTION

5. Design the project. **Design.**
   - *Consider how the project will look.*
   - Create an action plan. Assign roles. Create a timeline. Gather materials or supplies that are needed. Is there an organization, a non-profit, and/or a qualified person in the field that could help?

6. Do it. **Implement.**
   - *Consider action.*
   - Execute your plan. Keep track of student involvement. Keep a log of how the project is going, including hours. Keep notes, records, and photos of activity and findings. Track progress with charts, graphs, and journals.

7. Regroup and share. **Reflect.**
   - *Consider how the project went.*
   - What worked? What didn't work? What could be changed? What could be done better? What other projects could be done?

8. Disseminate information. **Present.**
   - *Consider how you can share the project and who you can present to*
   - What platform makes the most sense—formal papers, documentaries, PowerPoints, or podcasts?

Presentations could consist of the following: introduction to the area of service and how they choose it; any pertinent information on their research; its impact on the community; its impact on them personally; and a summary of what was learned, what they would change, and what their next steps would be. Students can present their presentations to the class, grade, or school. Consider even presenting to other organizations, as well, that could potentially team up and help continue the project. Students can also share their work via an electronic format or on a poster/display board so that students from other classes can view it.

Sometimes a full community service-learning project just isn't realistic, given time constraints and other factors. In these cases, simply being involved in a community service project can be a tremendous learning opportunity for your students. Community service can be used in the lower grades as a precursor to Community service-learning projects that will be introduced as students move up to higher grades. That is not to say that community service should be limited to only the lower grades. Community service can be done schoolwide in conjunction with community service learning. It is a powerful way to build community and give back to the greater community at large.

Community service opportunities can include:

- **Collection opportunities.** Canned food drives, eyeglasses drives, winter coat drives, blanket drives, toiletry drives, toy drives, book drives, clothing drives, Thanksgiving Basket drives, Christmas basket drives
- **Volunteer Opportunities.** Community Clean-ups, Beach and Park Clean-ups, School Beautification Days, Tutoring/Reading to students, Visits to convalescent homes, Recycling Program, Community Garden, etc.

    A parent volunteer or a staff member can contact the agency that will be supported and organize the collection and distribution of donated items.
- **Organizations and non-profits that need support and volunteers include.** Food banks, the local Red Cross, veteran's organizations, hospitals, fire departments, animal shelters, animal welfare groups, animal rescue

groups, homeless shelters, convalescence homes, environmental groups, parks and recreation, churches, synagogues, mosques, advocates for the elderly, sanitation department, local politicians, Habitat for Humanity, Adopt-a-Highway, Race for the Cure, Meals on Wheels, Big Brothers Big Sisters of America, Special Olympics

Students can create posters and decorate collection boxes. They can create cards and help organize what has been collected. In this way, the entire class, grade level, or school can be involved. Community service and community service-learning projects are engaging and make a difference. The outcomes are often greater for the students who are giving rather than for the people or organizations who are receiving their help.

Community Service Hours Chart					
Name:			**School:**		
Type of Service	**Date(s)**	**Time In**	**Time Out**	**Total Hours**	**Supervisor's Signature**

Community
Service
Project

Community Service Hours Chart

Name:			School:		
Type of Service	Date(s)	Time In	Time Out	Total Hours	Supervisor's Signature

Science Overview

Science is often divided into different strands of instruction. For this section, we focus on Physical, Life and Earth Science. The depth of study is geared toward age-appropriate understanding. While certain areas of science instruction may appeal to you, your primary goal should be to teach what is laid out in your standards. This ensures a student's preparedness for the next layer to be added at its designated subsequent grade level. For example, simple machines may be introduced in first grade and then studied in more depth or continued in fifth grade.

Physical Science

Physical science is the study of physical phenomena that exist in nature. The following is a general list of Physical Science substrands that may be covered at your grade level or by grade-level standards.

Simple Machines   Sound   Magnets

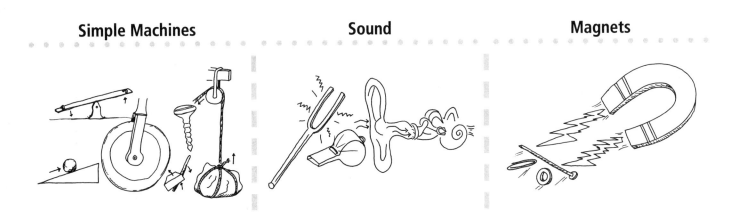

Electricity   Light   Energy and Matter

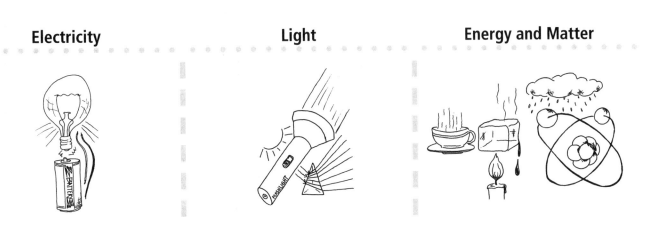

Life Science

Life Science is the study of everything pertaining to life. The following is a general list of Life Science substrands. Check your grade-level standards for specificity.

Birds

Mammals

Reptiles

Amphibians

Dinosaurs

Insects and Spiders

Fish

Carnivores

Herbivores

Five Senses

Human Body

Plants

leaf

stem

seed

root

Ocean Life

Food Chain

Earth Science

Earth Science focuses on the Earth and its physical structures, cycles, and relationships. Space Science can fall under this strand as it relates to Earth as a planet. The following is a general list of Earth Science substrands that may be covered at your grade level or by grade-level standards.

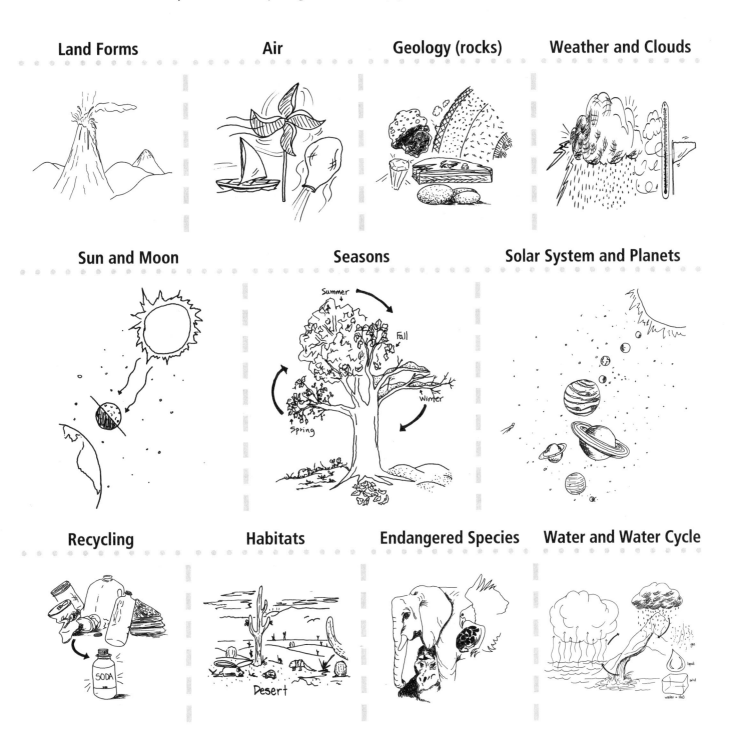

Land Forms

Air

Geology (rocks)

Weather and Clouds

Sun and Moon

Seasons

Solar System and Planets

Recycling

Habitats

Endangered Species

Water and Water Cycle

Engineering

Engineering is an important part of STEAM (Science, Technology, Engineering, Art, Math). More than ever, now we must give students time to problem solve and create. These days, many jobs are automated or outsourced; to succeed, students need the competitive edge as problem solvers and innovators. Young people need to know the right questions to ask and how to take the answers and apply them. In this learning process, they need to develop endurance and patience, and be able to handle unsuccessful outcomes as ways *not* to do something. Engineering opportunities offer students to exercise this cycle of design and redesign in order to succeed.

The basic cycle for engineering involves:

1. **Asking:** An engineer must identify a problem or need.

2. **Imagining:** An engineer must be able to envision and design a solution. Imagining requires the ability to think outside the box and to consider alternatives.

3. **Designing:** An engineer designs a solution or a model to solve the identified challenge. This is the planning phase of the process.

4. **Creating:** An engineer needs to be able to create. This is the building phase of the process. The engineer constructs a model.

5. **Improving:** An engineer needs to be open to change. Through testing and redesigning, the engineer's model is optimized. This is a critical part of the process. Learning how not to do something is the necessary mindset. It takes persistence.

6. **Sharing:** An engineer needs to be able to articulate their vision and process. Discussing the solution or model is the end goal for the engineer. The entire process has to be reflected to explain why conclusions and solutions work.

This can be a simple yet engaging product. Using everyday items, students can build and construct models that do a wide range of tasks, from launching a marshmallow into the air to suspending a tennis ball above a table. Whatever the activity, the learning experience isn't as much about the outcome as it is about the process. Giving students practice with problem solving and collaboration prepares them for the world beyond school. These opportunities lead to building the skills to be independent and confident.

Project Ideas:

Engineering projects, like any school activity, need to have a set intention/goal. These projects help solve a problem and involve trial and error and redesign. Listed are a few projects that can be used to solve a problem and will involve the process of redesign.

✓ Egg drop- create a container that could be dropped with an egg in it. Egg, paper, tape

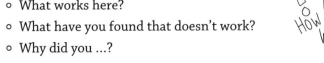

    ✓ Spaghetti/marshmallow tower challenge-pasta, marshmallows, tape, string

    ✓ Catapults for marshmallows-craft sticks, tape, marshmallows

    ✓ Paper airplane design- paper

    ✓ Film canastor rockets- film canisters, alka-setzler, paper, tape

    ✓ Structures- clothes pins, craft sticks, paperclips

✓ Bridges- straws, tape

✓ Gumdrop/marshmallow toothpick structures

✓ Marble roller coasters- paper tubes, card stock, tape

    ✓ Powered cars- balloons, rubber bands, card stock, bottle caps, water bottle, tape, dowel sticks

    ✓ Wind turbines- clay, craft sticks, paper

    ✓ Boats- paper, tape

    ✓ Suspension of a book/basketball/tennis ball above the desk- paper

Project Management

- Groups are an excellent way to facilitate the engineering process. Not only is innovation needed, but the skill of collaboration is also an integral part of good design. More than one mind on a challenge teaches students to value all input. Constructive input adds to the project; such input can not only reinforce what works, but also emphasize what doesn't. In this manner, there are no mistakes. All contributions are a valuable part of the process.

- This is a chance for the teacher to let go. Your job is to facilitate your student engineers in the process of design and problem solving. To foster deeper thinking, ask questions such as:
  - How did you decide to ...?
  - What is another way you could ... ?
  - What works here?
  - What have you found that doesn't work?
  - Why did you ...?

Gently guide students to dive deeper in an understanding of the problem they are exploring. Encourage students to embrace failure.

Be prepared. Make sure that students have easy access to the materials they need. Consider making "STEAM Bag Challenges" with the materials inside and a description of their challenge taped to the outside.

- Have fun! Your students will be engaged in a hands-on activity that builds a love for learning and design experimentation. These simple activities will serve them with a passion for design, a confidence in taking on the unknown and a growth mindset—all that can only come from real world, hands-on engineering.

Suggested Websites

There are hundreds of ideas on the internet for STEAM projects, specifically engineering projects using everyday items. Listed are just a few website resources.

https://www.nationalgeographic.org/education/engineers-in-the-classroom/
www.teachengineering.org
https://www.eie.org/eie-curriculum/engineering-design-process
https://www.iteea.org/
https://www.exploratorium.edu
https://online.kidsdiscover.com/
https://paperrollercoasters.com/

Engineering Organizer NAME: _____

Use this organizer to help plan your project. Illustrate and label your ideas.

Ask   What is the problem or need?

Imagine and Design   Brainstorm solutions/designs/a model. Draw and label your best.

Create   List materials need. Build your prototype.

Improve   Test, redesign, modify. What went well? What didn't work?

Prototype 2	Prototype 3	Prototype 4

Engineering
Organizer

Engineering Organizer NAME:_____

Use this organizer to help plan your project. Illustrate and label your ideas.

Ask What is the problem or need?

Imagine What would your solution look like?

Materials needed to create:

Reflect and Improve Test, redesign, modify.

Went well:_____

_____

Didn't go well:_____

_____

This is the best solution because:_____

_____

_____

Technology

Technology continues to be an ever-growing part of our modern-day classroom experience. Most students have access to cell phones and thus hold a powerful educational tool in their hands. With thousands of educational apps available, we can speak the language of our 21st-century students, which can engage and empower them. Even with a limited number of devices, you can use them to create another significant layer to your instructional delivery. Students can manage this aspect of their learning, often showing teachers how to navigate the latest technologies. Monitoring your students is critical to not only keeping them on task but also to ensure that the lesson objective is accomplished.

As part of STEAM, the technology piece has several objectives. It serves as a tool that is used to research, design, and model solutions to the problems students are exploring. Technology is an excellent discipline for the dissemination of information on multiple platforms, requiring in-depth understanding and design. Coding, some argue, is as important as reading.

Technology is perhaps one of the easiest components of STEAM to incorporate into the classroom because it is so engaging for students from all backgrounds and levels. There are numerous ways to use technology with traditional instructional methods. With that said, technology can support all the other areas in the STEAM acronym (Science, Technology, Engineering, Art, and Math). Listed are a few:

Technology as a Support

Research: Use on-line resources from libraries, museums, universities, and educational sites

Skill Reinforcement: With apps and websites, there are numerous sites that support learning in creative ways. Engaging students in games can reinforce specific skills that students are learning.

Frontloading/Flipping the Classroom: Using videos and apps, such as Show Me, that allow you to film your lessons can prepare students for the next day's class. Students arrive with an idea of what will be covered and come prepared with questions.

Building Technology

Coding: The vital language of the twenty-first century: Students not only need to understand how to use technology but also how to build technology. Both girls and boys benefit from a deeper understanding of coding. There are numerous apps and websites dedicated to these skills, which program a computer to complete tasks. Students learn this best through play. Apps allow them to create simple projects and games that

they "code" what to do. This can lay the foundation for more intensive coding as they become more skilled. Any student with coding skills will have an advantage moving forward in education and into the career world. Because of this, numerous apps and websites are focused on ensuring that students will be ready. Starting as young as kindergarten, students can learn coding skills just as they learn reading and math skills. Listed here are a few websites and apps to introduce and inspire young coders:

Websites:

https://code.org/
https://studio.code.org/
https://www.allcancode.com/
https://world.kano.me/
https://www.thinkfun.com/
https://scratch.mit.edu/
https://hourofcode.com/
https://www.tynker.com/hour-of-code/
https://code.org/minecraft
https://www.kodable.com/hour-of-code

Apps:

LightBot
SpriteBox: Code Hour
Hopscotch: Coding for kids
Daisy the Dinosaur
Cargo Bot
codeSpark Academy
Mozilla Thimble

Obtaining Technology

If you are lucky enough to have technology available at your school, use it! If you are not comfortable with technology, ask your students to get it up and running. More than likely, they will jump at the chance. Such an experience teaches students how to manage and problem solve as they navigate to your objective. Your job is to monitor, circulate, and keep students on task. Ask other teachers which apps and websites they use, and research them. Be careful if students are inputting any personal information that would comprise their privacy and *never* allow students to use their full name. Creating a screen name assures anonymity.

If you don't have technology available, reach out and ask. Friends and family members or local businesses for donations can be a good start. Technology changes so frequently people are often eager to make donations of older computers and devices. There are also websites for people who will donate to help purchase equipment for classrooms. You sign up to receive such donations with a specific project and present an action plan for it. Once you receive a donation, make sure to always follow up with thank-yous and updates. It's easy and a great way to bring technology into your classroom. Here are a few websites for donations:

https://www.gofundme.com/
https://www.donorschoose.org/
https://www.adoptaclassroom.org/
http://www.classwish.org/
http://teacherwishlists.com/
http://www.digitalwish.com/dw/digitalwish/about
http://www.treasures4teachers.org/

Lastly, remember to be flexible and use a growth mindset to embrace technology in the classroom. Move with this force of your students' understanding of technology and incorporate it into your best teaching practices.

Art Overview

Art is a vital part of a child's education and personal creative expression. Many teachers think that if they can't draw then they can't teach art. Don't fall into this trap. You just need to provide the necessary environment, enthusiasm, materials, and motivation; your students will take care of the rest. The following is a brief summary of the elements of art and the principles of design. With an understanding of these concepts and the basic art materials found in the classroom, anyone can teach art. There are always those teachers who are very creative and artistic and do wonderful projects. Your students are quite capable and you'll be surprised by the results. Have fun with it.

Elements of Art

Color

Primary: red, blue, yellow
Secondary: orange, violet, green
Value = light or dark
Intensity = bright or dull

Line

Continued stroke
Types:

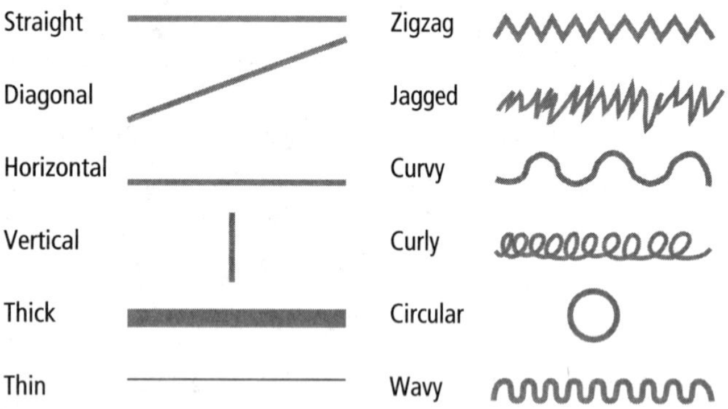

Straight	Zigzag
Diagonal	Jagged
Horizontal	Curvy
Vertical	Curly
Thick	Circular
Thin	Wavy

Form

Mass of an object (3-D)

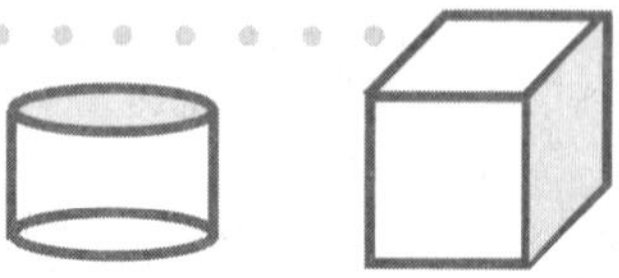

Shape

2-D geometric

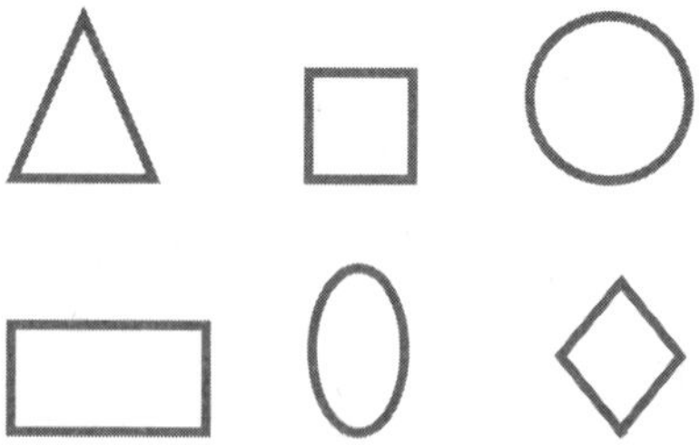

Texture

Quality of a surface

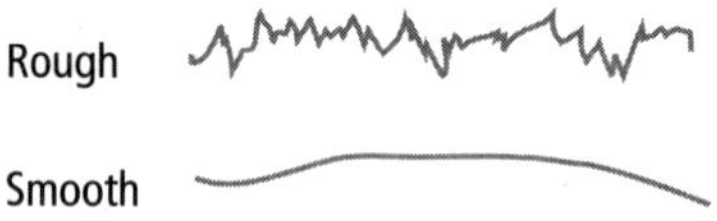

Rough

Smooth

Space

Area around an object

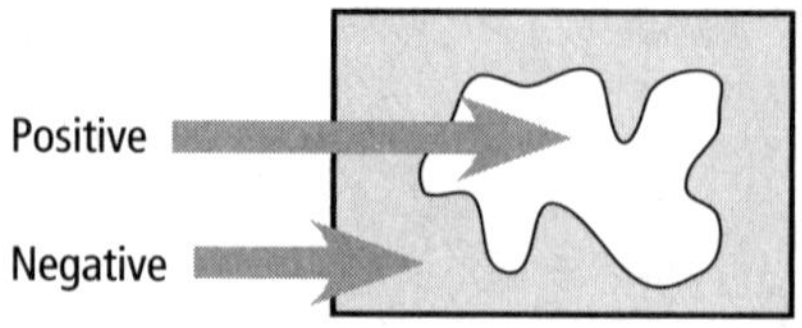

Positive

Negative

Principles of Design

Balance

Asymmetrical

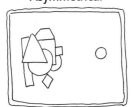

Balance

Radial

Balance

Symmetrical

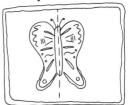

Theme

Common idea

Repetition

Repeating elements

Movement

How your eye travels
through an art piece

Contrast

Opposing aspects

Dominance

More emphasis on one part

Unity

Fitting together as one

Rhythm

Repeating flow of line or shape

Emphasis

Prominence

Basic Classroom Art Supplies

The following is a basic set of supplies that can be used in the classroom. Not all schools will have all supplies. Check to see what is available and permissible at your school.

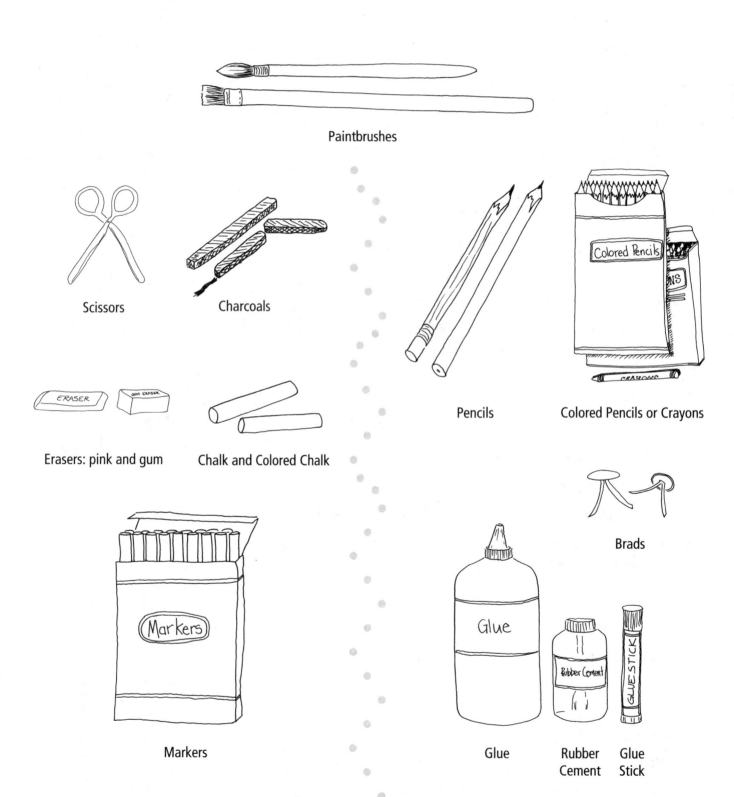

Paintbrushes

Scissors

Charcoals

Pencils

Colored Pencils or Crayons

Erasers: pink and gum

Chalk and Colored Chalk

Brads

Markers

Glue

Rubber Cement

Glue Stick

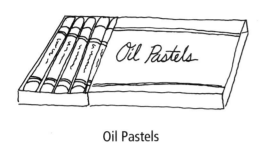

Oil Pastels

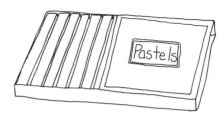

Pastels

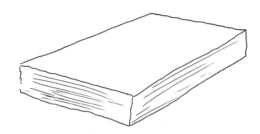

Paper: drawing and construction

Tissue Paper

Tape: masking, clear,
book-binding

Tempera Paint

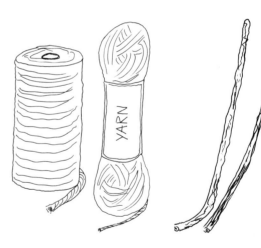

Cord or Yarn

Pipe Cleaners

Watercolor Paints

Color Wheel

Oone of the fundamental aspects of art is color. Students learn as early as kindergarten how to mix colors to create new ones. There are three primary colors, three secondary colors, and five intermediate colors. There are cool colors and warm colors. Colors that complement each other are complementary colors. One of the best ways to teach color is with a color wheel. The following page has a basic template for creating a color wheel. Here is a basic breakdown of color and suggestions for creating a color wheel.

Can be done with:

Crayons

Colored pencils

Pastels*

Paint*

*Heavier paper (paper plates work well, too)

Name: _____ Date: _____

Directions: (1) Color primary colors on every other wedge of the wheel.
(2) Color corresponding secondary colors between their primary colors.

RED
ORANGE
VIOLET
YELLOW
BLUE
GREEN

Color primary colors.

Then color the secondary colors.

Upper grades can show intermediate colors in between.

Mixing Colors

Directions: Color the missing colors.

+ = GREEN | + = ORANGE

+ = VIOLET

Blue + Yellow = Green
Red + Yellow = Orange
Red + Blue = Violet

Primary Colors

Red
Blue
Yellow

Secondary Colors

Violet
Orange
Green

Cool Colors

Blue
Violet
Green

Warm Colors

Red
Orange
Yellow

Intermediate Colors

Red-violet, Red-orange
Blue-violet, Blue-green
Yellow-orange, Yellow-green

Complementary Colors

(opposite sides of the color wheel)

Red → Green
Blue → Orange
Yellow → Violet

Name: _____ Date: _____

Directions: (1) Color primary colors on every other wedge of the wheel.

(2) Color corresponding secondary colors between their primary colors.

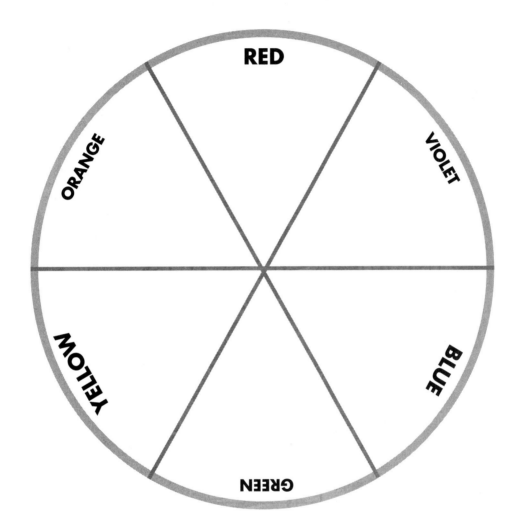

Mixing Colors

Directions: Color the missing colors.

+ = GREEN | + = ORANGE

+ = VIOLET

Music Overview

Music, like visual art, is an excellent creative outlet for students. Many teachers shy away from teaching music, but it doesn't have to be complicated. Again, look to the teachers who have strengths in this area for ideas and advice. Teaming is an excellent option. The following is an overview of some basic music terminology, some suggested activities, and basic classroom instruments.

Vocabulary

Beat: the pulse of music; can be clapped, tapped, etc.

Rhythm: the flow of the music, its movement with various sounds and rests; gives music its personality

Melody: unified tones or pitches that create a tune, have a rhythm

Pitch: high and low characteristic of a sound

Echo: repetition of a given sound

Rest: silent pause in music

Activities

Chart and Sing: Chart the words to a song and sing song while tracking words; very helpful in teaching a song. Also excellent for primary students to build print awareness and left-to-right tracking.

Play Along to a Song: Pass out some classroom instruments and allow students to play along to the beat or melody of a song. Try clapping to the song as a whole class first, then use instruments to play along to the song. Very simple, yet students love it. Try only a few instruments and rotate the instruments.

Pass the Beat: Sit in a circle or at desks. One person claps out a beat; then the entire class echoes the same beat. Each student takes a turn. Can add in actions, too. Try it with an instrument—students echo with clapping and the instrument is passed along to each student for his or her turn.

Basic Classroom Instruments

Classrooms are sometimes equipped with a basic set of instruments that can be used for music instruction. Check with your school and/or other teachers to see if any sets are available to be checked out or borrowed. If none are available, some of the basic ones can be made (see suggestions below). Always establish rules for using instruments to facilitate ease of instruction and maintain order. Oftentimes, especially with the primary grades, some free exploration time (five minutes) with the instruments helps take the edge off when students can get some play out of their system.

Suggested Rules:

1. Do not touch instrument until instructed to do so.
2. Only play instrument when instructed to do so.
3. Listen to and follow directions.
4. Pass instrument to next student when your turn is finished.

Not following the rules will result in you losing your turn with the instrument until the next rotation.

Maraca

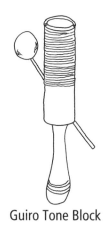

Guiro Tone Block

Jingle Clog

Jingle Bells

Hand Castanet

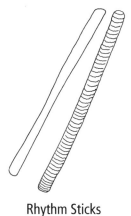

Rhythm Sticks

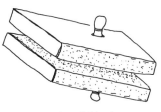

Sand Blocks

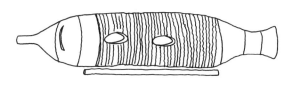

Guiro

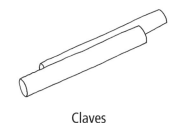

Claves

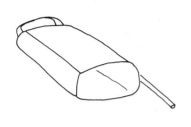

Cowbell

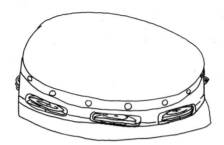

Tambourine

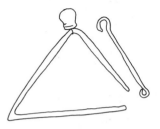

Triangle

Cymbals

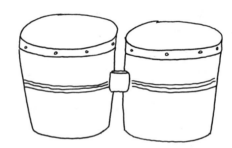

Bongos

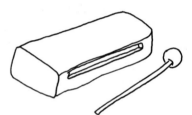

Wood Block

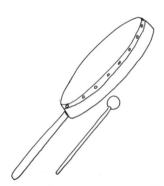

Hand Tom-Tom

Finger Cymbals

Slit Drum

Hand Drum

Do-It-Yourself Instruments

Soda-Bottle Shaker
- Use a plastic soda bottle.
- Fill with beans or rice.
- Cover or decorate with paper.

Kazoo
- Use a toilet paper roll.
- Put wax paper over one end.
- Secure with rubber band.
- Poke hole just below rubber band.
- Hum on open end.

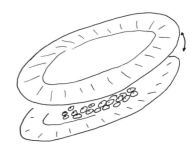

Paper-Plate Shaker
- Decorate and tape two paper plates together.
- Fill with beans or rice.

Rhythm Sticks

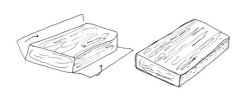

Sand Blocks
- Use two wood blocks and sandpaper.
- Cut sandpaper to wrap around three sides of blocks.
- Glue sides and attach.
- Staple to reinforce.

Bucket Drum

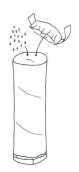

Paper-Roll Shaker
- Secure wax paper at each end.
- Fill with rice or beans.

Finger Cymbals
- Use small jar lids.
- Secure elastic strap through a hole.

Mallet
- Attach a cork to a pencil.

Coffee-Can Drum
- Empty a can and remove both ends.
- Cover one end with wax paper, vinyl, or leather.
- Secure with heavy rubber band.

Physical Education and Games

Physical education is an important part of a child's education and well-being. It can clear the mind and refresh the body. It's clearly a part of the secondary curriculum and students usually have organized PE every day but in the elementary grades, often it is hard to find the time to squeeze it in to your schedule with all the other mandated curricular areas. The following are some suggested activities/games that you can use with your students depending on your school policies. Always consult your standards (for skills and required minutes) and select games that support your students' level. Ask other teachers how they fit physical education into their daily/weekly schedule and what activities they use. Most schools provide equipment and have designated play areas. Physical education is an excellent break from the classroom and can build great peer-to-peer relationships as well as teacher-to-student relationships. It can also provide another venue for students to succeed in and build self-confidence. Try it and have fun!

Games can be played collectively as a whole class, in smaller groups, or individually. There are also many games that can be played indoors on inclement weather days.

The following are lists of some suggested games that can give you some options to start with.

Small Group Outdoor Games

- Four Square
- Hopscotch
- Handball
- Tetherball
- Jump rope

Whole Class Outdoor Games

- Cat and Mouse
- Steal the Bacon
- Red Light, Green Light
- Duck, Duck, Goose

Indoor Games

- Hunter and Prey
- Seven-Up
- Sparkle
- Around the World
- Learning Relay

Outdoor Games

(Small Group)

Four Square

Description: small-group game

Skills: bounce-serving a ball, bounce-returning a ball

Rules:

1. The game is played on a large square that is divided into four equal smaller squares. A standard soft red rubber 8½-inch kickball is used.
2. Four players each take a square with one being designated the "king" (the #4 square) and the others are numbered off 1–3 around the square. The object is to advance to king (square #4) and stay there.
3. The king serves the ball with one bounce in his or her square and then hits it (with one or two hands) into one of the other three squares.
4. The receiving player hits the ball into any of the other squares after one bounce in their square.
5. Play continues until one player is "out." A player is out when:
   - A serve is unsuccessful (i.e., doesn't bounce into other square)
   - The player hits or is hit by the ball prior to its bouncing in his or her square
   - The ball bounces twice (or is not hit)
   - The ball is hit with a fist
   - The player hits the ball out of bounds (not bouncing in a square)
   - The player momentarily holds the ball
   - The ball bounces over the player's head (the "hitter" is out)
6. The "out" player proceeds to the end of the line and a new player enters the game at the lowest square with the other players rotating to fill in the vacant square.

Hopscotch

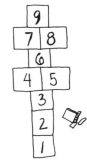

Description: skill and coordination game

Skills: hopping, balancing, tossing accuracy

Rules:

1. Played on a hopscotch grid.
2. Each player has a small object that can be tossed to land on grid (beanbag, rock, etc.).
3. Players hop down and back on the grid to start the game. (Single squares are landed in with one foot, doubles with two.)
4. Players who successfully complete their trips then take turns tossing objects onto each numbered square (starting with #1), one at a time. They then hop down the grid, always skipping over the square with the object in it. When players reach the #9 square, they turn on one foot and hop back down the grid while pausing to retrieve object.
5. Players must always:
   - Only toss object into consecutive square without it touching any lines
   - Land themselves only in the squares without touching a line, lowering a raised foot, or switching raised foot

Handball

Description: two players bouncing a ball against a wall

Skills: bouncing and hitting a ball, returning a ball

Rules:

1. Two players stand between six feet (the service line) and fifteen feet from the wall.
2. One player serves the ball by hitting it in a bounce to bounce on the ground inside the service area and up to the wall. The ball must then bounce from the wall to the serving area to be counted (must land between six and fifteen feet). Two attempts can be taken.
3. Player 2 then hits the ball on the bounce to the ground and up to the wall. It cannot bounce twice.
4. Play now continues with each player taking turns. At this point, the ball can hit anywhere in the court and even be hit on the fly.
5. Play continues until:
   - A good serve is not made in two tries
   - The serve doesn't rebound into service area or is hit on the fly
   - The ball is hit after bouncing twice
   - A player interferes with (fouls) another player
   - A ball bounces out of the court
6. Then a new player rotates in and the existing player serves.

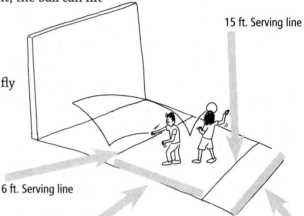

15 ft. Serving line

6 ft. Serving line

Serving area

Baseline

Tetherball

Description: two players serving and hitting a ball attached to a pole

Skills: serving and hitting a moving ball

Rules:

1. Two players play on a tetherball court.
2. One player serves, the other player gets to (1) dictate the direction of the serve and (2) choose his or her side of the court.
3. The server tries to hit the ball around the pole again and again to wind it around the pole.
4. Ball is officially in play when the receiver hits it and then tries to unwind the rope by hitting the ball in the opposite direction and wind it back around in this opposite direction.
5. The player who completely winds the rope and ball around the pole is the winner.
6. Play is stopped if and forfeited if:
   - A player hits the ball with anything other than his or her hand.
   - The ball or rope is caught or held in play.
   - The pole is touched.
   - A player steps in the neutral zone
   - The ball is completely wrapped around pole on serve and the receiver has not had an opportunity to hit the ball.

Neutral zone

Jump Rope

Jumping rope is an excellent cardiovascular and coordination activity. Most schools have standard equipment. A plastic rope can be purchased, or a rope can be made from a heavy cotton rope. As with any game, supervision is important. Working with students on taking turns and proper conduct is the key to independent success. The following are some jump-rope variations.

Single Jump Rope

- Single rope (shorter)
- One jumper
- Jump or skip, stationary or moving

Single Rope Paired

- Single rope
- Two turners
- One or two jumpers
- Fun with jump-rope rhymes

Double Dutch

- Two ropes simultaneously
- Two turners
- One or two jumpers
- Fun with jump-rope rhymes

Group Jump

- Single rope
- One student in the center of a circle
- Several jumpers in a circle
- Center student spins the rope around the circle.
- Students jump over rope as it passes them.
- Supervision is recommended.

Outdoor Games

(Whole Class)

Cat and Mouse

Description: a circle game with up to twelve players

Skills: running and dodging; tagging

Rules:

1. Students form a circle by joining hands.
2. One student is selected to be the "cat," another to be the "rat."
3. The cat starts outside the circle with the rat inside the circle.
4. The cat tries to catch or tag the rat.
5. Students assist the rat by raising and lowering joined hands so the rat can move in and out of the circle.
6. Students prevent the cat from catching or tagging the rat by lowering and raising their hands, whichever is necessary.
7. Once the rat is caught or tagged, both choose replacements to play again.

Tips:

- Have two cats or rats.
- Have students unclasp hands if game is too slow.
- As with any game, *discuss safety* to avoid unnecessary accidents.

Steal the Bacon

Description: yard game with two teams of about eight players

Skills: running and dodging

Rules:

1. Two teams each number off and line up facing each other with same numbers at opposite ends (diagonal).
2. A beanbag, knotted rag, or stuffed animal—the "bacon"—is placed in the center.
3. Teacher calls a number and both players with the called number race to the center to retrieve the bacon and return it to their side without being tagged by the other player.
4. Players can run anywhere between the lines to avoid being tagged.
5. Once a player crosses the line or is tagged, the bacon is returned and both players return to their respective positions.

Tips:

- Players who steal the bacon without being tagged score 2 points.
- Players who successfully tag a player with the bacon score 1 point.
- Call two numbers at once (four players = two teams).
- As with any game, *discuss safety* to avoid unnecessary accidents.

Red Light, Green Light

Green Light!

Description: tag game

Skills: running and stopping on signal

Rules:

1. One student is chosen as "it" and the class lines up along a line facing the student, whose back is turned to the class (25 to 30 feet apart).
2. Selected student calls "green light" to start class running toward him or her.
3. Selected student calls "red light" to stop students and turns to catch any students that are moving (have not stopped).
4. Any students caught moving must return to the start line. The remaining students continue to play from their newly advanced position until one player makes it to the finish line.
5. The first player to reach the finish is then designated "it."

Tips:

- Increase or decrease the distance students travel.
- As with any game, *discuss safety* to avoid unnecessary accidents.
- Have students connect to honesty by being able to admit when they moved after the call to stop.

Duck, Duck, Goose

Description: running game, two at a time

Skills: listening, running around a circle, passing to the right

Rules:

1. Class sits in a circle, and one student is designated "it."
2. "It" student walks around outside of circle tapping each student and calling "duck."
3. "It" student taps a student and calls "goose" to stand and race him or her around the circle in the opposite direction back to the vacated spot.
4. The first student to reach the spot sits and the remaining student proceeds around the circle tapping students and calling "duck" until he or she selects the next goose.

Tip:

- As with any game, *discuss safety* to avoid unnecessary accidents.

Indoor Games

Hunter and Prey

Description: indoor game with two players

Skills: balance and coordination

Rules:

1. A designated traffic pattern around the room is established.
2. Two players are chosen to be "hunter" and "prey" and are placed at opposite ends of the classroom.
3. Each player balances an eraser or beanbag on his or her head and cannot touch it.
4. Both players start to walk, and the hunter must tag the prey without losing the balanced object from his or her head.
5. If the prey is tagged or loses the object, he or she chooses a new prey.
6. This new prey then chases the hunter.
7. Whoever is tagged and/or loses the object chooses a replacement and the chase is switched.

Tips:

- Make sure the traffic pattern is obstacle- and feet-free to avoid tripping.
- As with any game, *discuss safety* to avoid unnecessary accidents.

Seven-Up

Description: tagging and guessing game

Skills: none

Rules:

1. Seven players are chosen to stand in front of the classroom and a group leader is appointed.
2. The group leader calls to the remaining seated students "Heads down!"
3. Students close their eyes, lower their heads, and leave one arm raised.
4. The seven chosen students circulate and each taps one student, who then lowers his or her hand, and the player returns to the front of the room.
5. When all seven players have returned to the front of the class, the leader calls "Heads up, seven-up!"
6. All seated students raise their heads and the seven "tapped" students stand beside their desks.
7. The leader asks each player to guess who tagged them.
8. A correct guess exchanges a student and his or her tapper. If the guess is incorrect, the student remains in his or her seat and the player retains his or her position in the seven.
9. The game continues once all guesses and exchanges have been made.

Tips:

- The leader needs to make sure all seven players have been tapped and their hands are lowered.
- Peekers can be eliminated from the game.
- Incorrect guessers can leave a thumbs-up so that others can have a turn to be tapped.

Sparkle

Description: spelling game

Skills: spelling and concentration

Rules:

1. Teacher calls out a word to be spelled and selects a student to give the first letter.
2. Student says first letter. Teacher points to another student to give the second letter.
3. Continue until entire word is spelled.
4. If a student misses a letter, he or she sits, and another student is called to give the letter.

Around the World

Description: reading game

Skills: word recognition

Rules:

1. Teacher has a set of words written on flash cards.
2. A student is selected to stand behind another student.
3. A word from the card set is shown to both students, and the first to read it moves behind the next student.
4. The next word is shown, and the first to read it advances.
5. The goal is to make it around the entire classroom (around the world).

Learning Relay

Description: math and spelling game

Skills: computation and spelling

Rules:

1. The class is divided into two teams, evenly broken down and mixed by student ability.
2. A student from each team is selected to start the game. They are called to the board, which has been divided in half.
3. Teacher calls out a math fact to be solved or a word to be spelled.
4. Players race to write and solve the problem or spell the word on their respective side of the board.
5. First player to finish successfully wins a point for his or her team.
6. Both players then select the next player from their team to go. Points are tallied.

Bilingual Overview

It is not uncommon to have students whose primary or first language is not English. These students are often categorized as English Language Learners (ELLs). Depending on the ELL population at your given school, you may or may not have a designated bilingual program or an instructional support plan. The following is a simple overview of an ESL (English as a Second Language) program and instructional strategies. Your school or district should have a specific program that they follow, along with support curriculum and assessments. Check with your school's administration and other teachers for guidelines and strategies.

Common Acronyms and Terms in a Bilingual Program

ELL: English Language Learner

ESL: English as a Second Language

ELD: English Language Development

SDAIE: Specifically Designed Academic Instruction in English

TPR: Total Physical Response

Comprehensible Input: Information delivered on a level that is understandable for a given ELD level

Reminders:

- Be sensitive and create a supportive environment.
- Access prior knowledge and make connections to a student's background, culture, and life experiences (creates meaningful learning).
- Pull the key vocabulary and skills to simplify content.
- Increase level of interaction (class, groups, partners) to promote practice through discussion (creates purposeful learning).
- Allow for plenty of speaking and writing time (multiple opportunities).
- Provide comprehensible input (gear instruction to meet the needs specific to the ELD level).

In your school or district, there may be specific strategies along with an adopted ESL program that can assist you in meeting the needs of your ELL students. Be sensitive to the needs of ELL students—learning a new language is a process, not a barrier. It takes real experiences and opportunities to learn a second language.

SDAIE (Specifically Designed Academic Instruction in English)

- SDAIE is strategic instruction that layers lessons to review vocabulary and concepts according to a student's needs. It can target and narrow a lesson's focus, making it easier for the ELL student (comprehensible input). This is an excellent strategy that shouldn't be limited to just ELL students.
- Helps students gain access to information (specifically at the higher ELD levels [3–5])
- With this strategy, the teacher understands the students' struggles, what they know, and what they need to know.

Realia (part of SDAIE)

- Tangible items that can be used to introduce vocabulary (e.g., plastic fruit, items of clothing, etc.)
- Students can touch, hold, and role-play to create "real" learning experiences.

Preteach/Reteach (part of SDAIE)

- Involves preteaching a lesson's vocabulary or concepts to the ELL students
- Increases familiarity/builds background knowledge
- Involves reteaching the key vocabulary and concepts after the lesson has been taught
- Reviews and reinforces

TPR/Role-Play (part of SDAIE)

- Total physical response involves physically executing described actions.
- "Sit down and open the book" = sitting down and opening a book
- Role-playing involves acting out and practicing real-life scenarios and practicing dialogue situations.
- Real learning experiences

Pictures/Graphic Organizers (part of SDAIE)

- "A picture is worth a thousand words."
- Pictures of individual items or of story scenarios
- Graphic organizers to simplify information

In more practical terms, teachers use the following levels of ELD. These levels help you, the teacher, understand a student's language capabilities. The goal is to move at least one ELD level per year, eventually redesignating into a "fluent English speaker" status. The following is a very simplified look at each level. If engaged in a lesson, students would communicate by:

ELD 1

- responding nonverbally to using a few words.
- pointing to pictures to respond.
- drawing pictures to communicate.

ELD 2

- giving verbal responses of one to two words.
- using yes/no responses.
- writing phrases with invented spellings.

ELD3

- giving verbal responses in short phrases (omitting words or verbs).
- responding to "whys?"—can elaborate.
- writing phrases to simple sentences (conventional spelling starts).

ELD 4

- conversing verbally with few errors.
- answering in discussion.
- writing related sentences with strong vocabulary and few errors.

ELD 5

- responding verbally like a native speaker.
- having discussions like a native speaker.
- writing with the ease of a native speaker.

English Language Development (ELD) Levels

There are three important components necessary to consider in when working with English language learners. ELD instruction and its delivery is often geared toward meeting the needs of students at their ELD proficiency level—**Emerging, Expanding**, or **Bridging**.

1. Know who you are teaching and their individual ELD level.
2. Create an optimal and welcoming environment for language learning.
3. Design high-quality, relevant, and engaging lessons for language development.
4. Adapt lesson planning, delivery, and assessments, as needed.
5. Consistently monitor, assess, and reevaluate student-language development.
6. Engage and collaborate with colleagues and specialists to share ideas for implementation.

All of these work in tandem together. It's not enough only to create strong lesson plans if you don't know who you are teaching. ELD Levels 1-5 are the most common way to designate proficiency levels, however a more simplified system of just 3 levels has also come into practice. Emerging, Expanding, and Bridging comprise this new leveling system.

Three Proficiency Levels

- **Emerging.** This is the first level of language acquisition. Much happens here, as students quickly begin to learn basic vocabulary and how to express themselves and meet their needs. This extends into the classroom, where they are starting to understand and use academic language. This level is a collaborative level, where students can start to engage in conversation with their peers.

- **Expanding.** This second level of language acquisition stretches the students into more advanced vocabulary and the application of higher-level linguistic structures, which more closely align to their grade level. Students can dive deeper into concepts and have increased academic confidence, which they can apply to everyday speaking and learning. This level is more interpretive in that students not only communicate but now can start to comprehend and analyze both written and spoken text.

- **Bridging.** This final level of language acquisition "bridges" students into full participation in a variety of academic activities and endeavors. This level involves continued growth and application to an even higher level of vocabulary production and linguistic skills across all academic areas. Students comprehend with confidence and can produce and share advanced texts, which demonstrate a full engagement across the grade-level curriculum without needed support. This level is productive. Students can now produce both written and spoken presentations, which demonstrate a command of their language acquisition.

At all three levels, language acquisition involves:

Conversation
Comprehension—both written and spoken
Creation—both written and spoken

Regardless of the students' level, best practices in language acquisition are necessary so that students can and should fully participate to the best of their ability with appropriate differentiation and scaffolding to support them. Sheltered English, front-loading lessons, use of images/video, and so on, can all serve as excellent methodologies to support English language learners.

Sponge Activities

Sponge activities are a fun, productive way to make use of down time or those five- to ten-minute gaps in the day before a transition (lunch/recess) or at the end of the day. They challenge students to think in a fresh, "out of the box" way that is purposeful. The following are some suggested sponge activities that can be used.

Primary-Grade Sponges

- Be ready to tell one playground rule.
- Be ready to tell me the names of the students in our class whose names begin with *P* or *M* (etc.).
- Be ready to draw something that is only drawn with circles.
- Be ready to tell a good health habit.
- Have a color on the board. Have students draw something with that color.
- Say numbers, days of the week, or months, and have children tell what comes next.
- "I went to the sporting goods store and I bought . . ."—each child names an item.
- What number comes between these two numbers: 31–33, 45–47 (etc.)?
- What number comes before or after 46, 52, 13 (etc.)?
- Have a word written on the board. Students make a list of words that rhyme.
- Have a word written on the board. Students make a list of words that have the same long or short vowel sound.
- Put spelling words in *abc* order.
- Count to 100 by twos, fives, tens, etc.—either orally or in writing.
- Use T-squares to drill math fundamentals.
- Think of animals that live in the jungle, on a farm, in the mountains, in water, etc.
- Give the names of fruits, vegetables, meats, etc.
- Play hangman using the names of students in the class, colors, numbers, etc.
- Play Simon Says.
- Play I Spy.
- List things you can touch, things you can smell, big things, small things, etc.
- List the colors you are wearing.

Primary-Grade Dismissal Sponges

- I Spy—who can find something in the room that starts with *M, P* (etc.)?
- Who can find something in the room that has a short **a** sound, a long **o** sound, etc.
- Count in order by twos, fives, tens, etc.
- Say the days of the week, the months of the year, etc.
- What day is it? Month? Date? Year? How many months in a year? Days in a week? Etc.?
- Use flash cards. The first correct response leaves first.
- Review the four basic shapes by having each student point out an object in the room that names the shape it represents.
- Say a word that begins or ends with certain consonants, blends, etc.
- Dismiss by color of eyes, clothes, shoe types, month of birthday, season of birthday, beginning letter of name, etc.
- "What did we learn today?" Student identifies one lesson from the day.

Upper-Grade Sponges

- List the continents of the world.
- Make up three names for rock groups.
- Name as many kinds of natural disasters as you can.
- Take a number. Write it. Now draw a face from it.
- Name as many gems or precious stones as you can.
- Write the names of all the girls or boys in the class.
- Write the names of as many teachers in this school as you can.
- List as many states as you can.
- Write as many as you can: (a) abbreviations; (b) Roman numerals; (c) trademarks; (d) proper names (biographical); (e) proper names (geographical).
- How many countries and capitals can you name?
- How many baseball teams can you name?
- Write down as many cartoon characters as you can.
- List as many kinds of flowers as you can.
- List all the things in your living room.
- Write what you would do if you saw an elephant in your backyard or on your street.
- Name as many kinds of ice cream as you can.

Upper-Grade Sponges (continued)

- List five parts of the body above the neck that have three letters.
- List one manufactured item for each letter of the alphabet.
- List as many nouns in the room as you can.
- List the mountain ranges in the United States.
- Write the twelve months of the year correctly. Stand up when you are done.
- Make a list of five things you can do outside after school.
- List one proper noun for each letter of the alphabet.
- Name as many holidays as you can.
- Write numbers by sixes as high up as you can.
- Name as many balls that are used for sports as you can.
- List as many U.S. presidents as you can.
- List all the work tools you can think of.
- List as many models of cars as you can think of.
- Name all the colors you know.
- How many parts of an auto or computer do you know?
- How many animals that begin with vowels can you list?
- List as many kinds of trees as you can.
- Name as many countries in the world as you can.
- Name as many personal pronouns as you can.
- Name as many kinds of transportation as you can.
- How many different kinds of languages can you name?
- Write as many homonyms as you can (e.g., past, passed).
- You have five children. Make up five names.
- Name as many things that are made of cloth as you can.
- List all the musical instruments you can think of.
- Name as many politicians as you can.
- Name as many wars as you can.
- Name as many types of dogs as you can.
- Scramble ten spelling words. Switch with someone. Unscramble the words.
- List as many things that make people the same as you can.
- List as many things that make people different as you can.
- List as many kinds of soup as you can.
- List all the places you find sand.
- List as many breakfast cereals as you can.

Independent Work Ideas

Independent work is important and gives you a chance to meet with individual students or small groups. Training students to work independently is important to minimize interruptions of instruction. Establishing a consistent routine helps as well as having a set of rules and norms in place. Because students work at different levels and speeds, it is important to provide a routine that meets the needs of a diverse student population. The following is a list of suggested activities and a suggested implementation to assist in the facilitation of independent work time.

Must Dos and May Dos

- Decide on your Must Dos and May Dos according to your instructional goals.
- Use chart paper or dry erase board.
- Gradually introduce activities until students can work independently on them (especially in primary grades). Practice before you attempt to work with a group—make sure they have it.
- Have templates, copies, and paper ready in a designated location.

Suggested Activities

- Write sentences with designated words.
- Write and illustrate designated words.
- Write a story from a given title using a set of designated words (e.g., using spelling words, try to write a story entitled "My Trip to the Beach").
- Alphabetize a set of words.
- Find rhyming words for a set of designated words.
- Find synonyms or antonyms for words.
- Add prefixes or suffixes to words.
- Look up words in the dictionary.
- Find words or vocabulary and cite an example from a story.
- Read a designated story.
- Write a book report.
- Select an activity from the extra work basket (always run off extra work or assignments and make them available).
- Write questions with *who*, *what*, *when*, *where*, *why*, and *how* that ask about a story or topic (can also partner trade).
- Write a number as many ways as you can think of (e.g., $9 = 4 + 5$, $13 - 4$, 3×3, etc.).
- Write and illustrate story problems with designated problems or numbers.

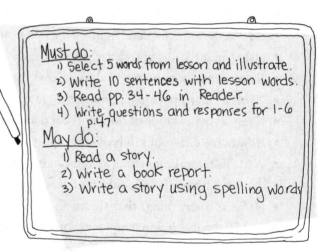

Must do:
1) Select 5 words from lesson and illustrate.
2) Write 10 sentences with lesson words.
3) Read pp. 34-46 in Reader.
4) Write questions and responses for 1-6 p.47

May do:
1) Read a story.
2) Write a book report.
3) Write a story using spelling words

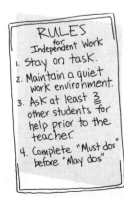

RULES for Independent Work
1. Stay on task.
2. Maintain a quiet work environment.
3. Ask at least 3 other students for help prior to the teacher.
4. Complete "Must dos" before "May dos"

Suggested Rules

- Use indoor voices and keep a quiet environment.
- Stay on task.
- Ask at least three other students for assistance prior to interrupting the teacher with a question.
- Complete Must Dos prior to starting May Dos.

Book Reports

Book reports are an excellent way to reflect and build comprehension. Reports can be used to evaluate your students' comprehension and understanding. Your students can respond to specific questions, write about a character from the book, retell the story, etc. The following are three book-report forms you can use to get started. Choose the report that best meets the needs of your students and supports the standards. As always, check with your school for any school adopted book report forms as well as with other teachers.

Beginning Book Reports

This is the most basic of reports. Kindergarten students can even dictate their book reports and then illustrate them. Here is a list of the key components found in a beginning report:

    Name
    Date
    Title
    Author
    Illustrator
    Three sentences on what the book is about
    Student's illustration

Intermediate Book Report

An intermediate book report goes beyond a simple summary and asks for the student's favorite part. Here is a list of the key components found in an intermediate report:

    Name
    Date
    Teacher
    Room
    Title
    Three sentences on what the book is about
    Three sentences on student's favorite part
    Student's illustration

Advanced Book Report

Here is a list of the key components found in an advanced report:

    Name, Date, Teacher, Grade, Room
    Title, Author, Illustrator, Copyright, number of pages
    Genre
    Outline
    Student's report
    Student's illustration

Book Report

Name: _____

Date: _____

Title: _____

Author: _____

Illustrator: _____

Write three sentences telling what the book is about.

_____

_____

_____

_____

_____

_____

_____

_____

_____

_____

_____

_____

Draw a picture about the story (on the back). Include characters in the setting.

Book Report

Name: _____

Date: _____

Teacher: _____

Room: _____

Title: _____

1. Tell what the book is about (three or more sentences):

_____

_____

_____

_____

_____

_____

_____

_____

2. What was your favorite part (three or more sentences)?

_____

_____

_____

_____

_____

_____

_____

_____

3. Draw a picture about the story (on the back).

BOOK REPORT

Name: _____

Date: _____

Teacher: _____

Grade: _____

Room: _____

BOOK INFORMATION

Title: _____

Author: _____

Illustrator: _____

Copyright date: _____

Number of pages: _____

Genre: ☐ Fiction ☐ Nonfiction ☐ Fable ☐ Fantasy

☐ Fairy Tale ☐ Expository ☐ Biography ☐ Autobiography

BOOK REPORT OUTLINE

Select an outline to assist you in writing your book report.

☐ 1. (a) State subject. (b) List three facts you learned. (c) Describe the most interesting part.

☐ 2. Describe: (a) the main characters (b) the setting (c) the conflict or problem (d) the resolution

(e) a personal connection or opinion.

_____

_____

_____

_____

_____

_____

_____

_____

_____

_____

_____

_____

_____

_____

_____

_____

_____

_____

_____

Draw a picture of your favorite part of the story (on the back).

Journals

Journals help students to reflect on learning across the curriculum. They give students the opportunity to summarize, predict, record, illustrate, and demonstrate what they have learned in a purposeful way. Journals can be easily assembled by stapling the desired journal pages together with a cover sheet (construction paper, student-designed cover, etc.). You may even color-code them for their specific subject (e.g., green for science or red for math). Journals keep an ongoing record of what is being covered in a particular subject. They can be used at conference time to show parents what is being taught and how their child is participating in the process. You may find it easier, especially in the primary grades, to collect them and keep them in a designated location with an appointed journal monitor to distribute them as needed or keep in individual desks for easy access. Journals can be guided or independent. They can serve as a daily warm-up when set up prior to going home and then recorded in the next morning. The following journals have been included in this book for your use. Be creative—ask others how they use journals in their classrooms. Journals create powerful, meaningful learning.

In the News Journal

Current events

School events

Daily/Weekly lesson summaries

Response Journal

Response to literature

Response to events

Response to lessons

Math Journal

Story problems

Problem explanations

Vocabulary/illustrations

Science Journal

Observations

Predictions

Summaries

Data

Labeled illustration

Social Science Journal

Historical events

Holidays

Customs

Traditions

Blank Journal

Story writing

Quick writes

Daily journal

In the News
Journal

In the News Journal

Name: _____ Date: _____ Class: _____ Room: _____

Name: _____ Date: _____

Response
Journal 2

Name: _____   Date: _____

Math
Journal

Name: _____   Date: _____

Science
Journal 1

Name: _____ Date: _____

Name: _____ Date: _____

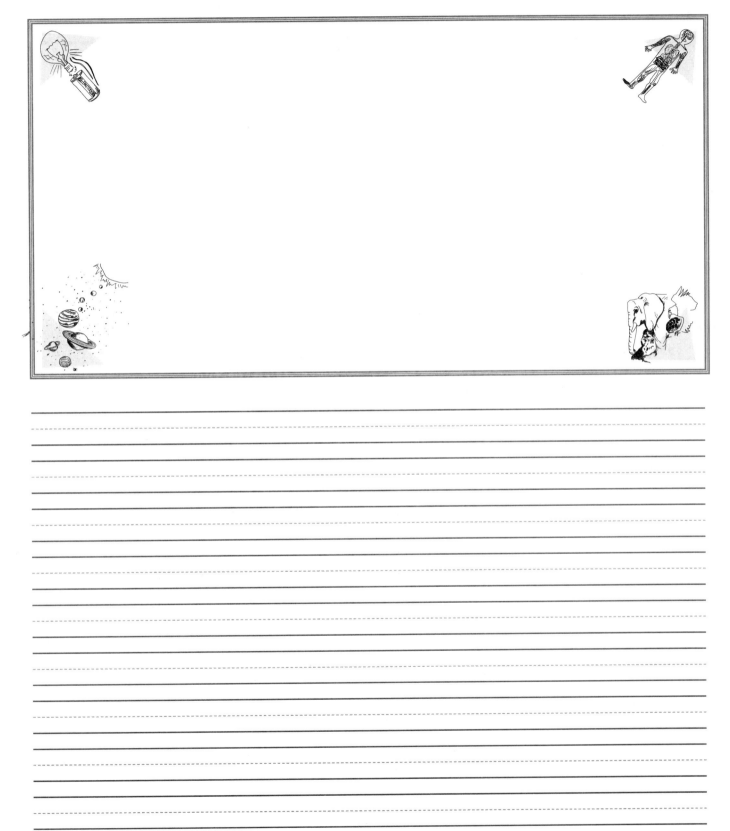

Name: _____ Date: _____

Name: _____   Date: _____

Journal

Name: _____ Date: _____

Bibliography

As most teachers know, the current mandated language arts programs and social studies texts are not enough to teach children all they need to know about history and keep them enthused about reading. With this in mind, it is imperative that teachers maintain a varied classroom library of picture books ranging from informational books, folktales, poetry, realistic fiction, fantasy, biographies, and historical fiction stemming from today's multicultural selections. Such a library will enhance the mandated curriculum and bring it to life. More important, a theme-based library makes the books more accessible and readily available. When a child can see himself or herself in the books being read in class, he or she is more likely to stay engaged, ask critical questions, and gain a deeper understanding of the content. Children learn to enjoy books when books of interest are available to them.

Children's Literature by Theme or Topic

Family

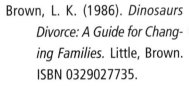

Adoff, A. (1973). *Black Is Brown Is Tan.* Harper & Row. ISBN 0060200839.

Brown, L. K. (1986). *Dinosaurs Divorce: A Guide for Changing Families.* Little, Brown. ISBN 0329027735.

Bunting, E. (2001). *Jin Woo.* Clarion Books. ISBN 0395938724.

Bunting, E. (1989). *The Wednesday Surprise.* Houghton Mifflin Harcourt. ISBN 0395547768.

Ching, E. (1991). *Forgot the Turnips & Two Bushels of Grain: A Story in English and Chinese.* Wonder Kids. ISBN 1561620017.

Clark, Emma Chichester. (2004). *No More Kissing.* Random House. ISBN 0440417619.

Curtis, J. L. (1996). *Tell Me Again About the Night I Was Born.* HarperCollins. ISBN 00602528X.

Dorros, A. (1993). *Radio Man: A Story in English and Spanish.* Harper Collins. ISBN 006021547X.

Flournoy, V. (1985). *The Patchwork Quilt.* Dial Books. ISBN 0803700989.

Freidman, I. (1987). *How My Parents Learned to Eat.* Houghton Mifflin Harcourt. ISBN 0395442354.

Greenfield, E. (1980). *Grandmama's Joy.* Philomel Books. ISBN 0399210644.

Jones, R. (1995). *Great Aunt Martha.* Dutton Children's Books. ISBN 0525452575.

McKissack, P. (2000). *Ma Dear's Aprons.* Simon and Schuster. ISBN 0689832621.

Mem, F. (1985). *Wilfrid Gordon McDonald Partridge.* Kane/Miller. ISBN 0916291049.

Pellegrini, N. (1991). *Families Are Different.* Holiday House. ISBN 0823408876.

Similarities and Differences

Beaumont, K. (2004). *I Like Myself.* Harcourt Brace. ISBN 0152020136.

Bottner, B. (1998). *Two Messy Friends.* Scholastic. ISBN 059063285X.

Bunting, E. (2006). *One Green Apple.* Houghton Mifflin. ISBN 0618434771.

Bunting, E. (1994). *Smoky Night.* Harcourt Brace. ISBN 0152010351.

Cheltenham Elementary. (1991). *We Are All Alike . . . We Are All Different.* Scholastic. ISBN 0590491733.

De Luise, D. (1990). *Charlie the Caterpillar.* Aladdin Paperbacks. ISBN 0671796070.

Dorros, A. (1992). *This Is My House.* Scholastic. ISBN 0590494449.

Fox, M (1997). *Whoever You Are.* Harcourt Brace. ISBN 0152007873.

Gantos, J. & N. Rubel. (1998). *Back to School for Rotten Ralph.* Harper Collins. ISBN 0060275324.

Gliori, D. (1992). *When I'm Big.* Children's Press. ISBN 1564022412.

Heide, F. & J. Gilliland. (1990) *The Day of Ahmed's Secret.* Lothrop, Lee & Shepard Books. ISBN 0688140238.

Henkes, K. (1991). *Chrysanthemum.* Greenwillow Books. ISBN 0688096999.

Hoffman, M. (1991). *Amazing Grace.* Dial Books. ISBN 0803710402.

Kraus, R. (1971). *Leo the Late Bloomer.* Harper Collins. ISBN 0878070427.

Lester, H (1999). *Hooway for Wodney Wat.* Houghton Mifflin. ISBN 0395923921.

Lester, H. (1988). *Tacky the Penguin.* Scholastic. ISBN 0590994514.

Lovell, P. (2001). *Stand Tall Molly Lou Mellon.* Scholastic. ISBN 0439434521.

Madrigal, A. (1999). *Erandi's Braids.* G. P. Putman's Sons. ISBN 0399232125.

Max, K. W. (1998). *Halala Means Welcome! A Book of Zulu Words.* Hyperion Books. ISBN 0786804149.

Polacco, P. (2007). *The Lemonade Club.* Penguin. ISBN 0399245405.

Polacco, P. (2000). *The Butterfly.* Penguin. ISBN 0399231706.

Rathman, M. (1991). *Ruby the Copycat.* Scholastic. ISBN 0590437488.

Reitano, John. (1998). *What If the Zebras Lost Their Stripes?* Paulist Press. ISBN 0809166496.

Rohmer, H. (1989). *Uncle Nacho's Hat: El Sombrero del Tío Nacho: A Story in English and Spanish.* Children's Book Press. ISBN 0892390433.

Simon, N. (1979). *Why Am I Different?* Albert Whitman. ISBN 0807590756.

Smith, C. Jr. (2003). *I Am America.* Scholastic. ISBN 0439431794.

Soto, G. (1995). *Chato's Kitchen.* G. P. Putnam's Sons. ISBN 0399226583.

Steel, D. (1989). *Martha's Best Friend.* Delacorte. ISBN 0385298013.

Taylor, B. (1999). *The Best Sign.* Perfection Learning. ISBN 0789129000

Wells, R. (1998). *Yoko.* Hyperion Books. ISBN 0786803959.

Woodson, J. (2001) *The Other Side.* G. P. Putnam's Sons. ISBN 0399231161.

Immigration, Migration, and Language

Aliki, B. (1998). *Marianthe's Story: Painted Words and Spoken Memories.* Greenwillow Books. ISBN 0688156622.

Ancona, G. (1998). *Barrio: Jose's Neighborhood.* Harcourt Brace. ISBN 0152010491.

Bunting, E. (1988). *How Many Days to America? A Thanksgiving Story.* Clarion Books. ISBN 0395547776.

Bunting, E. (1992). *The Wall.* Houghton Mifflin Harcourt. ISBN 0395629772.

Bunting, E. (1997). *Day's Work.* Houghton Mifflin Harcourt. ISBN 0395845181.

Bunting, E. (2000). *Dreaming of America.* Bridge Water Paperbacks. ISBN 0816765219.

Freeman, R. (1980). *Immigrant Kids.* Puffin Books. ISBN 0140375945.

Iijima, G. (2002). *The Way We Do It in Japan.* Albert Whitman. ISBN 0807578223.

Jiménez, F. (1998). *La Mariposa.* Houghton Mifflin. ISBN 0395816637.

Lachtman, O. (1995). *Pepita Talks Twice: Pepita Habla dos Veces: A Story in English and Spanish.* Piñata Books. ISBN 1558850775.

Lakin, P. (1994). *When A Parent Doesn't Speak English.* Rosen Publishing Group. ISBN 082391691X.

Lawrence, J. (1993). *The Great Migration: An American Story.* Harper Collins. ISBN 0374351147.

Leitner, I. (1992). *The Big Lie: A True Story.* Scholastic. ISBN 0590455699.

Levine, E. (1989). *I Hate English.* Scholastic. ISBN 0590423053.

Levinson, R. (1985). *Watch the Stars Come Out*. Penguin. ISBN 0140555064.

Miller, Elizabeth I. (1999). *Just Like Home / Como en Mi Tierra.* Albert Whitman. ISBN 0807540684.

Nagano, E. (1994). *Chopsticks from America.* Polychrome Publishing. ISBN 1879965119.

Namioka, L (1994). *Yang the Youngest and His Terrible Ear.* Dell Yearling. ISBN 0440409179.

Parker, L. K. (2003). *Why Mexican Immigrants Came to America.* Rosen Publishing. ISBN 0823964590.

Pérez, A. (2002). *My Diary from Here and There: Mi Diario de Aqui Hasta Allá: A Story in English and Spanish.* Lee and Low Books. ISBN 1584300450.

Perez, A. (2002). *My Diary from Here to There.* Children's Book Press. ISBN 0892391758.

Pérez, L. (2002). *First Day in Grapes.* Lee and Low Books. ISBN 1584300450.

Rael, E. O. (1996). *What Zeesie Saw on Delancey Street.* Simon & Schuster. ISBN 0689805497.

Recorvits, H. (2003). *My Name Is Yoon.* Frances Foster Books. ISBN 0374351147.

Say, A. (1993). *Grandfather's Journey.* Houghton Mifflin. ISBN 0395570352.

Say, A. (1999). *Tea with Milk.* Houghton Mifflin. ISBN 0395904951.

Surat, M.M. (1983). *Angel Child, Dragon Child.* Scholastic. ISBN 0590422715.

Whitman, S. (2000). *Immigrant Children.* Carolrhoda Books. ISBN 1575053950.

Williams, S. A. (1992). *Working Cotton.* Harcourt Brace. ISBN 0152996249.

Customs and Traditions

Barasch, L (2001). *The Reluctant Flower Girl.* HarperCollins. ISBN 0060288108.

Bulion, L. (2002). *Fatuma's New Cloth.* Moon Mountain Publishing. ISBN 0967792975.

Chavarria-Chairez, B. (2002). *Magda's Tortillas.* Piñata Books. ISBN 1558852867.

Chavarria-Chairez, B. (2001). *Magda's Piñata Magic.* Piñata Books. ISBN 1558853200.

Cheng, A. (2000). *Grandfather Counts.* Lee and Low Books. ISBN 1584301589.

Chinn, K. (1997). *Sam and the Lucky Money.* Lee and Low Books. ISBN 1880000539.

Daly, N. (2001). *What's Cooking, Jamela?* Farrar, Straus & Giroux. ISBN 0374356025.

Fine, E. (1999). *Under the Lemon Moon.* Lee and Low Books. ISBN 1880000695.

Gray, Nigel. (1988). *A Country Far Away.* Orchard Books. ISBN 0531057925.

Hru, D. (1993). *Joshua's Masai Mask.* Lee and Low Books. ISBN 1880000024.

Kleven, E. (1996). *Hooray a Piñata.* Dutton's Children's Books. ISBN 052545658.

Lachtman, O. (1998). *Big Enough: Bastante Grande.* Pinata Books. ISBN 1558852212.

Parry, Florence. (1995). *Day of Ahmed's Secret.* HarperCollins. ISBN 0688140238.

Schotter, R. (1995). *Passover Magic.* Little, Brown. ISBN 0316774685.

Soto, G. (1997). *Snapshots from the Wedding.* G. P. Putnam's Sons. ISBN 039922808X.

Soto, G. (1996). *The Old Man and his Door.* G. P. Putnam's Sons. ISBN 0399227008.

Soto, G. (1993). *Too Many Tamales.* G. P. Putnam's Sons. ISBN 0399221468.

Uegaki, C. (2005). *Suki's Kimono.* Kids Can Press. ISBN 1553377524.

Multicultural Fairy Tales

Anderson, H. C. (1984). *The Princess and the Pea.* North South Books. ISBN 0030057388.

Climo, S. (1989). *The Egyptian Cinderella.* HarperCollins. ISBN 0690048246.

Climo, S. (1996). *The Irish Cinderlad.* HarperCollins. ISBN 0060243961.

Climo, S. (1999). *The Persian Cinderella.* HarperCollins. ISBN 0060267658.

Coburn, J. R. (1998). *Angkat the Cambodian Cinderella.* Shen's Books. ISBN 1885008090.

De La Paz, M. J. (1991). *Abadeha: The Philippine Cinderella.* Pacific Queen Communications. ISBN 0962925500.

Demi. (2000). *The Emperor's New Clothes.* Margaret K. McElderry Books. ISBN 0689830688.

De Paola, T. (2002). *Adelita: A Mexican Cinderella.* Penguin. ISBN 0399238662.

Flor, Ada A. (1998). *Yours Truly, Goldilocks.* Aladdin Paperbacks. ISBN 0689816081.

Huck, C. (1989). *Princess Furball.* Greenwillow Books. ISBN 0688078389.

Johnson, T. (1998). *Bigfoot Cinderrrrella.* Penguin. ISBN 039923021.

Kimmel, E. (1992). *The Four Gallant Sisters.* Henry Holt. ISBN 0805019014.

Kimmel, E. A. (1994). *The Three Princes.* Holiday House. ISBN 082341115X.

Louie, Ai-Ling, (1982). *Yeh-Shen: A Cinderella Story from China.* Philomel Books. ISBN 039920900X.

Lowell, S. (2001). *Dusty Locks and the Three Bears.* Henry Holt. ISBN 0805058621.

Martin, R. (1992). *The Rough-Faced Girl.* G. P. Putnam's Sons. ISBN 0698116267.

Minters, F. (1994). *Cinder-elly.* Hampton-Brown Books. ISBN 1563347237.

Minters, F. (1996). *Sleeping Beauty.* Penguin. ISBN 0670870331.

Osborne, M. (2000). *Kate and the Beanstalk.* Atheneum Books. ISBN 0689825501.

Salinas, B. (1998). *The Three Pigs: Los Tres Cerdos: Nacho, Tito, and Miguel.* Pinata Publications. ISBN 0934925054.

San Souci, R. (1988). *Cendrillon.* Simon & Schuster. ISBN 068980668X.

Steptoe, J. (1987). *Mufaro's Beautiful Daughters: An African Tale.* HarperCollins. ISBN 0618062238.

Stewig, W. J. (1995). *A Spanish Fairy Tale. Florecita and the Iron Shoes.* Apple Soup Books. ISBN 0679847758.

Young, E. (1989). *Lon Po Po: A Red-Riding Hood Story from China.* Scholastic. ISBN 0590440691.

Gender Roles

Allard, H. (1977). *It's So Nice to Have a Wolf Around the House.* Doubleday. ISBN 0385113005.

Allard, H. (1985). *Miss Nelson Has a Field Day.* Houghton Mifflin. ISBN 0395366909.

Beck, M. (1989). *The Wedding of Brown Bear and White Bear.* Little Brown. ISBN 0316086525.

Berry, C. (1990). *Mama Went Walking.* Henry Holt. ISBN 0805012613.

Brown, A. (2000). *My Dad.* Farrar Straus Giroux. ISBN 0374351015.

Brown, A. (1989). *The Tunnel.* Alfred A. Knopf. ISBN 039484852X.

Carlstrom, N. W. (1987). *Wild Wild Sunflower Child Anna.* Scholastic. ISBN 0590443461.

Corey, S. (2000). *You Forgot Your Skirt, Amelia Bloomer.* Scholastic. ISBN 0439079199.

Geeslin, C. (1999). *How Nanita Learns to Make Flan.* Atheneum Books for Young Readers. ISBN 0689815468.

Hilton, N. (1989). *A Proper Little Lady.* Orchard Books. ISBN 0531058603.

Moore, E. (1996). *The Day of the Bad Haircut.* Scholastic. ISBN 0590697706.

Munsch, R. N. (1980). *The Paper Bag Princess.* Annick Press. ISBN 0920236162.

Nolen, J. (1999). *In My Momma's Kitchen.* Lee & Shepard Books. ISBN 0688127606.

Pfanner, L. (1987). *Louise Builds a House.* Orchard Books. ISBN 0531057968.

Zolotow, C. (1972). *William's Doll.* Harper Trophy. ISBN 0064430677.

Alternative Families

Caines, F. (1982). *Just Us Women.* HarperCollins. ISBN 006020942.

Combs, B. (2001). *123: A Family Counting Book.* Two Lives. ISBN 0967446805.

Combs, B. (2001). *ABC: A Family Alphabet Book.* Two Lives. ISBN 0967446813.

DeHam, L. (2002). *King & King.* Tricycle Press. ISBN 1582460612.

Elwin, R. & M. Pause. (1990). *Asha's Mums.* Women's Press. ISBN 0889611432.

Krakow, K. (2002). *The Harvey Milk Story.* Two Lives. ISBN 096744683X.

Lindenbaum, P. (1991). *Else-Marie and Her Seven Little Daddies.* Henry Holt. ISBN 0805017526.

Loewen, I. (1996). *My Mom Is So Unusual.* Pemmican. ISBN 0919143377.

Newman, L. (1990). *Heather Has Two Mommies.* Alyson Wonderland. ISBN 15583180X.

Newman, L. (1993). *Saturday Is Pattyday.* New Victoria. ISBN 093468529.

Newman, L. (2002). *Felicia's Favorite Story.* Two Lives. ISBN 0967446856.

Okimoto, J. & E. Aoki. (2002). *The White Swan Express: A Story About Adoption.* Clarion. ISBN 0618164537.

Resier, L. (1994). *The Surprise Family.* Greenwillow. ISBN 068811671X.

Updike, J. (1999). *A Child's Calendar.* Holiday House. ISBN 082341440.

Vigna, J. (1995). *My Two Uncles.* Albert Whitman. ISBN 080755507X.

Willhoite, M. (1990). *Daddy's Roommate.* Alyson Wonderland. ISBN 1555831184.

Classroom Preparedness

Home-Study Folders

Home-study folders are very useful in helping students organize their homework assignments and keep track of any paperwork being sent home for parents. They are a good way to introduce parents to your expectations and also serve as a resource to students. They can be easily assembled using any common inexpensive two-pocket folder and then laminating it (later using an X-Acto® knife to open the folders). You may wish to have students color or write their own name on their folders prior to laminating it, making sure they don't color over the text portions. Introduce the folder and its components prior to sending it home, so students are familiar with it and can use it as a resource.

Front

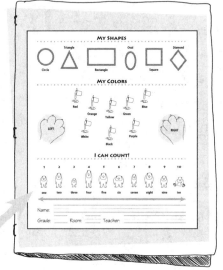

Rubber cement works well and doesn't bubble up.

Back

Inside Pockets

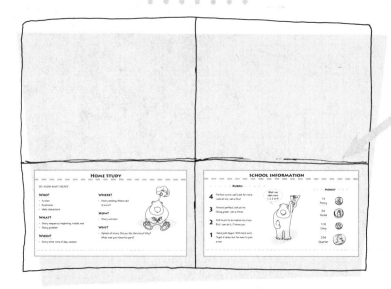

Slice inside pockets after laminating.

MY SHAPES

MY COLORS

I CAN COUNT!

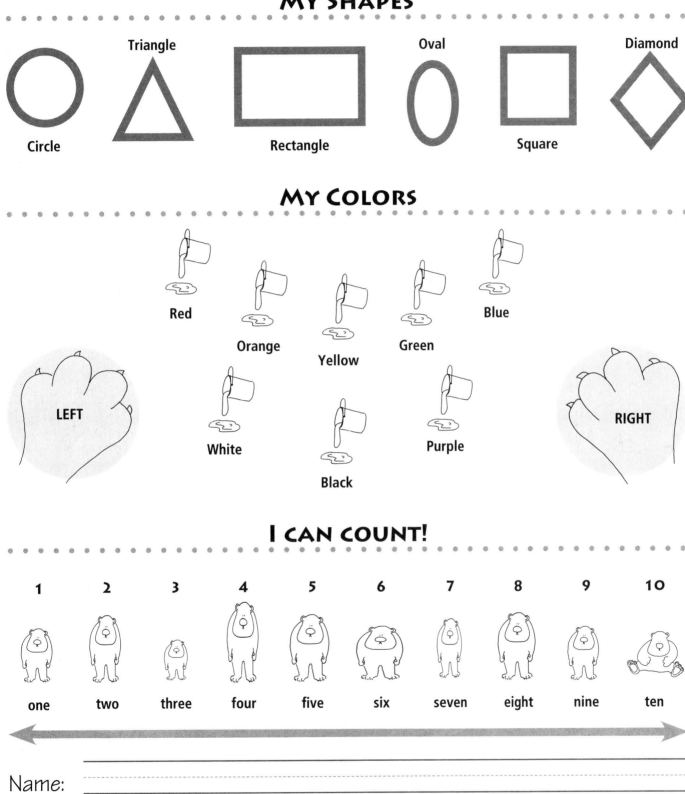

Name:

Grade: _____ Room: _____ Teacher: _____

217

HOME STUDY

DO I KNOW WHAT I READ?

WHO?

- Author
- Illustrator
- Main characters

WHAT?

- Story sequence: beginning, middle, end
- Story problem

WHEN?

- Story time: time of day, season

WHERE?

- Story setting: Where did it occur?

HOW?

- Story solution

WHY?

- Opinion of story: Did you like the story? Why? What was your favorite part?

SCHOOL INFORMATION

RUBRIC

4 Perfect score, can't ask for more. Look at me, I am a four!

3 Almost perfect, look at me. Doing great, I am a three.

2 Still much to do makes me a two. But I can do it, I'll show you.

1 I have just begun. With hard work, I'll get it done, but for now I'm just a one.

What's my rubric score: 1, 2, 3, or 4?

MONEY

1¢
Penny

5¢
Nickel

10¢
Dime

25¢
Quarter

Alligator

Bear

Cat

Dog

Elephant

Fish

Goat

Zebra

Yarn

X-ray

Horse

Igloo

Jet

I CAN READ MY SIGHT WORDS!

all	and	are	an	at	be	but	came
for	from	go	got	had	have	he	her
him	his	if	in	is	it	me	of
on	one	out	said	saw	she	so	that
the	their	there	them	then	they	this	to
up	was	we	went	were	with	you	your

I CAN COUNT!

1	2	3	4	5	6	7	8	9	10
11	12	13	14	15	16	17	18	19	20
21	22	23	24	25	26	27	28	29	30
31	32	33	34	35	36	37	38	39	40
41	42	43	44	45	46	47	48	49	50
51	52	53	54	55	56	57	58	59	60
61	62	63	64	65	66	67	68	69	70
71	72	73	74	75	76	77	78	79	80
81	82	83	84	85	86	87	88	89	90
91	92	93	94	95	96	97	98	99	100

Kite

Lion

Monkey

Wagon

Vacuum

Umbrella

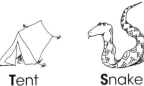
Tent

Snake

Robot

Queen

Pig

Octopus

Nest

Prefixes

anti-: against	*mid-:* middle
de-: opposite of	*mis-:* wrongful
dis-: not the opposite of	*non-:* not
en-: cause to	*pre-:* before
fore-: before	*re-:* again
in-: not/in, into	*sub-:* under
inter-: among, between	*un-:* not, opposite of

Suffixes

-able/-ible: able to do	*-like:* similar to
-en: made of	*-ly:* characteristic of
-er/-or: person that does	*-ment:* action or process
-est: most	*-ness:* a state of being
-ful: full of	*-ous:* full of
-ish: have likeness to	*-tion/-sion:* act or process
-less: without	*-y:* characterized by

Part of Speech	Definition	Example	
Noun	A person, place, or thing	**Tom** (person) sat on the **bench** (thing) in the **park** (place).	
Pronoun	Takes the place of a noun	Mary is my friend. **She** is tall. (I, he, she, it, we, you, they)	
		Sam's dog is big. **His** dog is big. (my, his, her, me, its, our, your, their)	
Adjective	Describes a noun	The man sat. The **large**, **old** man sat.	
Verb	An action word	The stallion **runs** fast.	
Adverb	Describes a verb	The tortoise walks **slowly**.	
Preposition	Relates nouns or pronouns to other words	The frog jumped **into** the pond.	
Conjunction	Joins words, phrases, or clauses	Sam read **and** Jan wrote a story.	

Name: _____

Grade: _____ Room: _____ Teacher: _____

220

Home-Study
Folder Inside
Pockets–Middle
Grades

Home Study

Comprehension Checklist

Who?
- Author
- Illustrator
- Main characters

What?
- Story sequence: beginning, middle, end
- Story problem

When?
- Story time: time of day, season

Where?
- Story setting: Where did it occur?

Why?
- Opinion of story: Did you like the story? Why? What was your favorite part?

How?
- Story solution

Writer's Checklist

Content
- ☐ I have a topic sentence.
- ☐ I have supporting sentences.
- ☐ I have used descriptive words.
- ☐ I restate the topic in the concluding sentence.

Mechanics
- ☐ I have indented my paragraph. ¶
- ☐ I have checked my spelling. thier = their
- ☐ I have used correct punctuation. . ? !
- ☐ I have subject/verb agreement. "they **are**"

The Writing Process

Prewrite → **Draft** **Edit** **Revise** → **Proofread** → **Publish** → **Share/Reflect**

School Information

Fractions

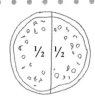  Numerator / Denominator

Units of Measure

1 pint = 2 cups | 1 quart = 2 pints | 1 half gallon = 2 quarts | 1 gallon = 4 quarts | 1 liter | 1 cup | 1 tablespoon | 1 teaspoon

Money

1¢ *Penny* heads | tails   5¢ *Nickel* heads | tails   10¢ *Dime* heads | tails   25¢ *Quarter* heads | tails

221

Home-Study
Folder
Back–Middle
Grades

Triangles

Isosceles
Triangle

Scalene
Triangle

Right Triangle

Equilateral
Triangle

Angles

Right Angle

Acute Angle

Obtuse Angle

Circles

Radius

Diameter

Multiplication Table

	1	2	3	4	5	6	7	8	9	10	11	12
1	1	2	3	4	5	6	7	8	9	10	11	12
2	2	4	6	8	10	12	14	16	18	20	22	24
3	3	6	9	12	15	18	21	24	27	30	33	36
4	4	8	12	16	20	24	28	32	36	40	44	48
5	5	10	15	20	25	30	35	40	45	50	55	60
6	6	12	18	24	30	36	42	48	54	60	66	72
7	7	14	21	28	35	42	49	56	63	70	77	84
8	8	16	24	32	40	48	56	64	72	80	88	96
9	9	18	27	36	45	54	63	72	81	90	99	108
10	10	20	30	40	50	60	70	80	90	100	110	120
11	11	22	33	44	55	66	77	88	99	110	121	132
12	12	24	36	48	60	72	84	96	108	120	132	144

Geometric Forms

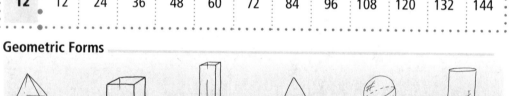

Pyramid   Cube   Rectangular Prism   Cone   Sphere   Cylinder

Place Value

Millions   Thousands

136,547,821.942

Hundreds Tens Ones Hundreds Tens Ones Hundreds Tens Ones Tenths Hundredths Thousandths

Formulas

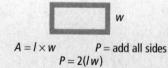

$A = \frac{1}{2}bh$ $A = l \times w$ $P = $ add all sides $C = 2\pi r$ $A = l \times h \times w$
$P = 2(lw)$ $(\pi = 3.14)$

Lines

 Line   Line Segment   Ray   Intersecting Lines   Parallel Lines

Shapes

Square

Rhombus

Rectangle

Parallelogram

Trapezoid

Quadrilateral

Pentagon

Hexagon

Octagon

Weekly Classroom Focus

The next two pages contain reproducibles you can use to send updates home to your students' parents/guardians. This update will let them know what standards you are focusing on in your classroom. This note should contain focus standards according to your state standards. These should be standards that you would like parents/guardians to be aware of and to focus on at home with their child. This sheet can be a valuable resource in helping the parents/guardians to understand specifically what their child is learning so that they can better support what's being asked of them! This will also make your job in the classroom easier and offer more clarity to students and their families.

Weekly Focus Standards

Here are the standards we are working on in class this week! These are things you can focus on at home with your child in order to help reinforce what we are learning in the classroom. Thanks for your support.

Writing/Language Arts *1.2 Use descriptive words when writing.*

Math *2.3 Identify one more than, one less than, 10 more than, and 10 less than a given number.*

Science/Social Studies *Students should know solids, liquids, and gas.*

Art *Your student should be able to recognize and use the different types of line in a drawing.*

*If you have any questions, please contact Mr./Mrs.(Ms.) *Wasley* at phone # *208.444.1000* .

- Check with your administration or go online to find your state's standards.

- This sheet is a valuable resource that can increase parental involvement in their child's education.

- Try to send this weekly or monthly via hard copy or e-mail.

- Review these standards and this sheet with your students before you send it home. A powerful teaching tool is letting the students know exactly what they are learning.

- Keep standards clear, concise, and focused. You can edit standards and reword them to be more parent friendly.

WEEKLY FOCUS STANDARDS

Here are the standards we are working on in class this week! These are things you can focus on at home with your child to help reinforce what we are learning in the classroom. Thanks for your support.

WRITING AND LANGUAGE ARTS _____

_____

_____

MATH _____

_____

_____

SCIENCE AND SOCIAL STUDIES _____

_____

_____

ART _____

_____

_____

If you have any questions, please contact Mr./Mrs./Ms. _____

at phone number _____.

MONTHLY FOCUS STANDARDS

Here are the standards we are working on in class this month! These are things you can focus on at home with your child to help reinforce what we are learning in the classroom. Thanks for your support.

WRITING AND LANGUAGE ARTS

_____

_____

_____

MATH

_____

_____

_____

SCIENCE AND SOCIAL STUDIES

_____

_____

_____

ART

_____

_____

_____

If you have any questions, please contact Mr./Mrs./Ms. _____

at phone number _____

Daily
Schedule

Daily Schedule

Teacher: _____   Room: _____

School: _____   Year: _____

Time   Subject or Activity

Teacher Signals

No matter if you're a new teacher or a veteran teacher, almost all of you in the teaching profession have a few tricks to get your students' attention. Here are a few signal ideas you may want to add to your repertoire.

1. **Turn off the lights.**
   This is universal and works with any age group. The response is instant.

2. **Clap.**
   This is another simple yet effective signal. Any simple rhythm or single clap, "clap once if you're listening!"

3. **Use a catchphrase.**
   This is more directed to primary-grade teachers, and an easy-to-learn phrase will do. A popular one among kindergarten teachers is "Crisscross applesauce!"

Criss Cross..!

4. **Ring a bell.**
   This one is easy and quick. The bell can work for all age groups and is an instant attention-getter. A whistle can be substituted for the bell.

5. **Give me five.**
   This is a nonverbal hand signal used to get students' attention when you don't want any noise. As you put up each finger of one hand, the following happens; one, stop; two, tell a neighbor to stop; three, look; four, listen; and five, wait for a cue or directions.

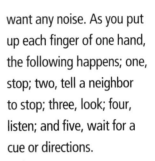

6. **Use nonverbal cues.**
   A couple of good nonverbal cues can be a lifesaver. If you are talking to a colleague or you simply don't want to yell, a nonverbal signal is great! One of the most common nonverbal signals is two fingers in the air, which is usually the sign for quiet. Experiment and see what works for you.

7. **Play favorite Music.**
   For transitioning from one subject/activity to another or for getting students ready for recess, lunch, or dismissal, turn on your music player to signal the transition.

Uses for Teacher Signals

Why use a teacher signal? What is its importance? These simple attention-getters have unlimited uses inside or outside of the classroom. The following are reasons teacher signals are necessary and useful for attention-getting in the classroom!

An Emergency

This is perhaps the best reason for a signal. In an emergency, a signal is needed for instant attention: stop, look, and listen.

Change of Subject

A signal to transition your class between two subjects can be a time-saver. This is a great place to include steps after the signal is given.

During a Directed Lesson

This can be a catchphrase or a simple clap. We've all had classes where when one student answers, the entire rest of the class feels free to add in their answers as well. When your students do this or are not all paying attention, try a quick attention-getter. A great signal is, "Clap once if you're listening!"

Guest in the Room

This is a great situation for a nonverbal signal. It could be a sign for the class to quiet down if you happen to be interrupted by a guest at the door. Usually, you're busy talking to the guest and need a signal that doesn't require you to speak.

Recess or Dismissal

Choose one signal that signifies when it's time to leave the room, be it recess, nutrition, lunch, or dismissal. Different signals cue different things; a great signal for this is to simply turn the lights off. It's easy and quiet and elicits an instant response.

Student Risk Factors

No matter where you teach, students come to school with their own sets of issues. This can mean anything happening in a child's life outside of school—some things good and some not so good. As teachers, we have an innate sense of when a student is going through adverse or hard times at home. These adversities show up in a variety of ways within the student. This page is a simple reminder of behaviors a student might exhibit when dealing with adverse happenings. These behaviors can often be a subconscious cry for help from the student. If you are experiencing any of these behaviors with a student, investigate and get information about the student. Before drawing any conclusions, talk with that particular student's previous teachers, check student records, get advice from your administrators, talk with the school psychologist and/or counselor, and possibly meet with the parents/guardians. Because a child exhibits one of the behaviors listed below, it doesn't mean you should push the panic button; it simply means you need to pay a little more attention to that student.

- Excessive Absences
- Low Self-Esteem
- Frequent Change of Residence
- Poor Peer Relationships
- Grade Retention
- Disruptive Behavior
- Inability to Tolerate Structure
- Frequent Health Problems
- Withdrawn

- Forgetful
- Single-Parent Family
- English Language Learner
- Immature, Easily Influenced
- Frequent Suspensions or Expulsions
- Easily Distracted

- Inattentive
- Poor Classroom Behavior
- Doesn't Complete Tasks
- Doesn't Submit Homework
- Alternative Living Situation
- Parent Work Schedule
- Sleepy
- No Appetite
- Other

Just to Let
You Know
Form

A Note
Home
Form

Just to Let You Know…

To the parent(s) of:

Date: _____   From: _____

Reason for the note:

☐ Exceptional Behavior   ☐ Incomplete or Missing Homework

☐ Super Listener   ☐ Poor Attendance or Tardiness

☐ Great Attitude   ☐ Not Following Directions

☐ Great Work   ☐ Unacceptable Behavior

☐ Excellent Homework   ☐ Other

Comments:

_____

_____

Please   ☐ Sign and return.   ☐ Talk with your child.

        ☐ Contact Mr./Mrs./Ms. _____   ☐ Arrange for a conference.

A Note Home …

To the parent(s) of: _____

Date: _____ From: _____

Reason for the note:

☐ Exceptional Behavior   ☐ Incomplete or Missing Homework

☐ Super Listener   ☐ Poor Attendance or Tardiness

☐ Great Attitude   ☐ Not Following Directions

☐ Great Work   ☐ Unacceptable Behavior

☐ Excellent Homework   ☐ Other

Comments:

_____

_____

Please   ☐ Sign and return.   ☐ Talk with your child.

        ☐ Contact Mr./Mrs./Ms. _____   ☐ Arrange for a conference.

Teacher's Aide

As the leader of the classroom, you are not only responsible for your students, you are also responsible for your aide. Depending on your school, the grade/subject you teach, and funding, you may or may not have an aide. If you are unfamiliar with what a teacher's aide is, this is a person who is hired to assist you in your classroom. If you have an aide, you might wonder what to do with your aide. Whether you have been in the class for two or twenty years, you may have questions on how to use your aide successfully. These are some ideas to get you started.

Helpful Tips:

1. Make clear what kind of work and participation you want done by your teacher's aide. Give him or her clear and concise direction on what needs to be done each day. Depending on experience, your aide may be very capable and used to working in a classroom setting; however, aides don't usually hold teaching credentials. Provide a to-do list each day/week so your aide knows what to do if he or she comes into the class while you are teaching.

2. Be friendly but also be sure to maintain a professional relationship, which makes things much easier when *you* are running a classroom.

3. Remember, you are the teacher! At the end of the day, the class is your vision and your responsibility, so make sure you are the one in charge. That's not to say you need to be disrespectful or dictatorial, it just means you need to be professional and provide your teacher's aide with kind guidance and your vision.

4. Be good to your teacher's aides. Try to smile and promote how helpful they really are. Like teachers, aides perform much better when they are appreciated!

Teacher's Aide Activities

Here is a list of productive activities that you can have your teacher's aide do within your classroom.

Review with Low-Achieving Students

An aide can be very effective working with low-achieving students on a daily basis. Establish a list of students and review skills to give your aide a clear task. This will give him or her a one-to-one relationship with the students, which will make the job more meaningful for your aide.

Small-Group Review

You may choose to have your aide pull together a small group of students to review particular skills they may need work on.

Assessments

Your aide can help you keep up with assessments. Whether it's recording the scores or actually giving the assessment, your aide can be a time-saver. The only time you would not want the aide to give an assessment is when you want to get a sense for yourself as to where your students are.

Individual Guidance

Even though an aide is not a one-to-one type of tutor, he or she can be helpful in keeping one or two students focused on you during a guided lesson. A great tool is to have your aide sit with the student(s) while you are giving the lesson.

Guide the Entire Class in a Lesson

If you as the teacher want to do individual review with students, then your aide could take the class in a guided lesson while you pull students for individual review. You may want to have your aide already trained to take the class in case you need to speak with a visitor or feel like doing individual review for a week or two.

Record Keeping

This is an activity that an aide could accomplish in a last-minute circumstance, possibly helping grade an assessment that is due. The other recommendations, however, are better choices for using an aide's time.

TEACHER'S AIDE WORKSHEET

Student's Name: _____   Grade: _____

Helper's Name: _____   Date: _____

Teacher's Name: _____   Room Number: _____

Date	Book Title and Author	Follow-Up Skill Activities Review	Focus Standard

Notes: _____

_____

_____

Extra Student Plan

From time to time, you may get an extra student in your class. This usually occurs when a teacher is absent and a substitute has not been obtained, so the absent teacher's class is usually broken up to various classrooms. This extra student can be in your room for a few minutes, a few hours, or a few days. If you find yourself in this situation, here are a few suggestions and ideas that can make having an extra student an easy adjustment.

- Have a routine that works when a student enters the room. Have a responsible student be the extra student's helper and guide. Have a place for the student to sit, a task for him or her to do, and extra work available.

- An extra set of workbooks is always an easy answer to an extra student; he or she can enter your room and work right along with your class. Of course, this works well for one or two extra students—if you get five or six, then you'll need to be creative! Having an extra set of workbooks put aside and easily accessible means you don't have to look for anything, and you're ready as soon as the student enters the room.

- Workbooks enable a student to work along with your class. Another good idea besides the workbooks is a folder with worksheets that a student can keep and stay busy with. This folder should be in an easy place to access. The worksheets should be simple for the student to complete without much guidance from you, and they should be fun for the student. These folders can be premade and ready for any extra students you may get.

- At the beginning of the year, it's always helpful to save a few copies of everything your students have worked on, including extra workbooks, in case your extra student becomes permanent!

Sub Folder

A folder for a substitute teacher is good to have in case you are absent. This sub folder can be used by a sub whether your absence is planned or unexpected. If your absence is planned, then you may have more precisely detailed plans; nonetheless, a good sub folder is always an excellent resource. You should keep your sub folder in a place that's easy to find, with simple directions for conducting class. Having a great sub folder will make life easier for your substitute, and your class can proceed as though you were present.

Sub Folder Cover

Your sub folder cover can benefit from a bright color that's easy to see. Bright yellow or gold is a great color!

First Page

This page is dedicated to the general information about the school, personnel, administration, etc.

Second Page

This page contains your daily class schedule. It is specific to your class and should be changed each year.

Third Page

This page contains your class seating chart.

Keep It Simple

Remember that, with a sub folder, less is more. A substitute is usually there for only a day or two. Make your plans clear and concise.

Activity Sheets

These pages should be activities that a sub can reproduce and use in case he or she has nothing to conduct the class with. Use three different subject areas, i.e., Math, Language Arts, and Science. You may also include emergency plans and extra student referral forms.

Sub Feedback Form

This sheet is designed for a substitute to leave feedback to you as to how the day went. This sheet holds students accountable for their behavior because they know that you will be getting feedback on how the day went.

General Information for Substitute

Welcome!

School: _____

Address: _____ Phone Number: _____

The Principal is: _____ The Vice Principal is: _____

The Counselor is: _____ and is located _____.

The Office Manager is: _____.

The Custodial Person for this building is: _____.

The Nurse is: _____ and is located _____.

School begins at _____ and dismisses at _____.

This general sheet is for room number _____ Mr./Mrs./Ms. _____
last updated _____.

Two teachers who can be asked for help or answer any questions are: _____,
room number _____ and _____, room number _____.

The location this class will arrive for school is: _____.

The lunch area is located: _____.

The dismissal location for this class is: _____.

Two students who can assist you with class operations and general knowledge are: _____
_____ and _____.

My teacher's aide is _____ and arrives at _____.

Notes _____

_____

_____

_____

Phone Extensions

Office: _____ Library: _____ Nurse: _____

Counselor: _____ Teacher #1: _____ Teacher #2: _____

Emergency: _____ Fire: _____ Police: _____

Other: _____ Other: _____ Other: _____

Sub Feedback Form

Name: _____ Employee Number: _____ Phone Number: _____

The Day

Things we accomplished:

Things we didn't get to:

The Class

Helpful hands:

Anecdotal

Concerns or Issues:

Name	Concern or Behavior	Action

Thanks for your help!

Seating
Chart

Seating Chart

Teacher: _____   School: _____

Year: _____   Room Number: _____

Classroom Map and Seating Chart

Notes, Special Needs, Etc.

Teacher Evaluation Environment Guide

Here are some recommendations of things you can be aware of within your room before being evaluated. Not all administrators are the same, and, depending on your administrator, these things might not carry as much weight. Regardless, it is nice to be able to check your room organization against this checklist and see how you're doing. This list shouldn't serve to make every room the exact same, but you can use this list to take you to a higher level in your teaching. It always helps to have ideas about what your administrator may be looking for.

☐ Contents of students' desks neatly arranged

☐ Tops of student tables neat and clean

☐ Floors clean and free of paper debris

☐ Top of closets clear of clutter and boxes

☐ Students' coats and backpacks hung in closet

☐ Clean and neat closets

☐ Clean work tables

☐ Clean sink area

☐ Bookcases arranged neatly

☐ Class schedule posted

☐ Teacher's desk neat and organized

☐ Weekly lesson plan visible and on the desk

☐ Print-rich environment (charts and graphs)

☐ Furniture arrangement facilitates instruction

☐ Independent reading area

☐ Bulletin boards display students' work.

☐ Captions on boards promote critical thinking.

☐ Generally neat and clean learning environment.

☐ Teacher's name and teacher's aide name posted

☐ Emergency bag in easy location to access

Teacher Evaluation

H ere is a list of *all* the areas that you will be expected to juggle in this profession. Remember, don't get overwhelmed, just do your best and keep adding to the list of things you're already doing. Good luck!!

Planning and Preparation
- Weekly plans w/objectives
- Long-range planning
- Planning for T.A.
- Appropriate curriculum
- Field trips, technology labs, etc.

Room Environment
- Evidence of standards
- Print-rich environment
- Great-looking bulletin boards
- Daily class schedule posted
- Clean and neat furniture

See Evaluation Checklist

Instructional Strategies
- Directed lessons
- Small vs. large group
- Use of different learning modalities
- Ongoing assessments
- Use of technology
- Student-driven activities

Classroom Management
- Students are on task.
- Clear expectations of student behavior
- Students follow directions.
- Students transition easily.
- Students are aware of standards.
- Students take responsibility.
- Good leadership

Record Keeping
- Student records up to date
- Student attendance accurately recorded
- Evidence of assessments
- Title I identification paperwork
- Referrals to the student success teams
- Any state paperwork completed
- Your credentials kept current

Reminder

Be strong and brave during your evaluation. An OK administrator will reprimand you if you need improvement, but a great administrator will help you get stronger in your weak areas. Don't be too hard on yourself; know that you're doing your best!

Professional and Adjunct Responsibilities
- Good attendance
- Attend staff meetings
- Extracurricular activities
- Attend professional development
- Neat and clean appearance
- Begin and end class on time
- Show leadership
- Evidence professional growth

Parent/Guardian Involvement
- Home contact
- Parent volunteers
- Parent conferences
- Open house/back to school
- Parent workshops

Helpful Tips
- Find a mentor teacher—a teacher who has been in the classroom for a while can be an excellent source of support and advice.
- Keep a portfolio of your work; this can be a great tool for personal growth!

Evaluation Checklist

Most districts have a formal evaluation process that is required every year to a few years, depending on your status. New teachers are usually evaluated annually for the first few years. This can be a stressful event for even the most seasoned teacher. It is a good opportunity to focus on your room environment, planning, and teaching, and it can be a positive experience. The key here is to be prepared, organized, and focused on your lesson's objective.

☐ **Clean Room Environment**
A clean, inviting, child-centered room goes a long way and leaves a good impression, even when things are hectic.

☐ **Current Student Work Displayed**
Current bulletin boards are necessary. Try to rotate them, choosing a new board every two to three weeks. This way they will stay current and aren't stressors. Check with your school for what needs to be displayed:

☐ Standards
☐ Open-ended question
☐ Board title
☐ Rubric
☐ Teacher comments
☐ Rubric score

☐ **Student Work Sample Folders**
- Collecting work samples is a good idea to keep as evidence of a student's performance.
- Some administrators will want to see them. Check with other teachers at your school.

☐ **Student Portfolio Box**
- Different from work samples (is a living collection that is updated by students)
- Collection of a select few work samples chosen by students (up to about ten)
- Check with other teachers for portfolio ideas.
- Keep a current collection of student work.

☐ **Current Lesson Plans**
- Keep up with weekly lesson plans!
- Ask other teachers how they plan.
- Check with your evaluating administrator on his or her expectations.

☐ **Long-Range Lesson Plan**
- It is a good idea to have long-range plans available.
- Some administrators may request them. Ask other teachers and your administrator.

☐ **Assessments**
- Assessments are very important, and most administrators will want to see evidence.
- Find out which district and/or school assessments are required. House them together.
- Find assessments that you are comfortable with for your own use.

☐ **Grade Book**
- Evidence of grades is very important and should also be available.
- Ask other teachers how they keep their grades, and find a system that works for you.

Tips for Back-to-School Night

This page is designed to assist you with back-to-school night. This sheet should serve only as suggestions for what you might want ready for the parents/guardians. Depending on your school or your own personal flair, your list may vary. A great idea is to discuss the areas listed below during the parent visitation.

Rubrics

These should be in plain view and easy to read. If you or your district doesn't use rubrics, this is a type of chart describing how you grade the academic performance of each student as well as assignments.

Literature

Back-to-school night gives parents/guardians a chance to see what types of books and texts their children are using. This display of books and texts will serve as a great way to not only reinforce what is being read in class but also provide parents/guardians with ideas of what to buy their child for their own home libraries!

Refreshments and Snacks

Using treats and refreshments at back-to-school night is a super way to begin any meeting. Everyone likes some type of snack, and eating makes people smile. When parents/guardians smile, that is a key to your success at back-to-school night.

Class Rules

Any great classroom has some type of class rules chart. There are many styles for this chart, but it should be very easy to understand and easy for students to follow.

Student Work or Portfolios

If possible, it's nice to have any current assessments and student work folders out on the desks and accessible to the parents/guardians. Parents/guardians will want to see how their child is doing so far. If time permits, you can have a more complete discussion with any parents/guardians you feel the need to talk to.

Educational Materials

All educational enhancements should be posted, and all your class bulletin boards should reflect the work being done in class. Think about an organized and colorful display that can really "wow" the parents and make you look great!

Class Expectations

A great way to start off the year is to explain exactly what you expect from the parents/guardians. A powerful way to reinforce this is to type out your expectations and give a copy to each parent. Getting off on the right foot with parents/guardians can save you a lot of time and can enhance their child's academic performance.

Activity or Learning Centers

Learning centers should be neat and clean. These centers will benefit from a label and instructions on how to use the materials. As with the books in the room, these centers provide a visual for the parents of what type of learning is going on in your classroom.

Back-to-School-Night Checklist

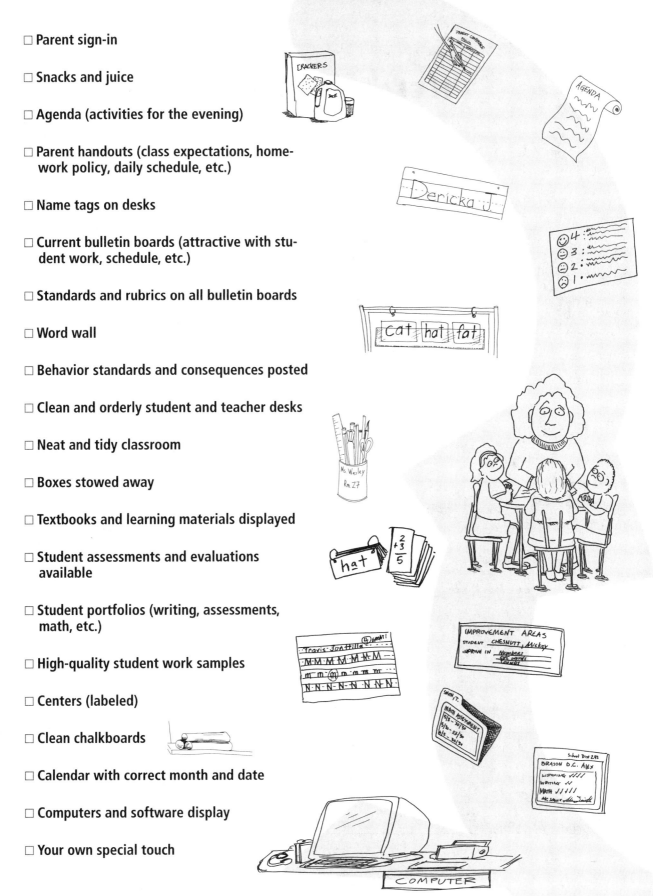

- ☐ Parent sign-in

- ☐ Snacks and juice

- ☐ Agenda (activities for the evening)

- ☐ Parent handouts (class expectations, home-work policy, daily schedule, etc.)

- ☐ Name tags on desks

- ☐ Current bulletin boards (attractive with student work, schedule, etc.)

- ☐ Standards and rubrics on all bulletin boards

- ☐ Word wall

- ☐ Behavior standards and consequences posted

- ☐ Clean and orderly student and teacher desks

- ☐ Neat and tidy classroom

- ☐ Boxes stowed away

- ☐ Textbooks and learning materials displayed

- ☐ Student assessments and evaluations available

- ☐ Student portfolios (writing, assessments, math, etc.)

- ☐ High-quality student work samples

- ☐ Centers (labeled)

- ☐ Clean chalkboards

- ☐ Calendar with correct month and date

- ☐ Computers and software display

- ☐ Your own special touch

HELLO, PARENTS!

Date: _____

Dear Mr./Mrs./Ms. _____ ,

I would like to invite you to back-to-school night. I want to take just a few minutes to discuss expectations for the year, homework, and academic goals. Your attendance at this meeting would be greatly appreciated and extremely beneficial to your child's success! The date and time are

_____ . See you then.

Thanks,

(Please fill out and return to school.)

- -

☐ Yes, I will be there!

☐ No, I can't make it.

Name: _____

Phone Number: _____

Student's Name: _____

Back-to-School Night Sign-in Sheet

Teacher: _____ Room Number: _____

Date: _____ Grade: _____ Time: _____

Date	Student's Name	Parent's Name	Comments

Parent Conference Reminders

The following is a list of reminders for you to consider during parent conferences. Parent conferences can be a great opportunity for you, the student, and the parents. Parent conferences help you obtain additional information about the student from the parents. They allow you to share information with the parents/guardians about their child, discuss any concerns about the student, and, most important, enlist the cooperation of the parents/guardians in addressing the student's education.

- Try to establish a positive relationship with the parents/guardians before presenting any concerns.
- Allow the parents/guardians to talk.
- Avoid telling the parents/guardians what the student does not do in a negative way.
- Have your assessments, sample work, and report card ready to share with the parents/guardians.
- Avoid lecturing or talking down to the parents/guardians.
- Try to obtain the cooperation of the parents/guardians when dealing with the student's education.
- Do not use words with negative connotations, like *dumb*, *lazy*, *stupid*, or *bad*.
- Remember, be as positive with parents/guardians as possible. Parents/guardians can be a great asset to your educational program!

Conference Week Master Calendar

Time	Monday	Tuesday	Wednesday	Thursday	Friday
(_____ min.)	Date: _____	Date: _____	Date: _____	Date: _____	Date: _____
A.M.					
P.M.					

Teacher Reminders:

☐ Check with school for times and possible off-limit days.
☐ Fill in dates and times on template.
☐ Send home sign-up page.

☐ Assign conferences.
☐ Be prepared.
☐ Enjoy!

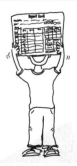

Conference
Week Calendar

Conference Week Calendar

Dear Parent/Guardian:

We are scheduling conferences to meet and discuss your child's academic progress. Your child and I look forward to sharing all that we are learning in school. It is an important chance for all of us to get to know one another and to give your child recognition. I hope you can make it. To help me schedule you, please sign up for the most convenient times that you are available. Fill in your first, second, and third choices in the corresponding box and time, and I will do my best to accommodate you. I will send this schedule back with your child's name in the box of their assigned conference. Thank you for your support. I look forward to meeting you. Sincerely yours,

_____ Room Number _____

Time	Monday	Tuesday	Wednesday	Thursday	Friday
(_____ min.)	Date: _____	Date: _____	Date: _____	Date: _____	Date: _____
A.M.					
P.M.					

The Writing Process

Organizing the writing process can help facilitate your students' writing and organize where they are in the process. Students can independently maintain an ongoing writing assignment while you assist individual students. The following is a way to organize your writing process and maintain a level of consistency. (*Note:* Upper-grade forms have different graphics.)

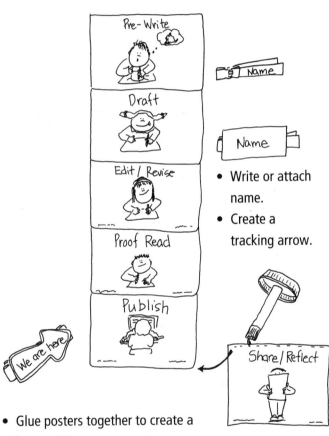

- Write or attach name.
- Create a tracking arrow.

- Ongoing writing folder matches forms and posters.
- Students can move paper clip down the side to track where they are in the process.
- Folder houses papers from each phase.
- Use folder for the year—laminate it.

- Glue posters together to create a long writing process poster.
- Track each student with clothespin.
- Helpful for conferencing—move clothespin once you have conferenced with student.

- Writing templates give consistency.
- Templates match posters.
- Have a supply of each form available.

Writing in Progress

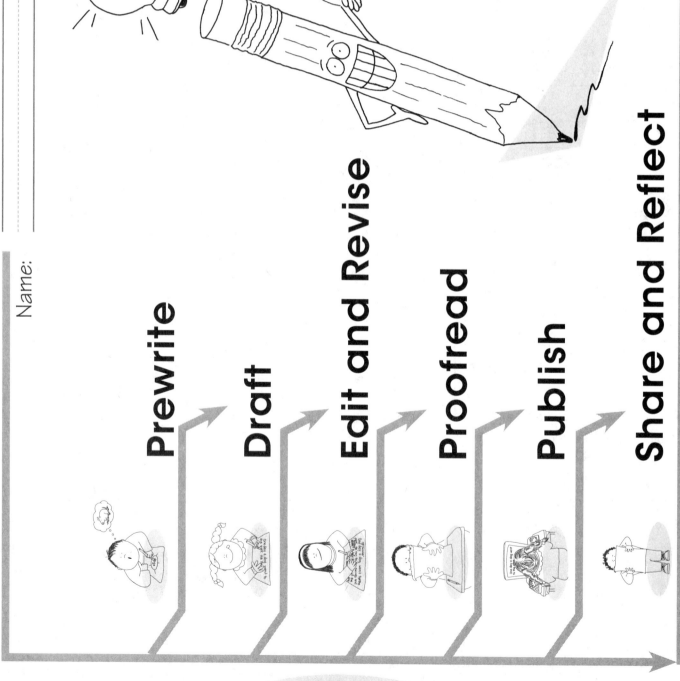

Name:

Prewrite

Draft

Edit and Revise

Proofread

Publish

Share and Reflect

Prewrite

Draft

Edit and Revise

Proofread

Publish

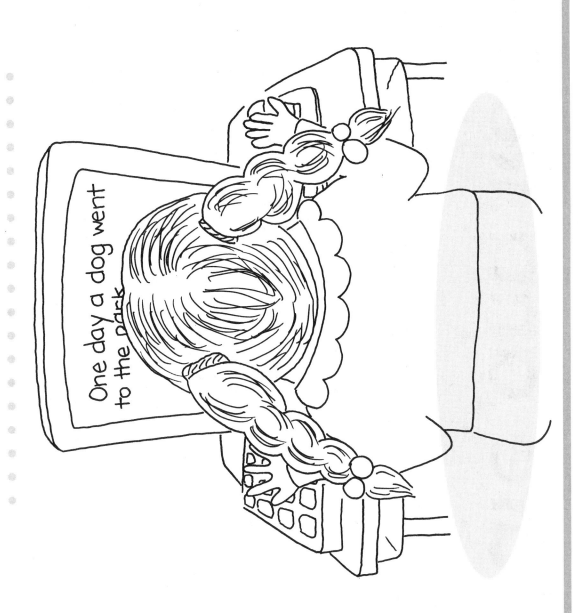

One day a dog went to the Park

Share and Reflect

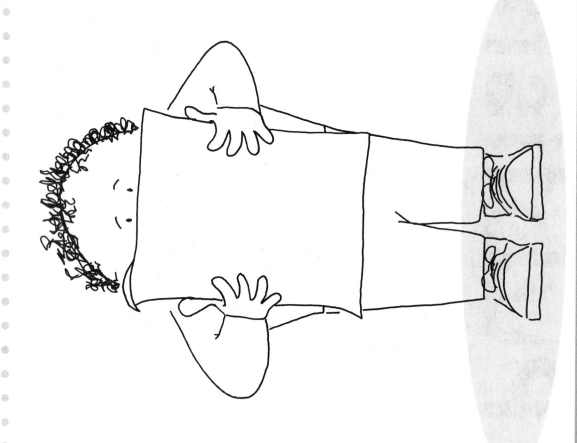

Name: _____

Date: _____

 Prewrite

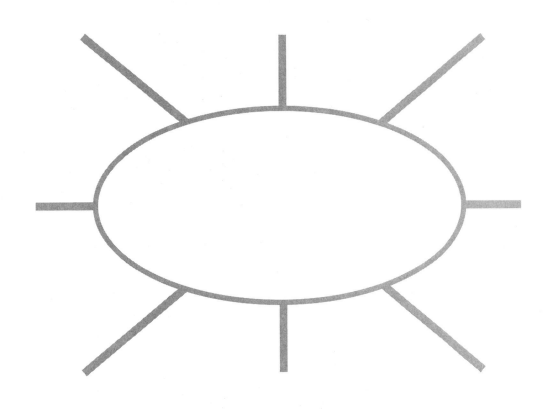

Name: _____

Date: _____

Draft

☐ Edit and Revise   ☐ Proofread

Draft (continued)

☐ Edit and Revise   ☐ Proofread

Final Draft
Template–Lower
Grades

Name: _____

_____

Date: _____

Rubric Score ____ / ____ / ____ / = ____

Final Draft

Final Draft (continued)

Name: _____

Date: _____

My Story

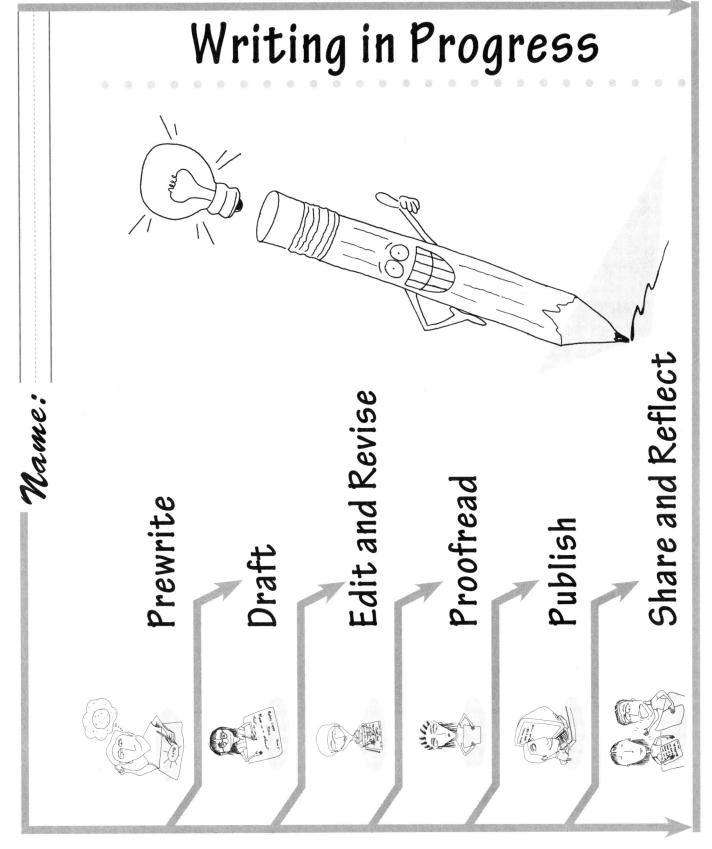

Writing in Progress

Name:

Prewrite

Draft

Edit and Revise

Proofread

Publish

Share and Reflect

Prewrite

Draft

Edit and Revise

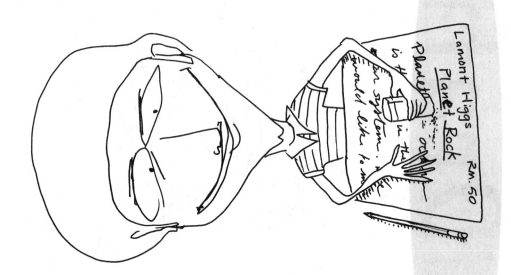

Proofread

Publish

Share and Reflect
Poster–Upper
Grades

Share and Reflect

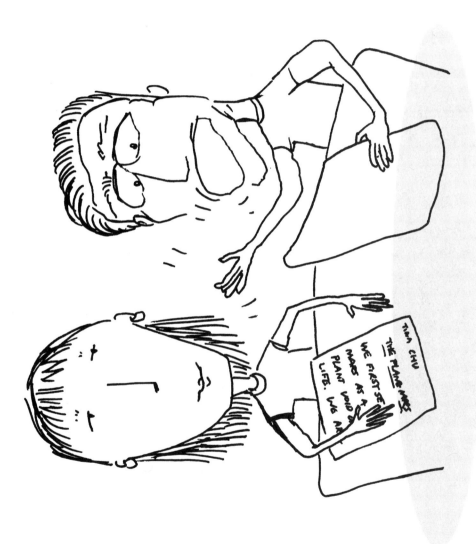

Name: _____

Date: _____

Prewrite

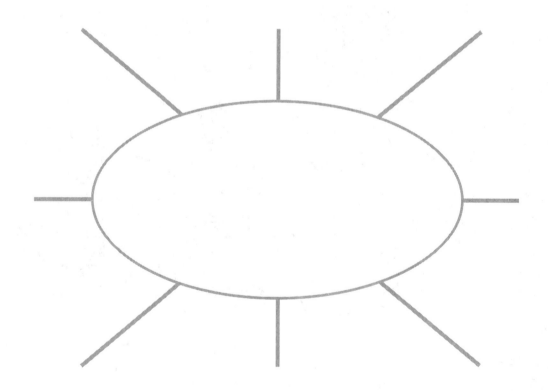

Name:

Date:

Draft

☐ Edit and Revise   ☐ Proofread

Draft (continued)

☐ Edit and Revise   ☐ Proofread

Name: _____

Date: _____

Final Draft

Rubric Score

___ / ___ / ___ / = ___

Final Draft (continued)

Name: _____

Date: _____

My Story

My Story (continued)

Bulletin-Board Checklist

Contents for a Great Bulletin Board

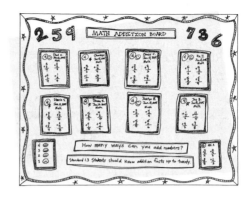

☐ Title (theme of the board)

☐ Students' work (with corrections, rubric score, and positive feedback)

☐ Open-ended question (extending their learning)

☐ Rubric (a rubric you develop identifying the criteria for the assignment)

☐ Standard (the standard you are teaching based on your state standards)

☐ Teacher work example (a model example for students to achieve)

Supplies to Complete the Board

Paper (colorful and fadeless, if possible)

Roll Paper (to back the board; chart paper if available)

Tag Board or Sentence Strips (for writing the question and standard)

Markers

Scissors

Stapler

Borders (make your own or buy from a local education supply store)

Students' Work

Tips for Superior Bulletin Boards

- Some administrators like all boards in the room to be the same colors.
- A great way to zest up your boards is to go for three colors instead of one.
- Mount students' work on two color sheets instead of one.
- Kid-friendly writing is always a brilliant idea.
- Boards should be consistent (questions and standards in the same place on each board).
- Try letting the students direct how the board should look.

Bulletin-Board Diagram

Rubric Score

Title or Theme

Border (two colors)

Student Work
(double-mounted
on colored paper)

Pictures
or Added Artwork

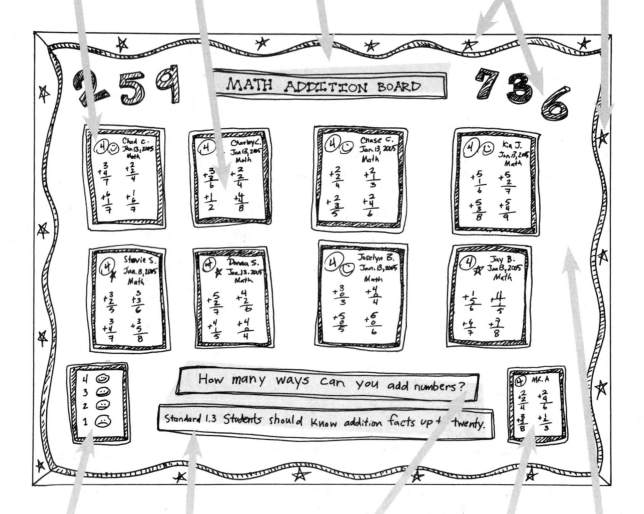

Teacher-Created,
Student-Friendly Rubric

Teacher Work Example

Open-Ended Question

State Standard

Fadeless Background
Paper

Word Walls

Word walls can work for any student from kindergarten through twelfth grade. These word walls should contain words that are relevant to the work being done in your class. Word walls can go as far as your imagination can take them and can be put in several places in the classroom. As far as the word list itself, a good practice is to rotate your words at a consistent pace, not too fast and not too slow. Take your time and get a sense of what works best for your group of students. Every class is different, so what works one year may not work the following year. Word walls serve as a continuous reference point while the students master the words and definitions. Words posted on the wall or on a chart are a great way to make language fun, make words important, and get kids excited about learning vocabulary.

- Try to use the word wall frequently—the more you use the word wall, the more your students will refer to it.
- Word walls can be an effective way to spotlight particular words that you want students to focus on.
- Not all words on the word wall have to be new; some words may repeat or stay up for a longer time.
- Have fun with this. Make it an easy and powerful way to enhance students' vocabulary.
- If possible, make the students responsible for changing and editing the list. Give your students ownership of the word wall!

- Use these sources:
  - Math vocabulary
  - Reading vocabulary
  - Sight words
  - Spelling words
  - Word families
  - Rhyming words
  - Thematic unit words
  - New vocabulary for curricular areas

- Not all words need to stay up for a long time; if the class has mastery of a word, then change it out for a new one.

Activities for Word Walls

1. **Students can illustrate each word.** For those who struggle with writing, an illustration still shows their understanding.

2. **Use in daily oral activity—students can use the words in a sentence.** Use this practice if students finish work early or as a way to release students to recess/lunch.

3. **Put the words in ABC order.** Students can do this on their own in writing or with a pocket chart and sentence strips.

4. **Quiz the students on the words.** Like a spelling test, have students write the corresponding word for the definition you call out.

5. **Define each word.** Students can write their own definition for each word.

6. **Discuss each word daily.** Before lessons begin, review relevant/corresponding words from the word wall.

7. **Have students create their own flash cards.** The students can write the word and draw an illustration on one side and write the definition on the other.

8. **Use in class recital or read-aloud.** The teacher calls out a word and the students repeat.

Placement Ideas for Word Walls

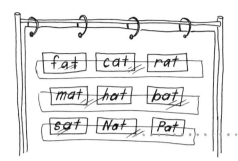

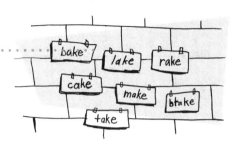

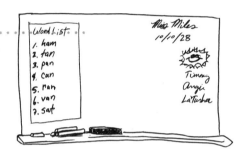

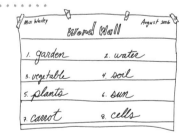

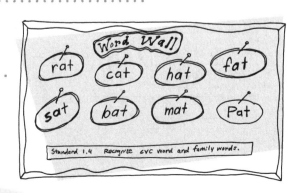

- Wall
- Chart Rack
- Chalkboard
- List Paper
- Journal Page
- Closet Door
- Bulletin Board
- Easel
- Label Room Items
- Other?

Field-Trip Checklist

Trip: _____

Location: _____

Date: _____ **Time:** _____

Adults: _____

Six Weeks Prior

- □ Get permission from district—purpose, destination, and plan.
- □ Request transportation.

Two Weeks Prior

- □ Notify cafeteria
  - □ sack lunches needed
  - □ will purchase/provide (none needed)
  - □ complete lunch request (if required)
- □ Confirm bus.
- □ Remind administrator.
- □ Letter home to notify parents of upcoming trip.*
- □ Invite any parent chaperones.
- □ Connect to theme or unit.

  * Refer to school-trip policy.

Three Days Prior

- □ Send parental consents home.
  - Leave in office (parent release)
  - Take on Trip (student emergency contact)
- □ Prepare name tags.
- □ Discuss trip, safety, and procedures.

Trip Day

- □ Finalize count.
- □ Distribute name tags.
- □ Leave name list and consents in office, site information.
- □ Take parent and emergency contact information on each child.
- □ Use restroom.

- □ Assign trip buddies.
- □ Review trip procedures (times, restrooms, safety, etc.).
- □ Periodically take head count.

Follow-up

- □ Share, discuss, or write
  - □ Write a story (favorite part, describe an attraction).
  - □ Sequence the trip.
  - □ Relate to theme.
  - □ Compare and contrast what was seen.
  - □ Draw a picture.
  - □ Create a class mural.

Reflection and Notes: (What went well? What would you do differently? etc.)

_____

_____

_____

_____

The following is a weekly checklist that can help you prepare for the start of the week. It is an excellent way to make sure you haven't forgotten anything.

Am I ready for the week?

- ☐ Lesson plans
- ☐ Attendance cards or roster
- ☐ Calendar
- ☐ Lesson materials: _____

_____

_____

- ☐ Spelling words
- ☐ Home study prepared
- ☐ Pencils sharpened
- ☐ Chalk or markers
- ☐ Paper

Week of: _____

- ☐ Art supplies: _____

_____

_____

- ☐ Trips or assemblies: _____

_____

_____

- ☐ Daily agenda
- ☐ Notices to go home
- ☐ _____
- ☐ _____

_____

Am I ready for the week?

- ☐ Lesson plans
- ☐ Attendance cards or roster
- ☐ Calendar
- ☐ Lesson materials: _____

_____

_____

- ☐ Spelling words
- ☐ Home study prepared
- ☐ Pencils sharpened
- ☐ Chalk or markers
- ☐ Paper

Week of: _____

- ☐ Art supplies: _____

_____

_____

- ☐ Trips or assemblies: _____

_____

_____

- ☐ Daily agenda
- ☐ Notices to go home
- ☐ _____
- ☐ _____

_____

Test-Taking Overview

Standardized tests are given in most school districts starting in first grade. Every district is different, and procedures vary from state to state. Check with your school to find out what tests are administered and when they are given. The following tips can assist in the preparation for and administration of tests. Follow your curriculum and standards as outlined by your district, and your students will be prepared. Start early in challenging them to be critical thinkers by giving them various opportunities to practice test taking. Standardized tests can be a stressful time for you and your students. The key is being ready.

Checklist:

☐ **Test guide booklet**

☐ **Test booklets**

☐ **Pencils (No. 2)**

☐ **Eraser(s)**

☐ **Scratch paper**

☐ **Student dividers**

☐ **Student markers**

☐ **Door sign**

☐ **Approved mathematical instruments**

☐ **Testing organizer**

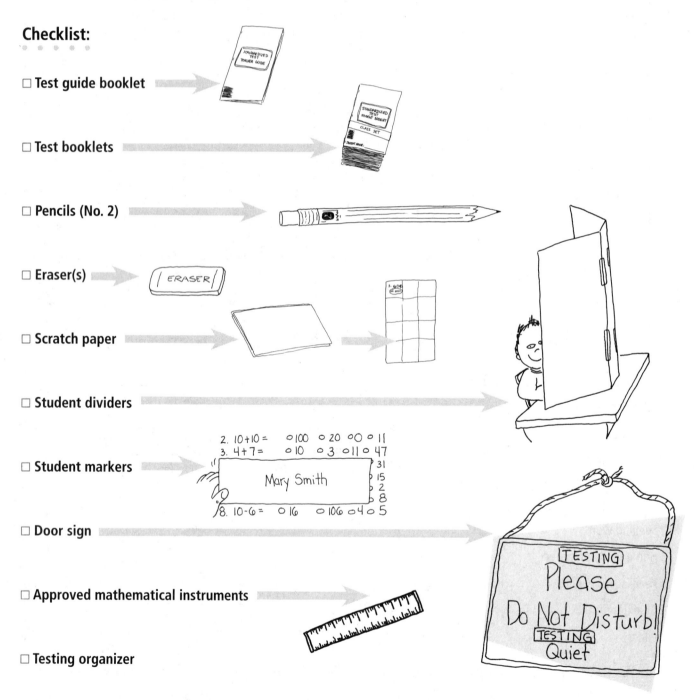

Test-Taking Tips:

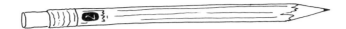

- Create dividers with chipboard and book-binding tape (every other student).

- Practice test taking; create multiple-choice assessments throughout the year (with bubbling in).

- Practice using scratch paper to transfer math problems for calculations (folding in half three times makes eight boxes).

- Provide students with markers to track problems (use a word card, construction paper, or index cards).

- Practice comprehension throughout the year. Write questions for anything read. Students can copy and answer—this teaches them to look back in the text for answers.

- Practice testing atmosphere whenever you are assessing to create a familiarity.

- Sit students where they will sit when taking test to familiarize them with their seating arrangement.

- Teach students to trust their first instinct.

- Teach students to quickly preview questions prior to reading a comprehension passage.

- Teach students to avoid stray marks on the actual test. All work must be done on scratch paper.

- Early finishers can read a book or draw on their scratch paper.

- Account for all testing materials daily (even scratch paper). You may have to actually sign them in and out.

- Take students to restroom prior to testing.

- Always have extra pencils and scrap paper ready.

- Know your students. Check to see if anyone requires special testing accommodations or has a parental exclusion signed.

- Make sure all tests are properly labeled and distributed. Account for all of them when finished.

- Always preview what you will test prior to administering the test. Be prepared!

- Get to know your proctor prior to testing. Establish a testing routine.

- Send a note home prior to testing that asks parents/guardians to have students at school on time, well rested, well fed, and dressed in comfortable clothing on the day of the test.

Test-Taking Strategies

Much success in test taking lies in understanding how to take a test. Students can improve their scores with simple strategies. Following are a handful of strategies that students can use while taking a standardized test.

- Respond to every question even if you have to make an educated guess; you aren't penalized for incorrect answers.
- Glance through the test quickly and answer the easiest questions first.
- If you can't answer a question within a minute or less, skip it and come back to it later.
- Eliminate answer choices if possible. Some are obvious and can be eliminated as possible choices. Narrow your selection.
- Watch the signs/symbols and wording. Are you adding or subtracting? Do they want the antonym or synonym?

- Keep your work on scratch paper as neat as possible so you don't misread your work.
- Read each question twice. Identify key words that indicate what is being asked.
- Don't answer until you have read all the answer choices. Even if one looks good, read through them all before going with that answer to make sure.
- In reading, go back to the text to find answers; mark/highlight/underline them if allowed.
- Read through questions prior to reading a passage to know what to look for in the passage.

- Always check your answer number against the number on the scantron to avoid misnumbering.
- Always check after doing a calculation to see if the answer is reasonable/logical.
- For math, fold scratch paper three times to create eight boxes to work in. Number your work so you can revisit it to double-check if you have time.
- For math, when solving a story problem write down information that is important and ignore extra information that doesn't relate to a specific problem.
- Whenever possible, draw pictures to help visualize the problem.
- When you finish the test, go back and recheck your answers.

TESTING ORGANIZER

Use these two sheets to plan your testing schedule and student's needs.

Teacher: _____ Grade: _____ Room: _____ Date: _____

MONDAY					TUESDAY					WEDNESDAY					THURSDAY					FRIDAY			
Section(s)			Minutes		Section(s)			Minutes		Section(s)			Minutes		Section(s)			Minutes		Section(s)			Minutes
Materials	#	Out	In		Materials	#	Out	In		Materials	#	Out	In		Materials	#	Out	In		Materials	#	Out	In
Test					Test					Test					Test					Test			
Books					Books					Books					Books					Books			
Test					Test					Test					Test					Test			
Manual					Manual					Manual					Manual					Manual			
Scantrons					Scantrons					Scantrons					Scantrons					Scantrons			
Absent Students					Absent Students					Absent Students					Absent Students					Absent Students			

MONDAY					TUESDAY					WEDNESDAY					THURSDAY					FRIDAY			
Section(s)			Minutes		Section(s)			Minutes		Section(s)			Minutes		Section(s)			Minutes		Section(s)			Minutes
Materials	#	Out	In		Materials	#	Out	In		Materials	#	Out	In		Materials	#	Out	In		Materials	#	Out	In
Test					Test					Test					Test					Test			
Books					Books					Books					Books					Books			
Test					Test					Test					Test					Test			
Manual					Manual					Manual					Manual					Manual			
Scantrons					Scantrons					Scantrons					Scantrons					Scantrons			
Absent Students					Absent Students					Absent Students					Absent Students					Absent Students			

Testing Organizer

287

Testing Organizer

Teacher: _____ **Grade:** _____ **Room:** _____ **Year:** _____ **Test Coordinator:** _____ **Test Proctor:** _____

Testing Checklist

☐ Testing Meeting (Date: _____ Time: _____)   ☐ Signed Affidavit   ☐ Test pick-up/return (Room: _____ Time: _____)

☐ Test labels/hand completed student information   ☐ Practice Tests (Date: _____ Time: _____)

Materials   ☐ Pencils   ☐ Erasers   ☐ Scratch paper   ☐ Rulers   ☐ Dividers   ☐ Door sign   ☐ Timer

STUDENT NAME	ACCOMMODATIONS (LANGUAGE, ALLOTTED TIME, READ ALOUD, ONE ON ONE, ENVIRONMENT, ETC.)

TESTING MAKE-UPS   **TEACHER:** _____   **GRADE:** _____   **ROOM:** _____   **DATE:** _____

Student Name(s)	Testing Section	Date	Student Name(s)	Testing Section	Date

Lesson Planning

Unit Plan Overview

This sheet is designed to help you plan for an entire unit. Using this sheet can be a great way for you to make sure that you cover major portions of the curriculum when designing a unit. An example is included below to show you what you should be including in your unit plan. Remember to link your unit across the curriculum and include as many subjects and corresponding standards as possible.

- Be sure to include specific literary sources and books that you may be using in this unit.

- Keep this with your weekly lesson plans as a guide to where you are going with your instruction, as well as evidence of planning. Your administrator will be happy to see this!

Unit Plan

Teacher: _J. Zavaleta_   Grade: _1st_   Room: _24_   Date: _April 4, 2024_

Subject: Reading

- Read aloud--summarize /predict/sequence
- Big book/projector--track the text, students follow along, choral reading experience
- Read pages--students act out with fruit and caterpillar puppets as read

Materials: A copy of The Very Hungry Caterpillar

Subject: Writing

- Create a flipbook to show the sequence of the story
- Students write a sequel for the butterfly: Where does it go? Where does it live? What does it eat? Who are its friends?
- Write a letter to the hungry caterpillar

Materials: Premade flipbook of paper and/ or construction paper

Subject: Math

- Count the number of holes punched out for each day
- Greater than and less than--ask questions such as, "Did the caterpillar eat more or less on Tuesday than Friday?"
- Math problems (+/−) with fruit manipulatives
- Story problems

Materials: Pictures from the book, fruit manipulatives

Theme: Perseverence
Weeks: 2–4 Weeks

Subject: Science

- Life cycle of the butterfly--pictures from the story; relate to other life cycles
- Plants--seeds to fruit, needs
- Health-food pyramid--where do food items fit, discuss importance, illustrate favorite.
- Make a fruit salad--vocabulary (ESL)

Materials: Food pyramid and pictures of the lifecycle of the butterfly from the book, fruit items

Subject: Social Studies

- Community helpers who assist with our nutritional needs--farmer, baker, chef, grocery store employee, doctor, nutritionist, and so on; list/discuss
- Commerce cycle--farm, boat/plane, truck, store, table

Materials: Pictures of community members, cycle template

Subject: Art

- Mixing colors—primary colors of tissue paper layering—e.g., blue and yellow to make green
- Collage/torn art of Eric Carle's style—caterpillars using torn construction paper and glue
- Create fruit/caterpillar puppets with popsicle sticks and paper

Materials: Tissue paper, popsicle sticks, construction paper, glue

Unit Plan

Teacher: _____ Grade: _____ Room: _____ Date: _____

Subject:

Materials:

Subject:

Materials:

Subject:

Materials:

Theme:
Weeks:

Subject:

Materials:

Subject:

Materials:

Subject:

Materials:

Sample Direct-Instruction Lesson Plan

Title: _The Very Hungry Caterpillar_   Unit: _Number Sense_   Grade Level: _First_

Teacher: _Persiani_   Suggested Time: _45 Minutes_

1. Anticipatory Set and Scaffolding:

Grab students' attention; then relate new objectives to past learning.

- _Using a caterpillar puppet as the voice, read aloud the story_ The Very Hungry Caterpillar _by Eric Carle._
- _Using the text and pictures from the story, sequence the events from the story in time order sequence (first, second, third, fourth, and so on)._

Objective:

By the end of the lesson students will:

- _Demonstrate their understanding of less than, equal to, or greater than (<, =, >) by using the symbols properly in class and for homework._
- _Explain their reasoning of less than, equal to, or greater than when presenting their findings on the board and in small groups._

2. Presentation and Procedure:

List the sequential steps for the lesson you will model.

- _Along with the students, count the number of holes punched out on the pages in the actual storybook for each of the days the caterpillar eats through foods. For Saturday, have the students count the different types of foods the caterpillar ate._
- _Using the text from the book, review a couple of examples of greater than and less than by asking students questions such as, "Did the caterpillar eat more or less on Tuesday or Friday?"_
- _In small groups, using the additional pages from the text, have students identify the number of holes eaten in each of the fruits/foods and then compare given days._
- _Students will complete a worksheet asking them to compare given numbers (<, =, >)._

3. Guided Practice:

The students and teacher work together to carry out an example or activity to match the objective.

- _During the read-aloud, the teacher will pause to ask students to summarize and predict the events of the story while drawing their attention to the number of holes eaten into each piece of fruit._
- _As a whole class, the teacher and students will put the events into time-order sequence. The teacher will model less than, equal to, or greater than (<, =, >), and then students will work in small groups to identify and compare the rest of the holes found in the pieces of fruit._
- _The teacher will circulate to note whether or not the students understand the concept._

4. Check for Understanding:

Use a quick and simple assessment to confirm students' understanding.

- _During the read-aloud, the teacher will pause to ask students to summarize and predict the events of the story and assess whether or not students understand the story._
- _After reviewing the story the teacher and students will put the events of the story into time-order sequence, orally and/or with prepared picture cards._
- _When students work in small groups to identify and compare the holes found in the pieces of fruit, the teacher will circulate to note whether or not the students understand the concept. They can record this on a worksheet that designates each page number, the food item, and a blank for the number of holes._

5. Independent Practice:

Students work independently on a task that meets the objective.

- *Students will be given a worksheet asking them to compare given numbers by using the symbols less than, equal to, or greater than (<, =, >).*

  Examples:
  8___4
  7___7
  6___9

6. Assessment, Homework, or Project:

Choose the method you will use to be sure students continue to understand the objective.

- *Using pictures of the fruit from the story, students will match the fruit on one side of the paper with the ordinal number of holes found in each piece on the other side of the paper. Students will also compare given numbers by using the symbols less than, equal to, or greater than (<, =, >).*

7. Content Standards:

Number Sense

- *Students understand and use numbers up to 100.*
- *Count, read, and write whole numbers to 100.*
- *Compare and order whole numbers to 100 by using the symbols for less than, equal to, or greater than (<, =, >).*

8. Modifications, Special Needs, or Technology Component:

- *ELLs—Place students of lower ELD levels with higher ELD levels, offer several opportunities for hands-on experiences, and use picture cues for time-order sequence and names of fruits.*
- *Special Needs—Be sure to offer extra time for those who need it, work one-on-one with those students who benefit from explicit instruction, and seat students with peer tutors for support. Preview the story with those who need preteaching (struggling readers, limited attention, etc.).*

9. Materials:

- *The Very Hungry Caterpillar by Eric Carle*
- *Pictures of each piece of fruit with the number of holes found in the book*
- *Teacher-made worksheets to match the story*
- *Picture cards of the fruit*

Direct-Instruction
Lesson Plan

Direct-Instruction Lesson Plan

Title: _____ Unit: _____ Grade Level: _____

Teacher: _____ Suggested Time: _____

1. **Anticipatory Set and Scaffolding:**
   * Grab students' attention; then relate new objectives to past learning.

   Objective:
   * By the end of the lesson students will:

2. **Presentation and Procedure:**
   * List the sequential steps for the lesson you will model.

3. **Guided Practice:**
   * The students and teacher work together to carry out an example or activity to match the objective.

4. **Check for Understanding:**
   * Use a quick and simple assessment to confirm students' understanding.

5. Independent Practice:

- Students work independently on a task that meets the objective.

6. Assessment, Homework, or Project:

- Choose the method you will use to be sure students continue to understand the objective.

7. Content Standards:

8. Modifications, Special Needs, or Technology Component:

9. Materials:

Week at a Glance

The best way to be organized on a weekly basis is to map out your week. Being organized and prepared helps you to meet your unit goals, your student's needs, and help them progress to meet the standards. This "Week at a Glance" template is a great tool for organizing your week. Lesson-plan books can often be detailed and hard to read, so mapping your week out by writing just the main objectives can be much easier to track.

Instead of having to read through the steps and standards of a lesson, which you would keep in a formal lesson plan book, on this page you would write a condensed version, such as "adding fractions" or "subtracting integers." In this manner, what you are setting out to accomplish in the week is easier to track at a glance. You can also schedule in any meetings, professional developments, lunch or recess duties, conferences, etc., so that everything is in one place and easy to read. Being prepared for each week is an essential part of being successful in the classroom.

WEEKLY PLANNER Week						
Monday						
Tuesday						
Wednesday						
Thursday						
Friday						

Home Study

Home study, or homework, is very important. It gives students a chance to practice and reinforce skills that have been covered in class. It also provides parents/guardians with an opportunity to take part in their child's education. Homework should be a review of skills covered that day and should be self-explanatory and focused. It is a strategic part of your planning. You can plan a week in advance and prepare a sheet to be sent or e-mailed home on Mondays that lists the homework for the week. There are a number of activities that can be done without having to run off copies. The following are some suggestions.

Spelling-Word Template

- Fill out template and send home weekly.
- Supplement with any additional homework.

Name:

Weekly Spelling List

1. bake
2. rake
3. take
4. sail
5. pail
6. snail
7. shout
8. trout
9. sprout
10. bridge
11. ledge
12. badge
13. judge
14. their
15. there
   Bonus
   sailboat

Date:

Directions:
Complete daily assignments.
Return daily.

Monday:
- Write sentences with words 1-5.
- How many ways can you say 8?

Tuesday:
- Write sentences with words 6-10.
- How many ways can you say 9?

Wednesday:
- Write sentences with words 10-15.
- Write 3 story problems with the numbers 8 & 9.

Thursday:
- Put words in alphabetical order. Study words for test.
- How many ways can you say 10?

Friday:
- Write a story with as many words as you can.
- Write 3 story problems that equal 10.

© Springer/Alexander 2004

Math Activities

- Write problems to represent a number, "Ways to say a number."
- Create story problems.
- Write out fact families for a number.
- Count in various ways.

Spelling-Word Activities

- Write sentences with the words.
- Write synonyms or antonyms for the words.
- Alphabetize words.
- Write rhyming words.
- Illustrate the words.
- Write a paragraph with the words. Challenge students by giving them a title to use (e.g., "My Day at the Beach").
- Write a story using as many words as you can.

Weekly Spelling
List (10 Words)

WEEKLY SPELLING LIST

1. _____

2. _____

3. _____

4. _____

5. _____

6. _____

7. _____

8. _____

9. _____

10. _____

BONUS

_____

Name: _____

Date: _____

DIRECTIONS: Complete daily assignments. Return daily.

MONDAY: _____

_____

_____

_____

TUESDAY: _____

_____

_____

_____

WEDNESDAY: _____

_____

_____

_____

THURSDAY: _____

_____

_____

_____

FRIDAY: _____

_____

_____

_____

Weekly
Spelling List
(15 Words)

WEEKLY SPELLING LIST

1.

2.

3.

4.

5.

6.

7.

8.

9.

10.

11.

12.

13.

14.

15.

BONUS

Name:

Date:

DIRECTIONS: Complete daily assignments.
Return daily.

MONDAY: _____

_____

_____

_____

TUESDAY: _____

_____

_____

_____

WEDNESDAY: _____

_____

_____

_____

THURSDAY: _____

_____

_____

_____

FRIDAY: _____

_____

_____

_____

WEEKLY SPELLING LIST

1. _____
2. _____
3. _____
4. _____
5. _____
6. _____
7. _____
8. _____
9. _____
10. _____
11. _____
12. _____
13. _____
14. _____
15. _____
16. _____
17. _____
18. _____
19. _____
20. _____

Bonus

_____

Name: _____

Date: _____

DIRECTIONS: *Complete daily assignments. Return daily.*

Monday: _____

_____

_____

_____

Tuesday: _____

_____

_____

_____

Wednesday: _____

_____

_____

_____

Thursday: _____

_____

_____

_____

Friday: _____

_____

_____

_____

Portfolios

Student Assessment Portfolio Cover

Assessment folders can provide you with a comprehensive means of tracking student performance and student growth as well as providing valuable information for report cards and grading. On the following page, you will find a portfolio cover sheet to place on your assessment folders. You may also want to enhance and create your own cover to fit your specific class needs. The cover below has been filled out as an example to show what one might look like. Use one folder per student. A nice touch is using the colored folders you can purchase at your local office supply store. Making a few extra blank folders will save you time if you get a new student during the year.

Write the name of your assessments here.

Student's name

Month the assessment is given in.

These boxes are to record your assessment scores. Assessments should be given three times a year (beginning, middle, and end).

Year

Student Alexander, London   **Year** 2024-2025

Assessments

	Sept.	Dec.	May	Growth Totals	
				Sept. - Dec.	Dec. - May
Phonics	91/200	124/200		33	
Oral Reading	2A	3		1	
High Frequency Words	87/100	92/100		5	
Totals (3 assessments)	180	219		39 +	

	10 wds.	20 wds.	30 wds	40 wds		
Reading	1 min ✓	1 min ✓				

Math Assessments	Sept. 75/100	Dec. 88/100	May

Total points achieved (for all assessments)

Math assessment scores

Extra boxes (for other assessments or district-required information)

This sheet can be glued on a colored folder for that extra touch!

Growth totals (beginning-middle and middle-end)

STUDENT: _____   **YEAR:** _____

ASSESSMENTS

	MONTH/DATE	MONTH/DATE	MONTH/DATE	GROWTH TOTALS
PHONICS				
ORAL READING				
HIGH-FREQUENCY WORDS				
TOTALS (THREE ASSESSMENTS)				

MATH ASSESSMENTS

WRITING PORTFOLIO

BEGINNER

STUDENT'S NAME: _____

ROOM: _____ TEACHER: _____

WRITING ASSESSMENTS

DATE

TOPIC/GENRE

UNIT NARRATIVES

DATE

THEME/PROMPT

FRIENDLY LETTER

DATE

PURPOSE

STRATEGIES:

CONVENTIONS:

WRITING PORTFOLIO

INTERMEDIATE

STUDENT'S NAME:

ROOM: _____ TEACHER: _____

WRITING ASSESSMENTS

DATE

TOPIC/GENRE

UNIT NARRATIVES

DATE

THEME/PROMPT

FRIENDLY LETTER (date, salutation, body, closing, and signature)

DATE

PURPOSE

STRATEGIES:

CONVENTIONS:

EXPOSITORY

DATE

SOURCE

Writing Portfolio
(Advanced)

WRITING PORTFOLIO
ADVANCED

STUDENT'S NAME:
ROOM: _____ TEACHER: _____

UNIT WRITING ASSESSMENTS

DATE

TOPIC/GENRE

NARRATIVE

DATE

THEME/PROMPT

DESCRIPTIVE

RESPONSE TO LITERATURE

DATE

PERSUASIVE

LETTER

DATE

PURPOSE

RESEARCH/EXPOSITORY

DATE

SOURCE

STRATEGIES:

CONVENTIONS:

Math
Portfolio

MATH PORTFOLIO

STUDENT'S NAME: _____

ROOM: _____ TEACHER: _____

NUMBER SENSE
(counting, adding to 20, comparing values, „ „ 5, the value of coins, ones and tens)

(WEEK 6)	(WEEK 12)	(WEEK 18)	(WEEK 24)	(WEEK 30)	(WEEK 36)

ALGEBRA AND FUNCTIONS
(number sentences, 5, 1, 2, adding and subtracting)

MEASUREMENT AND GEOMETRY
(length, weight, time, shapes, planes and solids, directions)

STATISTICS, DATA ANALYSIS, AND PROBABILITY
(sorting, comparing, graphs, patterns, tally charts)

MATHEMATICAL REASONING
(using tools [e.g., a ruler], sketches, justifying, making decisions on problems)

ELD Portfolio

ELD
PORTFOLIO

Student Name _____ ID Number _____

Birth Date _____ Age _____ Grade _____ Class _____

Current ELD Level (1–5 or Emerging, Expanding, Bridging) _____ Date Designated: _____ Home Language: _____

State/District Testing/Assessment Scores Speaking: _____ Listening: _____ Reading: _____ Overall: _____

SPEAKING
(pronunciation, accent, grammar, details, question, etc.)

DATE	OBSERVATION/ASSIGNMENT	SCORE

LISTENING
(attentive, follows directions, restates, active participant, etc.)

DATE	OBSERVATION/ASSIGNMENT	SCORE

WRITING CONVENTIONS
(spelling, grammar, punctuation, etc.)

WRITING APPLICATIONS
(writing genres, vocabulary, expression, etc.)

READING: WORD ANALYSIS/VOCABULARY/FLUENCY
(self-correction, pronunciation, cadence, sounding out, blending, etc.)

READING: COMPREHENSION/UNDERSTANDING
(main idea, author's purpose, cause and effect, inferences, etc.)

Assessments

Assessments

Assessments are an integral part of your instructional program. They allow you to identify your student's strengths and areas of need for specific skills as well as what gains they have made. Many districts or schools have set assessments and/or use curricular assessments to evaluate their students. These are very important; however, there are times when you may need to assess students on a specific skill or skills. There are many excellent assessment resources available, and you should ask other teachers what they use. Then you can try a few of them and find out which ones work for you. Keep assessments short and focused. The following are templates that can be used to create your own assessments. Use your school's designated curriculum to create tailored assessments.

Math Assessment

Math Assessment Name:	
Focus: double digit +/− Date:	

1. 37 +43	2. 65 −37
3. 87 −35	4. 31 +19
5. 23 +80	6. 97 −39
7. 40 −17	8. 63 +17

Score: ___/___ Observation:

© Springer/Alexander 2004

Math Assessment
- Select up to eight math problems.
- Focus on a particular skill or standard.

Sight-Word Assessment

Sight Word Assessment Name: Date:

the	no	this
a	was	said
is	here	of
on	an	my
are	too	do
you	says	does
see	can	we
have	like	they
but	with	where
she	it	were

Score: ___/___ Observation:

© Springer/Alexander 2004

Sight-Word Assessment
- Write in targeted sight words.
- Students can read and be scored on the correct number read.

Reading Assessment

Reading Assessment Name: Focus: short vowels /sight word Date:

The Cat

One day a cat went to the park. He saw his friends the bird and the dog. They played in the sun. They napped under a tree. After their nap they ate a snack. They ate chips and drank milk. They were full. It was late so they said good bye and went home. It was a good day. They were happy. They will play again.

(line numbers: 2, 10, 19, 27, 35, 42, 50, 58, 66, 68)

Observations:

Time:

© Springer/Alexander 2004

Reading Assessment
- Write or photocopy a passage or write sentences.
- Target specific spelling patterns or level.
- Students can be timed (e.g., one minute) to see how many words they can read in a designated time period (fluency).
- Students can be timed as they read a passage.
- Number words per line for ease of scoring.

Subject Assessment

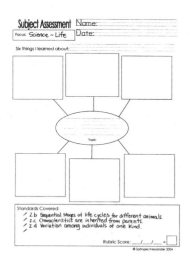

Subject Assessment Name: Focus: Science ~ Life Date:

Six things I learned about:

Topic

Standards Covered:
✓ 2.b Sequential stages of life cycles for different animals.
✓ 2.c Characteristics are inherited from parents.
✓ 2.d Variation among individuals of one kind.

Rubric Score: ___/___/___ = ___

© Springer/Alexander 2004

Subject Assessment
- Social Science or Science
- Students write up to six things they have learned about a topic.
- List the standards covered.

Dictation Assessment

Dictation Assessment Name: Date:

Word dictation:
1.
2.
3.

Sentence dictation:
1.
2.
3.

Score: Word dictation: ___/___ Observation:
Sentence dictation: ___/___ Observation:

© Springer/Alexander 2004

Dictation Assessment
- Target specific spelling patterns.
- Dictate words and sentences.
- Score the assessment.

Name: _____ Date: _____

Focus:

1.	2.
3.	4.
5.	6.
7.	8.

Score: _____ / _____   Observations:

Sight-Word
Assessment

Name: _____ Date: _____

Score: _____ / _____   Observations:

Name: _____ Date: _____

Focus:

Time: _____   Observations:

Subject
Assessment

Name: .... Date: ....

FOCUS:

SIX THINGS I LEARNED ABOUT _____

TOPIC

Standards Covered:
-
-
-

Rubric Score: _____ / _____ / _____ =

DICTATION ASSESSMENT

Name:

Date:

WORD DICTATION:

1.

2.

3.

4.

5.

6.

7.

8.

9.

SENTENCE DICTATION:

1.

2.

3.

Score: Word dictation: _____ / _____   Observation:

Sentence dictation: _____ / _____   Observation:

Rubrics

Rubrics are a simple way to score your students' work. Generally, you can select three to five specific goals or targeted skills that you want an assignment to reflect. Your students are then scored on a scale of 1–4 based on their level of achievement for each skill. This can be as easy as a verbal explanation and circulating around the room marking student assignments as a 1, 2, 3, or 4. It can also be in the form of a written rubric that is posted on a bulletin board or other prominent area in the classroom. It is very important to have clear expectations so that students understand what they specifically need to achieve for a set score or you are able to explain why they received a set score. If you aren't sure where to begin, you can find a variety of rubrics online, but here are a few ideas to get you started.

4
- "Ultimate Goals"
- Three to five goals
- Explicit

3
- "Most Goals"
- Excellent attempt—needs a few minor corrections
- Use words like *most, no more than two mistakes*.

2
- "Some Goals"
- Attempted but needs support
- Use words like *some, three to four errors* (in regard to goal).

1
- "Minimal Goals"
- Minimal attempt, needs a great deal of support
- Use words like *no/little evidence of, minimal, more than five errors*.

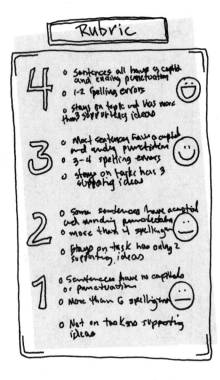

- Goals should be limited from three to five in an assignment.
- Goals should be explicit and specific.
- Goals need to be verbally communicated and explained to students.

- Graphics, like smiley faces, are helpful with primary students. Instead of a sad face, use a neutral one for "1," because a student shouldn't feel like an attempt is "sad" but rather that he or she needs support.

Example:

Goal: To have students use correct ending punctuation.

4 *All* sentences have the correct ending punctuation.

3 *Most* of the sentences have the correct ending punctuation (no more than two errors).

2 *Some* of the sentences have correct ending punctuation (no more than three to four errors).

1 There is *little to no evidence* of ending punctuation (more than five errors).

Demonstration Rubrics

You can create a demonstration rubric to illustrate how a rubric works and make them easier to understand. The following are three examples.

Hamburger Rubric

4
- Hamburger
- Bun
- Ketchup and mustard
- Lettuce and tomato

3
- Hamburger
- Bun
- Ketchup and mustard

2
- Hamburger
- Bun

1
- Hamburger

Pizza Rubric

4
- Pepperoni
- Mushrooms
- Cheese
- Tomato sauce

3
- Mushrooms
- Cheese
- Tomato sauce

2
- Cheese
- Tomato sauce

1
- Tomato sauce

4 Perfect score, can't ask for more. Look at me, I am a four!

3 Almost perfect, look at me. Doing great, I am a three.

2 Still much to do, makes me a two. But I can do it, I'll show you.

1 I have just begun. With hard work, I'll get it done, but for now I'm just a one.

What's my rubric score: 1, 2, 3, or 4?

- You can make these into posters.
  - Use construction paper for the hamburger.
  - Use a paper plate for the pizza, construction paper, and yellow yarn for cheese.

Sample Writing Rubric

Assignment: Write a one-paragraph personal narrative about your most memorable or a favorite time you had with a friend.

Include: The name of your friend, when and where the experience occurred, and why it was memorable. Be sure to write neatly and use correct punctuation, capitalization, and spelling. Also use descriptive words in your writing.

A specific number range is helpful if you are heavily targeting a skill. Words like few, several, or many allow you flexibility if you don't want as much emphasis on an area.

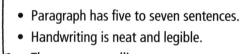

Friend Narrative

4
- Paragraph has five to seven sentences.
- Handwriting is neat and legible.
- There are no spelling errors.
- Correct punctuation and capitalization is used.
- Narrative fully addresses assignment and beyond.

3
- Paragraph has four to five sentences.
- Handwriting is neat and legible.
- There are few spelling errors.
- There are few errors in punctuation and capitalization.
- Narrative addresses assignment.

2
- Paragraph has three to four sentences.
- Handwriting is legible.
- There are several spelling errors.
- There are several errors in punctuation and capitalization.
- Narrative attempts to address assignment.

1
- Paragraph is less than three sentences.
- Handwriting is difficult to read and sloppy.
- There are numerous spelling errors.
- There are numerous errors in punctuation and capitalization.
- Narrative does not address assignment.

Sample Math Rubric

Assignment: Draw and solve a mathematical story problem.

Include: Illustrate the story problem clearly, showing how it can be solved mathematically. Write a sentence telling how the problem was solved.

Math may have fewer criteria in the rubric. Use standards to target specific skills.

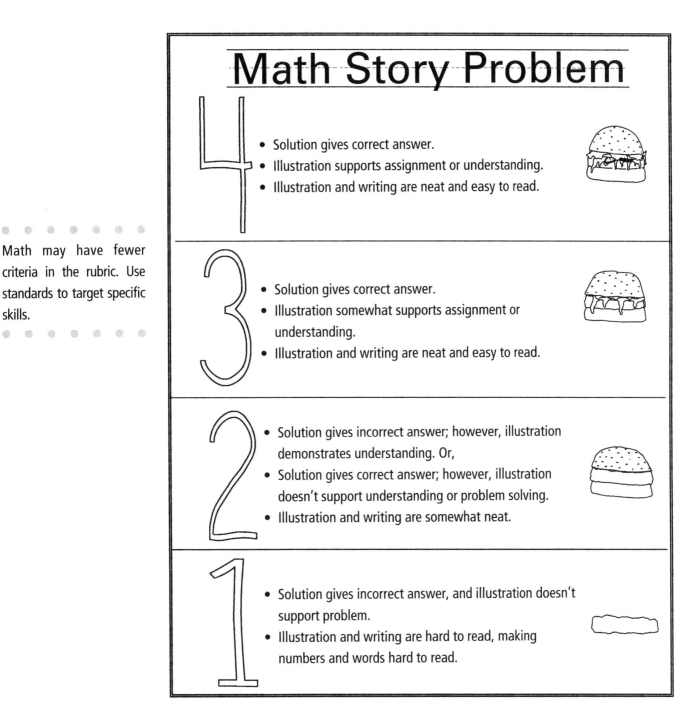

Math Story Problem

4
- Solution gives correct answer.
- Illustration supports assignment or understanding.
- Illustration and writing are neat and easy to read.

3
- Solution gives correct answer.
- Illustration somewhat supports assignment or understanding.
- Illustration and writing are neat and easy to read.

2
- Solution gives incorrect answer; however, illustration demonstrates understanding. Or,
- Solution gives correct answer; however, illustration doesn't support understanding or problem solving.
- Illustration and writing are somewhat neat.

1
- Solution gives incorrect answer, and illustration doesn't support problem.
- Illustration and writing are hard to read, making numbers and words hard to read.

Rubric
(Burger–Vertical)

Name:

4 · · · · ·

3 · · · · ·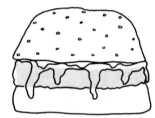

2 · · · · ·

1 · · · · ·

Name: _____

4 ⋮ 🍕

3 ⋮ 🍕

2 ⋮ 🍕

1 ⋮ 🍕

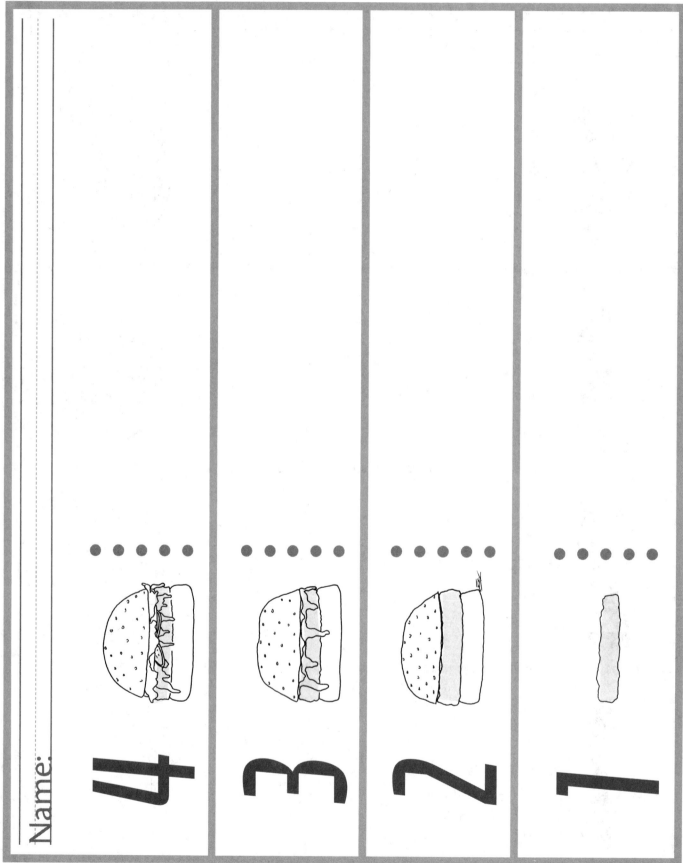

Name:

4

3

2

1

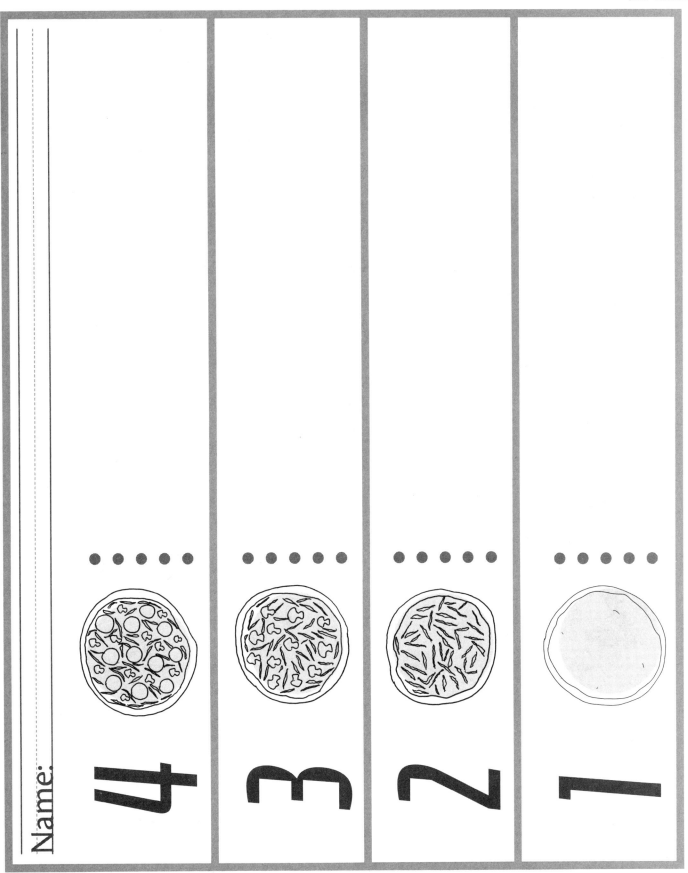

Name:

4

3

2

1

Rubric
(Blank)

Name:

4 • • • • •

3 • • • • •

2 • • • • •

1 • • • • •

Student Skills Review Sheet

The following page contains a sheet that you can use with your teacher's aide to focus on low-achieving students or students who may just need some review. You may want to design a sheet that will fit your particular program. Use these sheets as a starting place; then create your own. These practical sheets will give you a focus for your teacher's aide and will support your in-class instruction.

- List of students needing review

- Your aide can put a check mark after each time he or she has worked with a student.

- Name of month and the date

- Insert the codes of the skills that each student needs to review.

Student List for Skills Review

STUDENTS	July																			SKILLS
	1	4	5	6	7	8	11	12	13	14	15	18	19	20	21	22	25	26	27	28	
Kacee	✓+	✓+	✓+	/+	✓+	✓+															ABS
James	✓+	✓+	✓+	✓–	✓+	✓+															ABS
Xena	/–	✓+	✓+	✓+	✓+																BSD
Willy	✓+	✓+	✓+	NB	✓+																BSD
Kashala	✓+	✓+	/+	✓+	✓+																SDR

Notes

* Kacee needs more work on her CVC blending. (faster blending phonemes)

* Willy is close to dipthong & sight word mastery.

Key

A = alphabet
B = cvc words
S = sight words
D = dipthongs
R = reading

- You may want to assign a time limit to each student.

- Your aide can write notes about particular students and their progress.

- Enter the particular review skills with a corresponding code.

- Each month, you can evaluate your students' progress and make changes according to their growth.

- All students on the list should be seen daily.

- This sheet should be put in a folder along with the review material for your aide.

Student List for
Skills Review

Student List for Skills Review

SKILLS

STUDENTS

Month

Date

Key

Notes

Weekly Assessment Overview

This is an assessment that can be given weekly to help track your students' progress. This assessment is two-sided, with one side having spelling and behavior and the other side having a simple math assessment that you can create. It's a great idea to keep track of these scores on a grade sheet and have it available for conferences or administrators. Send this assessment home every Friday as a way to give parents/guardians feedback on their child's behavior for the week as well as their child's scores on the spelling and math assessments. Have students return it on Monday with a parent's/guardian's signature

- Spelling test with the score
- Spelling and math scores
- Behavior chart with the appropriate boxes checked
- Choose problems that reflect what the students have learned for the week.
- Math score

FRONT

BACK

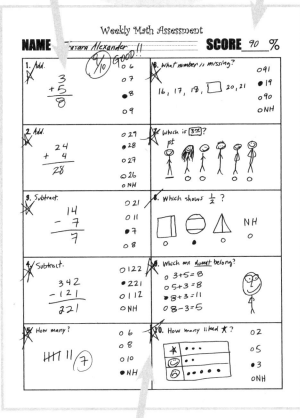

- Two practice sentences with corrections made
- A note to the parents/ guardians
- Parent's signature
- Math test that you create and grade (can be formatted to be like your state test)

Weekly
Assessment–Lower
Grades

Name:

WEEKLY SPELLING TEST

1.

2.

3.

4.

5.

6.

7.

8.

9.

10.

Date:

BEHAVIOR

	☺	☹
Attendance *(asistencia)*	☐	☐
Classroom Behavior *(comportamiento en la clase)*	☐	☐
Yard Behavior *(comportamiento en la yarda)*	☐	☐
Homework *(tarea)*	☐	☐
Work Quality *(cualidad de trabajo)*	☐	☐
Spelling *(deletreo)* _____ %	☐	☐
Math *(matemática)* _____ %	☐	☐

Comments *(comentario)*

_____

_____

_____

_____

_____

Parent's Signature *(firma del padre)*

_____

SENTENCE

Name:

Date:

WEEKLY SPELLING TEST

1. _____
2. _____
3. _____
4. _____
5. _____
6. _____
7. _____
8. _____
9. _____
10. _____
11. _____
12. _____
13. _____
14. _____
15. _____
16. _____
17. _____
18. _____
19. _____
20. _____

BEHAVIOR

	😁	😞
Attendance (asistencia)	☐	☐
Classroom Behavior (comportamiento en la clase)	☐	☐
Yard Behavior (comportamiento en la yarda)	☐	☐
Homework (tarea)	☐	☐
Work Quality (cualidad de trabajo)	☐	☐
Spelling (deletreo) _____ %	☐	☐
Math (matemática) _____ %	☐	☐

Comments (comentario)

_____

_____

_____

_____

_____

Parent's Signature (firma del padre)

_____

Sentences

Name: _____   Score: _____ %

1.	2.
3.	4.
5.	6.
7.	8.
9.	10.

Weekly Assessment Grade Sheet

Teacher:		Room:	Date:

STUDENT NAME	SKILL/STANDARD															
1.																
2.																
3.																
4.																
5.																
6.																
7.																
8.																
9.																
10.																
11.																
12.																
13.																
14.																
15.																
16.																
17.																
18.																
19.																
20.																

Notes

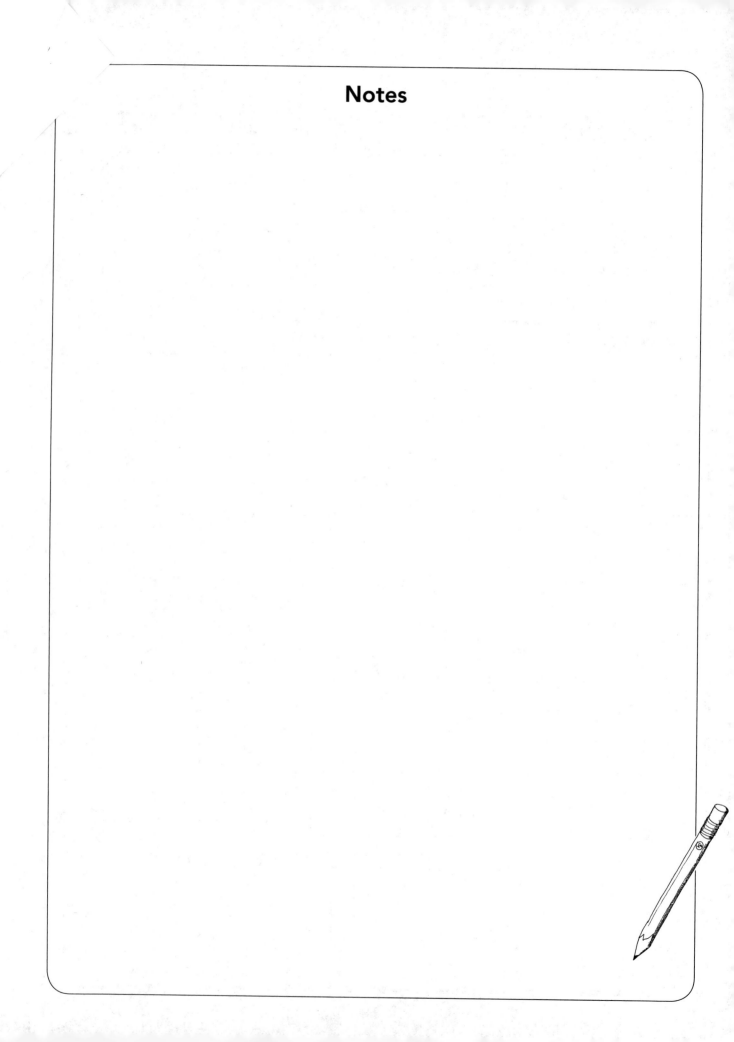

Notes

Notes